CONTENTS

Competence in Interpersonal Conflict

William R. Cupach
Illinois State University

Daniel J. Canary
Arizona State University

WAVELAND
PRESS, INC.
Long Grove, Illinois

For information about this book, contact:
Waveland Press, Inc.
4180 IL Route 83, Suite 101
Long Grove, IL 60047-9580
(847) 634-0081
info@waveland.com
www.waveland.com

ABOUT THE AUTHORS

WILLIAM R. CUPACH is Professor of Communication at Illinois State University. Bill earned his Ph.D. from the University of Southern California in 1981 and has since published numerous books and articles on the topics of conflict management, interpersonal competence, and face negotiation. Dr. Cupach also serves as the Associate Editor of Communication for the *Journal of Social and Personal Relationships*.

DANIEL J. CANARY is Professor of Speech Communication at Arizona State University. Dan earned his Ph.D. from the University of Southern California. Dr. Canary's research has focused on interpersonal conflict and argument, relationship maintenance behaviors, and sex differences and similarities. Dan also serves as an editorial board member of several journals that publish research about interpersonal communication.

PREFACE

Conflict between people is a natural feature of the human condition. When people interact and form relationships, disagreements inevitably emerge. Conflict presents us with both opportunities and challenges, in all types of interpersonal relationships. We experience conflict with friends and neighbors, spouses and best friends, parents and children, roommates and coworkers. How we manage our interpersonal conflicts powerfully affects our relationships, perhaps more so than any other kind of interaction behavior.

Conflict has both negative and positive consequences. Conflict can expose our greatest weaknesses, destroy our most valued relationships, and impart tremendous personal anxiety or fear. People often recall this negative side of conflict. Just as likely, however, conflict can help us solve problems productively, express strong beliefs and emotions, and solidify important relationships.

To understand interpersonal conflict, we need to recognize the ways in which communication conveys problems between people. Communication provides the means by which we recognize and express conflicts. In addition, communication most often distinguishes productive conflict from destructive conflict. People who manage their conflicts using appropriate and effective communication behaviors dramatically increase their chances of experiencing the productive aspects of conflict. Thus, we adopt an approach to managing conflict that values communication competence.

Throughout the book we focus on interpersonal conflicts. We concern ourselves principally with disagreements between individuals in a variety of personal and social relationships. There are two types of conflict that this book does *not* address. First, we do not concentrate on "intrapsychic," or internal, conflicts—that is, conflicts experienced by a single individual. Thus, we do not take up issues such as cognitive decision making, personal problems, or methods of dissonance reduction. We examine psychological features of conflict only to the extent that they relate to conflict between people. Second, this book does not address aspects of social conflict such as social movements, international disputes, or political diplomacy. Our focus remains on interpersonal conflict and how to manage it in an appropriate and effective manner.

The first two chapters of the book lay a conceptual foundation for understanding interpersonal conflict. Our opening chapter gives several reasons for studying conflict. We also present different ways of defining conflict and show that conflict is of various types and levels. As the reader will discover, conflict is a pervasive and important aspect of who we are and what our relationships become.

Chapter 2 presents a conceptual framework to organize ideas about interpersonal conflict and its management. We discuss communication competence and why it is central to conflict management. We also present a model of conflict that clarifies the antecedents and consequences of conflict from a competence focal point.

In Chapter 3 we describe the nature of conflict messages—the central feature of any conflict interaction. We survey the landscape of conflict topics and investigate the many possible message behaviors during conflict interaction. We describe these behaviors in terms of communication tactics, strategies, styles, and patterns. In Chapter 3, the reader will learn much about alternative communicative methods for managing conflict.

Chapters 4 and 5 outline what we refer to as "distal" and "proximal" influences on conflict interaction. Distal influences concern ways in which different types of people tend to approach and manage conflict. We cite several key relational background factors that give shape and meaning to specific disagreements. Proximal influences have to do with how people respond more or less spontaneously to conflicts. Anger and other kinds of negative stimuli can bring about reactions that people do not understand. We explore how people's instant interpretations of events can lead to different sorts of conflict communication. Finally, we examine how the partner's behavior provides an immediate source of feedback regarding one's own conflict messages.

Chapter 6 summarizes both short-term and long-term consequences associated with conflict interactions. These include blatant immediate outcomes such as thoughts and feelings. We also consider the more subtle processes in which the effects of individual episodes of conflict accumulate either to solidify or to undermine an interpersonal relationship.

Chapters 7 through 10 explore conflict in four unique settings. These chapters are contributed by well-respected scholars who are thoroughly familiar with their respective contexts.

In Chapter 7, Dr. Stella Ting-Toomey discusses the challenges of managing conflict in which the parties are from different cultures. After describing key concepts that explain cultural variability, Professor Ting-Toomey illustrates how cultural differences play out in conflict processes.

Drs. Michael Papa and Wendy Papa take the lead in discussing organizational conflicts in Chapter 8. Professors Papa and Papa explain the phases of conflicts experienced in the organization, and they illustrate how principles of competence apply to organizational conflicts between individuals, groups, and organizations.

Dr. Brian Spitzberg tackles the subject of violence in intimate relationships in Chapter 9. He debunks several myths about intimate violence and offers some thought-provoking analysis of the current research on this issue.

In Chapter 10, Professors Claudia Hale and Amy Thieme elucidate the process of mediation. In mediation an objective third party assists individuals who experience difficulty constructively managing a conflict on their own. The authors draw on their professional experiences to apply the principles of competence to conflict disputants and mediators.

Chapter 11 looks ahead to future conflicts you are likely to experience. We argue that adopting an ethical stance in managing your conflicts is both desirable and practical. We also offer general guidelines to assist you in grappling with your own conflicts in the future.

In sum, this book focuses on how you, the reader, can increase your competence at managing interpersonal conflicts in a variety of settings. We do not presume that you now are incompetent; we only hope to increase your present level of motivation, knowledge, and practical communicative skill at managing interpersonal conflicts.

ACKNOWLEDGMENTS

We owe a debt of gratitude to many people for their selfless efforts on our behalf—efforts that made this book stronger, clearer, and more relevant to our readers.

The following reviewers made helpful comments and suggestions: J. K. Alberts, Arizona State University; Denise Cloven, University of Wisconsin, Madison; Fran Dickson, University of Denver; William A. Donohue, Michigan State University; Karen R. Krupar, Metropolitan State College of Denver; Daniel Montgomery, Florida State University; Calvin Morrill, University of Arizona; Lawrence B. Nadler, Miami University; and Deborah Weider-Hatfield, University of Central Florida.

We want to express our appreciation to several people who provided important guidance and editorial assistance. In particular, we wish to thank Hilary Jackson, who acquired the project, and Marge Byers who inherited the project and saw it to completion. Bridgette Isaacson helped to smooth the transition between editorial teams, and Gwyn Meeks carried through on important details to the very end. We appreciate the efforts of Fran Marino and Valerie Raymond who worked as developmental editors, as well as Larry Goldberg who coordinated the project as editing supervisor. We are also grateful to Inge King for helping us obtain photographs. We owe a special debt of gratitude to Annette Bodzin and Stephanie Hiebert for their painstaking attention to manuscript minutae. Their efforts helped transform the book into a more coherent and informative text. To all these excellent editors, thank you.

Thanks to our students and colleagues for giving us fresh ideas and sustaining our enthusiasm for the study of conflict. We are indeed indebted to the SPCOM 404 students for providing feedback on a few of the chapters and facilitating the development of some exercises contained in the Instructor's Manual. We thank Duane Gustafson and Christine Roberson for their work on the Instructor's Manual, and Aimee Lanning for helping us compile the index. We sincerely appreciate the outstanding efforts of our contributing authors: Claudia Hale, Michael Papa, Wendy Papa, Brian Spitzberg, Amy Thieme, and Stella Ting-Toomey. We are fortunate, indeed, to have their engaging chapters in this book. Finally, thanks to Betty Cupach, Susan Messman, and Brian Spitzberg for giving us needed input and encouragement of various kinds at various stages of the book's development.

William R. Cupach

Daniel J. Canary

Competence in
Interpersonal Conflict

1

THE IMPORTANCE OF CONFLICT IN INTERPERSONAL RELATIONSHIPS

CHAPTER OUTLINE

You already know much about interpersonal conflict. You have been "trained" for thousands of hours about conflict strategies and tactics, and you have experienced many disagreements with relatives, friends, lovers, and others. These conflicts have ranged in importance from small disagreements (such as which college football team is the best) to critical disputes that may have determined the future of a job or an important relationship.

Your conflict management training began very early. By eighteen months of age, toddlers become more verbally expressive during conflict with parents (beyond saying "no"); by thirty-six months of age, children utilize different decision rules when responding to conflict (for example, rules about when to defend yourself, rules about how to obtain rewards, and rules about when it's all right to condemn others) (Dunn & Slomkowski, 1992). In addition, at about eighteen months of age, children learn that alternative types of reasons are appropriate and effective in different situations (Dunn & Slomkowski, 1992). For example, you learn that claiming "other children do it" does not satisfy your parents' desire for a reason why you put a dead bug in your younger sister's oatmeal or why you broke the CD player you were forbidden to touch.

As you proceeded through adolescence, you engaged in a different sort of conflict. You expanded your rights to take control over personal issues, such as your style of clothes, how to wear your hair, and how late to sleep in on Saturdays (Smetana, 1988, 1989). But most parents do not understand the importance of establishing rights over one's personal life. So the two of you (or three or more of you) argued and experienced tension like you have seldom felt since adolescence. People often do not understand that adolescents need to establish control over their own lives so that they can leave home and begin their own families (Robin & Foster, 1989). Your own children do or will strive for personal control, just as you did.

After you became an adult, you may have placed more emphasis on romance, your conflicts thus reflecting the issues that partners must face, especially issues of interdependence (Braiker & Kelley, 1979). As you become involved in intimate relationships, how you negotiate daily activities becomes an essential part of your relationships. Not surprisingly, and simply because you are not used to doing things with someone else, conflicts emerge. Your conflicts seem to involve mundane and seemingly unimportant issues, such as who drives the car, what type of groceries you purchase, how you spend your leisure time, and who watches the children while the other person folds the laundry. In addition, your conflicts can reflect more important relational issues, such as how you express yourself and show affection (including sex), how you get along with in-laws, and how money is spent.

Over time you have realized that interpersonal conflict is complex. It involves more than just a simple disagreement that can be repaired by one person apologizing and promising not to behave badly again. According to Selman (1980), people come to understand that interpersonal conflict involves a system of two people who have their own goals and perceptions of the issues at stake. You also realize that people are often inconsistent in their goals, beliefs, and behaviors. Perhaps most important, from an interpersonal perspective, is the fact that you have developed some preferred responses for handling your disagreements. If you already have learned a lot about conflict, then, you might wonder why you should study it more formally.

WHY STUDY CONFLICT?

Although some authors assume that people know nothing about conflict, we do not. We believe you are well on your way to being an expert on interpersonal conflict, although you are probably not acquainted with the language that scientists and other scholars use to explain conflict processes. So why should you study conflict? We can think of at least six reasons.

Reason 1: To Fine-Tune Your Expertise

One reason to study conflict is that you can fine-tune your ability to manage conflict situations. The information contained in this book is written for that purpose—to make you more competent in your interpersonal conflicts.

Competence in communicating refers to your ability to achieve your goals while you fulfill relational and situational expectations (Spitzberg & Cupach, 1984). Achieving your goals concerns your *effectiveness;* fulfilling other people's expectations concerns *appropriateness.* Interpersonal conflict involves two people who must somehow achieve goals that may appear incompatible.

People may sacrifice being appropriate in order to achieve their own goal; or they may be so concerned about offending someone that they do not pursue what they want. So interpersonal conflict often presents you with a quandary about how to behave in an interpersonally competent manner. This book provides you with principles based on research to help you increase your competence at managing interpersonal conflict.

Reason 2: To Learn That Conflict Is Common

Supposedly the only certainties in life are death and taxes. In our opinion, these are not all; the probability is 99.9 percent that you have experienced and will continue to experience interpersonal conflict. As Hocker and Wilmot (1995) have noted, conflict is an everyday, natural feature of everyone's interpersonal life. Findings from studies investigating different types of relationships support the view that conflict is pervasive.

Interpersonal conflict begins early and often with a parent. Dunn and Munn (1987) observed interactions between mothers and toddlers in age groups of eighteen, twenty-four, and thirty-six months. During each hour of observation, these interactions involved about seven to eight conflicts (that is, exchanges of disagreement), about half of which were extended disagreements and the other half short spurts of disagreement. Even if we count only the extended disagreements as "real" conflicts, parents and toddlers averaged three to four conflicts per hour. Although parent-toddler conflicts tend to be frequent, they are brief and unresolved (Eisenberg, 1992). Typically they do not lead to an escalation of negative feelings, and when negative emotions are involved in parent-toddler conflicts, they tend to occur at the beginning of the episode and then subside (Eisenberg, 1992).

Conflicts are routine for adolescents. In a study involving self-reports of their previous day, high school students reported an average of seven conflicts a day involving different types of relationships (Laursen, 1993). (These students also reported a large *range* in the number of conflicts in the previous day, from zero to thirty-nine.)

Adults report that their romantic involvements entail quite a bit of conflict. One study of college couples who were dating found an average of 2.3 conflicts per week (Lloyd, 1987). The amount of conflict depends partially on the couple's level of satisfaction and stability. One study found that unhappy married couples experienced an average of one conflict a day, but more satisfied and stable couples experienced one conflict only every five days (Vincent, Weiss & Birchler, 1975).

Although conflict is common, it does not have to be destructive. Conflict can be constructive (Deutsch, 1973). The competent management of interpersonal conflict can lead to stronger relationships, alternative ways of seeing a tough problem, and durable solutions. In this light, the frequency of conflict is probably less important than *how* people communicate during conflict (Straus, 1979).

Reason 3: To Understand That People Develop Individually through Conflict

Research in developmental psychology indicates that learning how to manage interpersonal conflict is necessary for personal growth. As Shantz said, "Conflict is a central concept in virtually every major theory of human development" (1987, p. 283). Research reveals that conflict is embedded within much of parent-child interaction. The child wants to expand her social world, and the parent "educates" the child about the limits of her social world. Through interpersonal conflict we learn early how to detect another person's thoughts and feelings, how to clarify the other's intentions for his or her actions, how to understand the social rules that indicate appropriate behavior, and how to use strategies to obtain personal goals (Dunn & Slomkowski, 1992).

It is important to understand that people's differences in thinking, behaving, and appearance often lead to interpersonal conflict. Conflict arises because of incompatibility between people (Deutsch, 1973). To have a conflict-free environment, you must be able to read minds and want to fulfill the other person's wants. Thus, a conflict-free environment is impossible, since no one is an accurate mind reader and we all vary in our wants. Such inevitable differences lead to conflict.

Unfortunately, most people do not seriously study the interpersonal skills that help them reconcile incompatible thoughts and behaviors between themselves and others. Here, communication in conflict plays a fundamental role in our personal and social development. If we learn how to manage conflicts competently, we can increase the likelihood of obtaining goals that are valuable to us without alienating people who are important to us. This reason for studying interpersonal conflict relates to the next.

Reason 4: To Promote Peace on Earth

Although most people manage their conflicts in ways that allow them to sustain their personal relationships, many do not learn how to manage conflict. For the latter, interpersonal conflict can be a very negative, and tumultuous, event. According to one review, 15 to 25 percent of parents complained about conflicts with their adolescents, and more than 20 percent of adolescents reported "tumultuous" growth marked by "many serious" disagreements with their parents (Montemayor, 1986, p. 18). These figures suggest that 20 to 25 percent of families with adolescent children experience disruptions that have emotional and psychological implications.

An extensive review by Marshall (1994) reported that about 20 percent of people in romantic involvements had experienced some form of physical violence in those relationships within the previous year. (Verbal and physical abuse are discussed in detail in Chapter 9.) As will become apparent throughout this book, the competent management of conflict helps people resolve issues so that they see a reliance on verbal or physical abuse as unnecessary and ineffective. In other words, clear education on interpersonal conflict can provide you with insights so that you have strategic, as well as personal, reasons to decide against abusive tactics.

Reason 5: To Maintain or Improve Your Physical Health

Learning how to manage conflict in a competent manner can reduce risks to your psychological and physical health. Substituting abusive behaviors with more productive ones should provide you with a safer social environment. Recent research also shows that the way in which people manage conflicts may directly affect their psychological and physical health. Cooperative and reasoned conflicts appear to be much more healthy than conflicts laced with negativity.

Kiecolt-Glaser and colleagues (1993) recruited happy couples in their first year of marriage to participate in a study conducted at a university medical center. The couples arrived early in the morning and had their blood checked. They then participated in a discussion of conflictual issues, and blood samples were taken at times during the discussion by an unobtrusive method (that is, participants were catheterized and did not know when their blood was being sampled). The couples stayed overnight in the hospital and had their blood sampled again the next morning before they left (about twenty hours after the conflict discussion). Kiecolt-Glaser and colleagues found that negative conflict behaviors (such as to criticize the partner, to deny responsibility for one's part of the conflict, and to put down the partner) adversely affected blood pressure during the talk, and they negatively impacted the immune system twenty hours later.

These results are clear evidence that negative conflict messages damage one's physical health, not only immediately, but for at least about a day. These findings are even more impressive when we realize that the conflictual conversations took place in a secure environment, that the couples reported high marital satisfaction, and that the individuals appeared to be well adjusted with no history of drug use or mental problems (for example, depression). Despite all these positive influences, at times the participants engaged in negative behaviors that resulted in damage to their health. Imagine the toll that naturally occurring, negative conflict behaviors take on people who are not in highly satisfying relationships, who may be already depressed or anxious about some event, and who may use drugs either socially or as a means of escape.

Another study examining how physiological responses connect to conflict was undertaken by Levenson, Carstensen, and Gottman (1994). On the basis of their results and other research, the authors reasoned that men are more aware than women of their own negative physical arousal during conflict. Although women experience more negative physiological outcomes, however, they are more likely than men to persist in conflict. Levenson, Carstensen, and Gottman concluded, "If sustained autonomic arousal is accepted as playing a role in the etiology of disease, then the health of women would be expected to suffer most in the most unhappy marriages, which are the marriages most likely to have intractable problems and repeated bouts of high-level conflict" (1994, p. 66). In short, the health problems that result from mismanaged conflict can be severe.

Reason 6: To Achieve Satisfying Relationships

A vast amount of research reveals that how you manage conflict powerfully affects your close, personal relationships. No other type of communication tests the character of one's relationship more than the interaction of interpersonal conflict (Canary & Cupach, 1988).

Many researchers have discovered that particular patterns of interaction separate satisfied from dissatisfied couples (see Chapter 3). For example, Ting-Toomey (1983a) found that one pattern among dissatisfied couples is a series of interactions in which one person complains and the other person defends himself or herself. Ting-Toomey found that dissatisfied couples often engaged in a long series of these complain-defend interactions; ten exchanges of such messages were not uncommon! She also found that satisfied couples

Do people really dislike conflict? (CALVIN AND HOBBES© 1994, 1995 Watterson Dist. by Universal Press Syndicate. Reprinted with permission. All rights reserved.)

do not engage in such patterns. Instead, satisfied couples engage in more confirming sequences of conflict interaction.

In this book we review other patterns, both constructive and destructive, to show how interpersonal conflict affects relationships. The work of many researchers attests to one simple principle: *How people manage interpersonal conflicts dramatically affects their close, personal relationships.*

DEFINING INTERPERSONAL CONFLICT

Scholars, like all other people, vary in their conceptions of conflict. These differences are due partly to the various levels of conflict we have discussed and partly to the fact that scholars have different research purposes. For example, some are interested in how conflict functions in the development of young children; others are interested in explaining marital problems. Each approach to defining conflict imparts something important about the topic; each approach stresses different ideas about how conflict is expressed or experienced. For this reason, we briefly look at the different approaches to defining conflict.

Definitions of interpersonal conflict vary on two features: *behavior* and *episode* (Canary, Cupach & Messman, 1995). First, some definitions of conflict specify particular kinds of behaviors that qualify as conflict, but other definitions do not limit conflict to specific behaviors. Second, some definitions describe conflict as a certain kind of interaction event, a distinct set of circumstances that produce conflict; other definitions of conflict do not describe the context surrounding disagreements. These characteristics lead to four definitional approaches, each of which indicates properties of interpersonal conflict.

Approach 1: Interpersonal Conflict as Pervasive

This first approach to defining interpersonal conflict indicates no behavioral or episodic features of conflict. In other words, *conflict is pervasive;* it can be manifested in all behaviors and regardless of situational factors.

According to this definition, people can convey disagreements with each other using a plethora of behaviors. In addition, this definition does not limit conflict to a particular kind of interaction. For example, Sprey claimed that "The family process *per se* is conceived of as a continuous confrontation between participants with conflicting—though not necessarily opposing—interests in their shared fate" (1971, p. 722).

This definition reminds us that conflict can emerge almost anywhere. As Sillars and Weisberg (1987) argued, interpersonal conflict contains a "surprise element." These scholars noted how conflict accompanies most of our activities. Conflicts cannot be separated from the experience of everyday living; their potential exists in every interaction we have.

Approach 2: Interpersonal Conflict as Explicit Disagreement

According to this definition, interpersonal conflict occurs in behavior but is not limited to a particular kind of situation. For example, Vuchinich defined verbal conflict as a "distinctive speech activity. . . . In verbal conflict, participants oppose the utterances, actions, or selves of one another in successive turns at talk. Linguistic, paralinguistic, or kinesic devices can be used to express opposition directly or indirectly" (1990, p. 118). Approach 2 says that interpersonal conflict occurs whenever people disagree with each other in a behavioral way, regardless of their emotional responses. This definition focuses our attention on the interaction of people.

Relying on this definition, scholars have examined many different behaviors that are said to constitute conflict. Some scholars refer to conflict behaviors as cooperative versus competitive strategies; others define conflict as confirming versus disconfirming behaviors. In addition, some researchers view conflicts simply as behavioral oppositions; others believe that some type of "significant disagreement" should accompany these behavioral oppositions. The point is that conflict emerges in a variety of messages (see Chapter 3).

Approach 3: Interpersonal Conflict as a Hostile Episode

A third category of definitions acknowledges that conflict entails perceptual parameters. Research shows that people can easily identify conflict episodes. *Episodes* are situations that have a recognizable beginning and end, which can vary widely in the minds of different people (Pearce, 1976). But people often use their definitions of the situation to locate the beginnings and endings of an interpersonal conflict.

People often identify conflict episodes by referring to their own feelings—hostility, depression, or some other emotion that causes them to recognize a situation as conflict. For example, the frustration we feel when another person prevents or delays us from achieving our goals is an experience that indicates conflict. Although interaction behaviors are not specified, they may be implied.

This approach reminds us that interpersonal conflicts are experienced in our perceptions of events. Of course, the prototype of this definition is when people disagree simply due to misunderstanding. Accordingly, this definition centers on the individual's experience more than on the relating of conflict. We all know that people can have different experiences of the same event. In addition, some people are more sensitive than others to negative feelings and thus might experience a conflict longer or with more feeling, and they may read more hostility into a conversation than was intended. Regardless of the intensity of feeling, people can experience interpersonal conflict over time, extending the conflict episode for weeks, months, or even years.

Approach 4: Interpersonal Conflict as Disagreement in Particular Episodes

This final definition specifies that interpersonal conflict must entail a behavioral form of disagreement. In addition, the conflict behaviors must occur within identifiable situations that are commonly understood as conflict episodes. This definition provides a central focus for the study of conflict at the interpersonal level. For example, Hocker and Wilmot offer the following popular Approach 4 definition of interpersonal conflict: *"an expressed struggle between at least two interdependent parties who perceive incompatible goals, scarce resources, and interference from the other party in achieving their goals"* [italics in original] (1995, p. 21).

This definition specifies conflict in terms of behavior (expressed struggle) and episode (perception of incompatible goals, scarce resources, and interference). Hocker and Wilmot's definition implies that people use particular behaviors when faced with incompatibility. In addition, this approach emphasizes conflict as something that is *communicated;* you must express your disagreement with someone to have an *interpersonal* conflict. Finally, this

TABLE 1-1
PROTOTYPICAL DEFINITIONS OF INTERPERSONAL CONFLICT

Approach	Definition and example
1	Interpersonal conflict concerns any incompatibility between people that can be manifested in any behaviors in any situation. For example, your successful older brother always finds a way to let everyone else know just how successful he is, which makes you crazy and spoils family reunions.
2	Interpersonal conflict refers to behaviors that explicitly show a disagreement between two people—for example, two consecutive oppositions.
3	Interpersonal conflict refers to situations that involve feelings of hostility between people. For example, you resent someone who broke up with you several years ago.
4	Interpersonal conflict refers to behaviors that explicitly show a disagreement between two people involved in situations marked by feelings of hostility. For example, you confront your nephew about his stealing money from your wallet.

Source: Adapted from Canary, Cupach & Messman (1995).

definition focuses on the division of scarce resources in close relationships that are marked by interdependence. Table 1-1 summarizes the four approaches to defining interpersonal conflict.

We have our own preference regarding an approach to defining conflict, but because we want to include various points of view, and for the sake of discussion, we refrain from offering our opinion. Instead, we would like you to determine for yourself which approach seems most insightful. You can refer to your own experience with interpersonal conflict, discuss the four definitional approaches with class members, and/or talk about these ideas with your instructor (who also probably has a preference on the topic of how to define conflict). The idea we wish to impart is that conflict is multifaceted, and much territory has been covered in the research literature.

FEATURES OF INTERPERSONAL CONFLICT

As we have seen, scholars differ in what they mean by the term *conflict.* In addition, different levels and types of conflict behavior are examined.

Levels of Conflict

Braiker and Kelley (1979) argued that conflict exists at different levels of interdependence. In other words, conflict arises when people try to coordinate actions and activities with one another. According to Braiker and Kelley, identifying where such problems arise reveals the following three different levels of conflict:

- Level 1 conflict refers to problems involved in coordinating *specific behaviors*. Interpersonal conflicts about specific behaviors refer to disputes over things such as which TV program to watch, how long to cook vegetables, and if you should mail a package overnight or by regular mail.
- Level 2 conflict concerns the coordination of *relational norms and roles*. At this level, you and your partner might disagree about what is expected from you in the relationship. Level 2 conflicts include disagreements such as whether one should share toys when asked, who should cook and clean, and whether the woman should take the man's last name when a couple marries. In other words, Level 2 conflicts entail disagreements about *relational rules*.
- Level 3 conflict regards *personal characteristics and attitudes*. These conflicts concern problems you might have with your partner's personality or beliefs. Examples of problems that might fuel conflict at this level include the behavior of an immature older sibling, the extreme jealousy of a romantic partner, and religious differences. Level 3 conflicts focus on someone's personality—the person's motives, qualities, faults, and (sometimes) strengths.

These three levels of conflict are often mixed during interaction. For example, you may disagree with your friend that she agreed to call you if she was going to arrive late (a specific behavior). You may also view her failure to call as part of a larger problem of not showing consideration as a friend (a relational rule). In addition, such instances of her treating you with a lack of consideration has decreased your liking of this person and your desire to spend any further time with her (a personal issue).

Types of Actual versus Perceived Conflict

In addition to having different levels, interpersonal conflict varies to the extent that it concerns actual differences or perceived differences. Conflicts can arise from real incompatibilities or from incompatibilities that are largely imagined (Deutsch, 1973). *Both* actual and perceived conflict represent legitimate bases for disagreement. No one's perceptions are 100 percent accurate, and perceptions differ in the extent to which they are anchored in reality.

An illustration can show how people might have different bases for conflict. Although many people think they can recall exactly who said what in a conversation, the research indicates otherwise. Stafford and Daly (1984) found that their participants could only recall about 9 percent of what they said the previous hour. Even when it comes to important issues, people only recall about 35 percent of what they talked about the previous hour (Sillars, Weisberg, Burggraf & Zeitlow, 1990). As you might have hypothesized, these

BOX 1-1

WORKING FOR MINIMUM WAGE: A CASE STUDY

Mike and Dave had different reasons for working part-time as janitors. Mike was a graduate student who needed tuition money. Dave had a family with four children and no permanent job, so he hoped this part-time job would turn into something better. They both worked for a large cleaning company, Zambam Inc., which won large contracts. But Zambam paid their employees as little as possible, which meant that Mike and Dave waxed floors and scrubbed toilets for minimum wage. Zambam also stretched its profits by underestimating how long particular jobs would take, thereby forcing employees to work fast and hard.

Zambam won a $10,000-a-month contract to clean a pharmaceutical firm (Sticka Pharmaceutical). After the initial cleaning, they put Mike and Dave on the account and allowed only four hours a night for them to clean the two office buildings and the factory. Mike would go before Dave and empty trash cans, clean ashtrays, and wipe off desks and railings. Dave watched out for the ever-menacing dust; he would dust, clean all air vents, and vacuum. They both cleaned the bathrooms in record time. Despite this system, they would miss one or two trash cans or an air vent.

Within a few days, Sticka started to complain that air vents and trash cans were not being cleaned, which was critical to that business. Zambam reminded Mike and Dave about their obligations to do a good job. So Mike and Dave worked faster—and longer than they were paid to. But that was not enough to do a thorough cleaning of these buildings. Sticka complained again to Zambam. Zambam warned Mike and Dave that they could lose their jobs.

Mike and Dave each felt the pressure. So they changed their routine to maximize their efficiency, and their new routine required split-second timing and coordination. Also, to keep their jobs, they put in twice the amount of work, without extra pay.

Mike knew he was working as hard as anyone could, and he was fast. Dave was not as fast, because he was concerned that they would miss an all-important air vent

low figures for conversational recall drop even lower over time. Given this research, it is ironic that many conflicts concern who said what to whom, why what the person said was merely in response to the other person's statement, and so forth. People sometimes state that they wish for a videotape to prove how accurate they are ("If only I had a videotape of this, you would see how right I am!"). However, it is likely that *neither* person recalled the conversation very accurately, and a videotape of their talk would show that inaccuracy.

Deutsch (1973) showed how interpersonal conflict differs depending on actual and/or perceived bases for disagreement, and whether the perceptions accurately represent the objective bases for conflict. Five types of conflict are possible:

• *Parallel conflict* (what Deutsch [1973] called "veridical" conflict) is a conflict that has an objective basis and is accurately perceived by both parties. For example, if Margo and Peter both agree that their conflict arises from the or an executive ashtray. Dave needed the money more than Mike. Mike began to complain that Dave was taking too long—and they weren't getting paid that much to work there all night. Dave would wipe the sweat from his eyes and remind Mike about missing certain ashtrays. They resented each other, despite the fact that they were friends.

One night, Dave spotted a full trash can that Mike had missed. He blew up, "What is wrong with you? Can't you see it doesn't matter how fast you go if you don't clean everything!"

Mike said, "Look, don't you give me that! I could get this place clean in plenty of time if I didn't have to drag you along all night!"

Dave replied, "Look, dummy, I have to clean things you miss, and that's what's slowing us down here! Now get it together or we'll lose this account."

Mike shot back, "Don't call ME stupid! At least I don't consider this a *career* opportunity."

Dave was so mad, all he could say was, "Watch yourself."

A week later they were called into Zambam's main office and told that they had lost the account. They were fired and handed their pay (minus their uniform fee) for the previous two weeks—$160.59.

Perhaps the real loss was the friendship. Mike and Dave lost contact with each other after a few months. Years later each of them would shake his head at how hard they had worked for so little.

Discussion Questions:

1. What is the *level* of conflict between Mike and Dave—behavioral, relational, or personal?
2. What *type* of conflict is this?
3. Was the conflict between Mike and Dave partly the company's fault for not providing enough resources for the account?
4. Did Mike and Dave manage the conflict in a productive way?
5. How would you deal with this issue if you were either Mike or Dave?

fact that Margo does not want to commit, whereas Peter does, then they have a verifiable basis for conflict and their perceptions parallel that basis.

• *Displaced conflict* is an instance in which someone might have an objective reason for conflict and perceives that a conflict exists but has perceptions of the conflict issue that are off target. Extending the previous example, Peter (who is uncertain of his relational future) may begin to withhold a full range of affection from Margo (from not sleeping with her to sulking). Margo may become upset at Peter and confront him about sulking around all the time. As long as they focus on the issue of sulking, the real conflict (about commitment) is displaced.

• Another form of conflict in which the objective basis for conflict is inaccurately perceived is *misattributed conflict* (Deutsch, 1973). In this case, however, the inaccuracy concerns *who* is in conflict. If Peter blames Margo's ex-lover for their problems, Peter may never confront Margo. Instead, Peter

TABLE 1-2
TYPES OF CONFLICT AT EACH LEVEL

Type of conflict	Example
Level 1: Specific behavior	
Parallel	At a party, your friend has consumed several drinks and wants to drive home. You do not want your friend to drive after drinking so much alcohol.
Displaced	You don't like the fact that your housemate talks nonstop. To drown out the talking, you turn on a football game. Your housemate doesn't like sports, so the two of you argue about what to watch on TV.
Misattributed	You discover the smell of cigarette smoke, which you hate, in your house. You think your daughter's boyfriend has been smoking, and you warn him to not smoke in your house. In actuality, your daughter was the person smoking.
Latent	You don't carry condoms because you think doing so is tacky. Your partner doesn't either, though you think he should. Several times now you have been frustrated because both of you want to make love, but you know you should practice "safe sex." Still, it's too embarrassing to discuss.
False	Two friends are in a heated debate about health care reform. They see their points as contradictory. In actuality, they both are advocating the same point of view but with different and even complementary evidence.
Level 2: Relational rules	
Parallel	You have received a job offer that requires you to move across the country. Your family doesn't want you to leave, and they plead with you to stay home. You really don't want to leave home, but this job is too good to pass up.
Displaced	Your parents have been having a lot of conflicts, which you can't stand. So you run away for the weekend in hopes of distracting their attention from their own problems.
Misattributed	You are very upset with your mother for breaking up the family by asking your father to move out. Your father indicates how sad he is to go, but your mother won't discuss the issue with you or your sister. Years later, you discover that your father had abused your mother.

may build a sincere hatred for the ex-boyfriend and pity Margo for her inability to make a commitment.

• *Latent conflict* refers to conflict "that should be occurring but is not" (Deutsch, 1973, p. 14). Although an objective basis exists for conflict, neither person perceives it. Such is often the case when couples have real differences in values but pretend that such differences do not matter. They continue to plan

Type of conflict	Example
Latent	You and your partner have been dating for about six weeks and you are falling in love. You do not want to date others and assume that your partner feels the same way. But he or she has just concluded an emotionally draining relationship and cannot fathom making another commitment right now and has plans to see other people when convenient.
False	You are unhappy with a friend who did not invite you to her wedding. She is unhappy that you did not attend her wedding. In actuality, the invitation was sent to your previous address but was not forwarded to you.
Level 3: Personality	
Parallel	An acquaintance advocates white supremacy. You are offended by this belief, and he is offended by your "liberal attitude."
Displaced	You find out that an instructor has been dating one of his former students. You think this behavior is unethical because you feel that there is a power imbalance in the teacher-student relationship that unprincipled male teachers can exploit. So you look for occasions to disagree with this "sleazy" teacher during lecture.
Misattributed	You heard a rumor about you that suggested you can't be trusted. In public, you confront the person you are sure began the rumor, someone you know to be a gossip and a liar. The person you confront easily dismisses your accusation and says you don't know what you're talking about. You never find out who initiated the rumor, though you often get embarrassed at recalling the event.
Latent	Your brother routinely uses drugs. The problem is that he cannot care for his two young daughters (ages two and four) when he is high. In fact, he likes to get high and take his daughters to the park to play. You hope he grows out of this phase.
False	You cannot understand why your roommate is so lazy. He sleeps until 10 A.M., complains about all the work that he never does, and likes to take naps in the middle of the day. In addition, he doesn't care that his courses are suffering this term. The two of you argue about it all the time, and he gets so depressed that he drops out of school. Later you discover that he has chronic fatigue syndrome and is under a doctor's care.

for the wedding and do not allow any serious talk about issues that might cause them to scrutinize exactly what they are getting into (as illustrated in the statement, "Oh, I know we're different, but that will change after we're married"). On the other hand, an important recent finding is that perceived agreement between people—and not actual agreement—is positively associated with relational satisfaction (Sillars et al., 1990).

- In *false conflict,* people disagree but have no objective basis for their disagreement. False conflicts are the result of misunderstanding. If I perceive that you dislike my best friend, but in fact you very much like my best friend, the conflict arising from my perception of you is a false one. A clear example of false conflict arises when a jealous lover imagines intrigue and guile that do not really exist. Jealous lovers may contribute to the conflict by using "detective" strategies, such as monitoring the partner by calling at unexpected hours, looking through the person's telephone bills and drawers, and other covert activities (Pfeiffer & Wong, 1989). Although such jealousies are often based more on imagination than on reality, the jealous person, who might even recognize the lack of factual data, may feel too insecure to admit his or her perceptual error.

In short, interpersonal conflicts differ in the extent to which they reflect real or perceived problems. Sometimes the perceptions of both parties match reality; in other instances conflict concerns the wrong issue. Seeing the issue accurately does not guarantee that the conflict will be reduced. In fact, sometimes knowing precisely where objective differences exist can hurt the relationship.

These various types of conflict also occur at different levels, from those about behavior, to those about relational rules, to those about personal evaluations. Table 1-2 illustrates the different levels of each type of conflict. The fact that conflict exists in different types and on different levels implies that we can expect interpersonal conflict to emerge in many different issues. The level of interpersonal conflict is tied to how the issue is framed. Some issues are seen as isolated events; others are seen as reflecting larger relational problems.

SUMMARY

You already have had much training in interpersonal conflict management. You have probably developed some very clear ideas about conflict and how you can effectively manage it. The purpose of this book is to help you refine your expertise by increasing your understanding of interpersonal conflict and how it can be competently managed.

Early in this chapter, we provided six reasons to learn more about interpersonal conflict: to fine-tune your expertise; to realize that conflict happens frequently; to see how conflict links to your development as a person; to promote peace on Earth; to maintain or improve your physical health; and to sustain positive relationships. We hope that each of these reasons provides you with enough incentive to learn more about the topic.

We offered four definitional approaches that researchers have used to study interpersonal conflict. Examining these alternative approaches helps us realize that conflict involves a multitude of factors, and each definitional approach stresses some of these factors. You must decide for yourself which approach is most informative.

In discussing the various levels and types of conflict, we noted that conflict issues range from those concerning behavioral differences to more serious disagreements about relational rules and personal characteristics. The various types of conflicts occur at different levels. Some conflicts are no more than minor disagreements that barely last a minute. Conflicts that concern fundamental issues about the relationship or about each other can last years.

Interpersonal conflict may appear to be unnatural and unfriendly. No one we know wakes up in the morning and asks, "Who can I get into a conflict with today!?" Most people prefer their lives and loves to continue in a smooth fashion. But neither life nor love is like that. Because we interact with others, conflict occurs. Some researchers see conflict as part of every conversation; others see it isolated to particular events within particular conversations. Regardless of the definition adopted, conflict represents a prominent and critically important experience in everyone's life.

DISCUSSION QUESTIONS

1 Recall the last time you had a significant conflict with someone close to you. What was the cause of the conflict? At what level, or combination of levels, was the conflict—behavioral, relational, or personal? Has the conflict been resolved?

2 The beginning of this chapter provides six reasons why people should study interpersonal conflict management. Which of these reasons represents the most convincing case, in your opinion? Can you think of other reasons that are not discussed here? Can you think of reasons why people should *not* study interpersonal conflict?

3 Please reread each of the definitions in Table 1-1. Which definition is the most insightful to you? Why?

4 Argyle and Henderson (1984) discuss different "rules of friendship." Several rules in particular were found to distinguish the quality of friendship. That is, if these rules were held, then the friendship was a good one. For example, consider the following rules:

a Standing up for the friend (to defend him or her) in his or her absence
b Sharing news of success with the friend
c Showing emotional support for the friend
d Volunteering to help the friend in time of need
e Striving to make the friend happy

Discuss a conflict that stemmed from one or both persons not following one or more of these rules. Also discuss other rules of friendship that are important to you. How do these rules differ from those in romantic relationships, such as dating seriously and marriage?

2

A COMPETENCE-BASED APPROACH TO INTERPERSONAL CONFLICT

CHAPTER OUTLINE

CRITERIA THAT GUIDE PERCEPTIONS OF COMPETENCE
Effectiveness
Appropriateness
The Relationship between Effectiveness and Appropriateness
Implications of Judging Competence
FACTORS THAT FACILITATE COMPETENCE
Knowledge
Motivation
Skill
AN EXPLANATORY MODEL OF INTERPERSONAL CONFLICT
Distal Context
Proximal Context
Conflict Interaction
Proximal Outcomes
Distal Outcomes
SUMMARY
DISCUSSION QUESTIONS

Our approach to understanding interpersonal conflict is based on a model of communication competence (Spitzberg & Cupach, 1984; Spitzberg, Canary & Cupach, 1994). A model that features communication competence is particularly helpful for understanding conflict management. Recall from Chapter 1 that competence is a judgment regarding the effectiveness and appropriateness of communication. Conflicts represent problematic situations that rigorously test our communication abilities. Getting what we want and simultaneously meeting others' expectations can be quite difficult. Thus, tension between the dual criteria of effectiveness and appropriateness is heightened in conflict situations and often becomes the focus of disagreement.

Research has shown the importance of competence judgments in interpersonal conflict (Canary & Cupach, 1988; Canary & Spitzberg, 1989). As we will show later, conflict behavior affects the relationship between conflict parties. The manner in which two friends manage disagreements, for example, influences their friendship. How a husband and wife deal with their inevitable conflicts affects the satisfaction of their marriage. In short, the perceived competence of conflict communication strongly influences whether conflict behavior will produce positive or negative relational outcomes. In technical terms, *perceived competence mediates the link between conflict behavior and relational outcomes.* In other words, conflict behavior affects judgments of competence, which in turn affect relational outcomes.

Figure 2-1 depicts a hypothetical example of the role of competence judgments. Ron is a salesman and Kathy is his supervisor. When Ron and Kathy have conflict, they implicitly judge each other's behavior. Ron assesses the competence of Kathy's conflict behavior. The more positive his judgments are, the more likely the relationship will be maintained. Similarly, Kathy's judgment of Ron's behavior filters the effects of Ron's behavior on Kathy's judgment of their interaction. If Ron and Kathy both see each other as managing conflict competently, their working relationship will be enhanced.

The perception of another person's competence is influenced partly by one's own behavior. Individuals are behaviorally interdependent when they communicate. Thus, they influence not only each other's perceptions through their behavior, but also each other's behavior during conflict interactions (Sillars, 1980a). If Kathy is particularly aggressive in her conflict behavior, Ron's aggressiveness may also surface. Thus, Kathy's own behavior indirectly affects her judgment of Ron's behavior, since she influenced Ron's behavior. The common tendency to mirror a conversational partner's behavior is called *reciprocity.*

Another reason for adopting the competence model is that it recognizes the complexity of conflict processes. Prespecified skills or behaviors cannot guarantee success in the management of conflict. It will become apparent, we hope, that communication behaviors do not possess intrinsic meaning or have

FIGURE 2-1
THE MEDIATING ROLE OF COMPETENCE JUDGMENTS IN CONFLICT SITUATIONS.

Ron's conflict behavior	⟶	Kathy's judgment of Ron's competence	⟶	Kathy's assessment of their relationship
↕				
Kathy's conflict behavior	⟶	Ron's judgment of Kathy's competence	⟶	Ron's assessment of their relationship

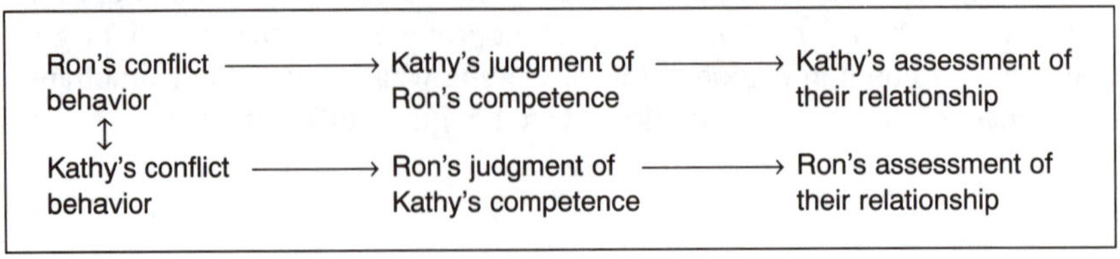

automatic outcomes. There is little value in preparing a cookbook of recipes for conflict success. The effects of conflict interaction depend directly on what the participants do mentally with conflict behaviors—that is, how they process and interpret those behaviors. Judgments of competence are made in terms of a communication context. Context generally is made up of the physical setting, psychological climate, and the goals and rules applicable to an interaction. In Chapter 5 we will discuss features of context that are particularly important in conflict episodes. We elaborate on the standards used for judging the competence of communication—effectiveness and appropriateness—in the following section.

CRITERIA THAT GUIDE PERCEPTIONS OF COMPETENCE

The quality of communication can be evaluated in many different ways. We define "good" communication using standards such as: Is it clear? Is it supportive? Is it eloquent? Different standards are more or less relevant in different communication contexts. However, two standards are prevalent: The criteria of *effectiveness* and *appropriateness* are general and apply to most instances of interpersonal communication (Spitzberg & Cupach, 1984, 1989), including those involving conflict. To reiterate our statement in Chapter 1, communication competence is a function of fulfilling *both* of these criteria. Here we consider how these two criteria are applied.

Effectiveness

Perhaps the most obvious benchmark for assessing communication is whether it is effective in accomplishing the goals of communicators. Goals represent the outcomes that people desire to achieve. To discern the extent to which communication is effective, we must know what goals motivate communication. While various classifications of goals have been offered by researchers, three general types of goals are present in all interpersonal situations: instrumental goals, self-presentation goals, and relational goals (Canary & Cody, 1994; Clark & Delia, 1979). Although all three of these types of goals are present in any conflict situation, the relative importance of each type varies.

   Instrumental goals are concerned with resources that we wish to acquire. Such goals include gaining compliance from another, changing another's attitude or beliefs, obtaining assistance or support, and so forth (Cody, Canary & Smith, 1994). Often the primary source of interpersonal conflict is the difference in the instrumental goals of two people. David wanted Mary to go away with him for the weekend, but Mary wants to stay home to finish a project for work. Mom wants little Jerry to come home to eat supper, but Jerry wants to stay out and play with his friends.

Self-presentation goals pertain to the personal image or persona we wish to present when we are interacting with others. We always want to leave a certain impression on those with whom we communicate (Schlenker, 1980). The identity we present and want others to accept during particular episodes of interaction is called *face* (Goffman, 1967). Most people want to be seen as intelligent and capable. Often, we wish to be perceived as likable and friendly. During conflict, there are numerous impressions we may want to sustain; we may want to appear trustworthy, credible, powerful, sincere, fair, or tough, for example. Successful accomplishment of our self-presentation goals can facilitate the accomplishment of instrumental goals. For example, if I think you are fair, I will be more likely to cooperate with you during conflict.

Sometimes conflict arises because our face is threatened by the actions of others (Cupach & Metts, 1994)—that is, because we perceive someone as interfering with our self-presentation goals. Whenever we are discredited—for example, if we are ridiculed or criticized publicly—our face is threatened. Others can unintentionally threaten our face by committing a faux pas or behaving foolishly. For example, if Ted brings his friend Tim to a party, and Tim gets drunk and makes a fool out of himself, Ted may feel guilt by association. Whenever we feel that our face is threatened, our self-presentation goals are being thwarted. The result can be conflict with the person responsible for our losing face.

Self-presentation goals sometimes interfere with instrumental goals, thereby complicating the management of conflict. For example, you may want help with your homework, but you don't want your roommate to think you are stupid. Or you may want to disagree with my opinion, but you don't want to seem arrogant. Or you may want to correct an erring employee, but you also want to be liked.

Relational goals pertain to the relationship status we wish to achieve or maintain with another person. Since interpersonal conflict is between two people, the relationship between them is always relevant to their mutual conflict. If Steve and Rachel are coworkers, the way they manage conflict with each other will be constrained by the desire to continue a smooth working relationship. And if Steve and Rachel are interested in pursuing a dating relationship, they may withhold disagreements about their attitudes to protect the fledgling relationship. Relational goals are often secondary, serving to constrain how instrumental goals are pursued (Dillard, Segrin & Harden, 1989). However, when two individuals disagree about how to *define* their relationship, then incompatible relational goals can emerge as the primary conflict issue. For example, Zeke and Paula want to date each other; Zeke wants an exclusive relationship, but Paula does not want to commit to Zeke. In this case, relational conflict seems inevitable.

Individuals impose hierarchical order on their interaction goals. At any given time, the most important goal has the strongest influence on our behavior, while the secondary goals qualify the manner in which the primary goal is sought (Dillard, 1990). If my primary goal is to convince you to take a cooking class with me, my behavior is motivated to overcome your resistance. The manner in which I try to influence you and my degree of persistence, however, will be tempered by my perceived risks to our relationship if I push you too hard. My relational goal constrains my actions directed at accomplishing the primary goal.

We normally think of goals as prospective; that is, we are cognizant of them prior to interaction, and we make plans and rehearse strategies for achieving them. However, this is not always the case. Much of the time we are probably only dimly aware of our goals. They exist, but we pursue them automatically and relatively thoughtlessly. Moreover, goals may be formulated and emerge during and after conflict interaction. Hocker and Wilmot (1991) call these *transactive goals*. The fluid and changing course of interactions, as well as the ongoing mutual influence that communicators have on one another, stimulates the emergence of transactive goals. Melissa may disagree with Hope about when to launch a new employee relations project in their work division. During their conflict Melissa may learn information from Hope that alters her original position. Melissa may even decide, as a result of the new information, to advocate scrapping the original idea. Hope may develop the goal of accommodating Melissa because Hope realizes during the interaction that she is going to need Melissa's support later for an unrelated project. Hope and Melissa may develop the mutual goal to get to know each other better socially because they seem to think alike and share some values. The development of transactive goals is consistent with the idea that competent communicators, above all else, must be adaptable to the dynamic circumstances of interactions.

Appropriateness

Most goals can be achieved by multiple paths, and usually we depend on other people in order to reach our goals. Thus, pursuing personal goals must take into account the following: (1) Our goals may conflict with the goals of others; (2) how we pursue our goals produces consequences for others, regardless of any real incompatibility. Thus, interpersonal competence demands that communication be not only effective but also appropriate. In other words, pursuing personal goals must take into account the expectations of others.

Communication *rules* constitute one basis for judging the appropriateness of communication. According to Shimanoff, rules "are followable prescriptions that indicate what behavior is obligated, preferred, or prohibited in certain contexts" (1980, p. 57). Although individuals are in the best position of identifying their own goals and the extent to which those goals are fulfilled, other people's judgments must be considered when evaluating what rules are relevant and whether they are followed.

Social rules are implicit in all social interaction. Although we do not think much about social rules, we certainly recognize them. In our society, we know that we are expected to treat others with politeness and civility. Questions are supposed to be met with answers. Interrupting a conversational partner is generally to be avoided. When rules are violated, conflict may occur. Conflict discussion may center on whether a rule was actually broken; whether the rule is legitimate; whether there is a relevant exception to the rule; whether there are other, more important rules; and the like (Newell & Stutman, 1988).

As interpersonal relationships develop history and intimacy, partners increasingly rely on their own interpersonal rules. Partners tacitly establish mutual guidelines for behavior in their relationship. When conflict arises in public, both social and interpersonal rules are in force. When conflict arises in a private setting, the interpersonal rules take precedence. Of course, individuals sometimes intentionally violate a known rule in order to escalate an emerging conflict. For instance, if you know that your children do not want you to date others (although your divorce is final), you may deliberately begin looking for someone to date. Other times, rules are unintentionally violated in the heat of interpersonal battle (for example, we might throw a glass of water at someone without considering the consequences of that action).

Some rules pertain specifically to conflict communication. These rules govern what behaviors people believe should or should not be enacted during conflict. For instance, a couple may adopt a rule of never going to sleep angry, or not arguing in public. Honeycutt, Woods, and Fontenot (1993) examined differences among married and engaged couples with respect to the endorsement of communicative rules for managing conflict (see Jones & Gallois, 1989). They found four different categories of rules governing conflict communication: *positive understanding* (for example, be able to say "I'm sorry," listen to the other); *rationality* (for example, don't get angry, don't raise voice); *conciseness* (for example, get to the point quickly, be consistent); and *consideration* (for example, don't make the other feel guilty, don't mimic or be sarcastic). Violation of rules such as these, when they are accepted by relational partners, can create a unique type of conflict: conflict about rules about conflict.

The Relationship between Effectiveness and Appropriateness

Put bluntly, effectiveness represents getting your way, and appropriateness reflects getting along with others. These criteria may seem incompatible, but often they are complementary. Getting what you want is often facilitated by getting along with others. Goals can be achieved efficiently because they are pursued within the limits of behavior defined by rules.

Of course, one can be personally effective while being inappropriate (for example, cheating to win at poker). Aggressively trying to meet goals at the expense of other people is personally effective, but interpersonally incompetent. By the same token, following rules and meeting the expectations of others show that one is willing to collaborate but are not sufficient for meeting one's own goals.

Implications of Judging Competence

Competence is not an absolute; it is not merely present or absent. Each person is relatively more or less competent in a given interaction. If a person achieves some of her goals, but not all of them, we would say that she is somewhat effective. If a communicator violates a minor rule, his or her behavior might be judged as momentarily improper. If someone frequently and flagrantly ignores an important rule, that person may be judged as severely inappropriate. Performing prohibited behaviors is likely to draw heavier sanctions than is failing to perform preferred behaviors (Shimanoff, 1980).

FACTORS THAT FACILITATE COMPETENCE

With occasional exceptions, we want to manage conflict competently. Nothing guarantees competence. There is no ideal personality type that is always competent. Nor can we specify certain behaviors that will always ensure that we simultaneously meet personal goals while accommodating the expectations of others. The nature of some conflicts is such that only one person can "win," or that each party can get only partially what he or she wants. Three ingredients, however, maximize your chances of being competent in any episode of conflict: knowledge, motivation, and skill (Spitzberg & Cupach, 1984; Spitzberg & Hecht, 1984). Developing all three of these components will help you be consistently competent in your management of conflict.

Knowledge

There are many types of useful information in a conflict encounter. Obviously, one must have knowledge of one's own goals, and one must be cognizant of the relevant social and relational rules in order to be competent. One must also know what behaviors are most likely to result in goal achievement, and what the unintended consequences are for various behaviors. In addition, knowledge of conflict situations in general, and awareness of our social environment in particular, allow us to discern when we are "in" a conflict situation. Being socially "intelligent" means having a sense of what motivates people, understanding what different verbal and nonverbal behaviors mean, and being able to predict fairly well what behaviors produce what consequences with what probabilities, under what circumstances.

Knowledge is learned, and experience is the best teacher. Observing and participating in productive and destructive conflicts is how we learn. Paying attention to all the consequences of our actions during conflict interactions helps us internalize typical conflict situations and appropriate and effective responses. Reading about the antecedents, processes, and effects of conflicts, as discussed in this book, should equip you with some knowledge to help you manage conflict.

Motivation

Knowledge is said to be power, but by itself, it is insufficient to produce competent behavior. You must also *want* to be appropriate and effective. The need for motivation raises the possibility that we sometimes choose to be *incompetent.* Have you ever felt strongly that your personal goals were very important—more important than being appropriate? You may have chosen to impose your point of view, knowing that you were abandoning tact and politeness. You may have felt pushed into being aggressive when the circumstances were strictly competitive. In this case, you were motivated to win the conflict; you were not motivated to be competent. Or at least, the other person interfered with your opportunity to be competent. Sometimes we choose the path of least resistance. For various reasons, we allow others to have their way at our expense; that is, we choose to be personally ineffective. We simply decide that some goals under some circumstances are not worth pursuing (for example, resolving a conflict when your partner is in an especially bad mood and snaps at you without provocation). Sometimes we make the choice to be incompetent.

Motivation can be stifled, even when we want to succeed. Fear of failure is probably one of the strongest psychological barriers to realizing motivation. If we believe we cannot be successful in a certain situation, we are said to lack *self-efficacy.* Diminished self-efficacy in conflict stems from two types of beliefs: (1) thinking that we are incapable of performing behaviors that will produce the outcomes we desire; and (2) thinking that even if we perform the relevant behaviors, the behaviors won't produce the desired consequences. The example in Box 2-1 illustrates the potential for frustration and communication incompetence when a lack of self-efficacy undermines our motivation.

Skill

Skill is reflected in the performance of communication behaviors. It is the *enactment* of knowledge and motivation. Without skill, we cannot be consistently competent. If you like to play poker and you meet with your friends regularly to do so, chances are you know how to play and are motivated to

---

BOX 2-1

LOW SELF-EFFICACY UNDERMINES MOTIVATION

Jennifer desperately wanted to confront her roommate Karen. Karen was always borrowing Jennifer's clothes without asking. This habit annoyed Jennifer, but she was reluctant to confront Karen. Having grown up in a household where people avoided conflict, Jennifer was not accustomed to assertively standing up for her rights. She was afraid she would look foolish trying to confront Karen because she wasn't sure *how* to confront her. Jennifer didn't think she could persuasively formulate what she should say. Moreover, Karen was very outgoing, articulate, and somewhat controlling, as well as very good at making excuses. Jennifer felt that even if she confronted Karen, her effort would be wasted because her confrontation would surely be too timid and Karen would probably continue to wear Jennifer's clothes without seeking permission anyway.

In the end, Jennifer said nothing, and when she complained to her friends about the problem, her friends replied that they never would have let Karen get away with it. Jennifer's parents advised her to turn the other cheek and hope that next year she could afford her own apartment. In short, Jennifer had an important goal (of getting Karen to stop wearing her clothes without asking), but her lack of self-efficacy in the situation prevented her from having sufficient motivation to pursue the goal.

---

win. Nevertheless, you may not be as skilled in playing the game as some of your friends. For example, you know that bluffing your opponents during bidding is both appropriate and effective. Even though you know what behaviors to perform in order to bluff, however, you can't seem to pull it off effectively. Your friends always see right through your attempts to bluff, so you rarely win at poker. Clearly, some people are better than others in translating knowledge and motivation into skilled action.

Perhaps the most important interpersonal skill is *adaptability* (Duran, 1992). This skill is general, yet complex. It involves tailoring communication behavior to the persons and the situation at hand. Every conflict situation presents a unique bundle of constraints and opportunities. Adaptable communicators avoid overly stylized and rigid communication patterns. They do not manage conflict in the same way all the time. Instead, they demonstrate behavioral flexibility. Adaptability requires having a diverse pool of communication strategies and tactics to draw from (see Chapter 3) and being able to perform the right behaviors at the right time in the right context.

Most of the skills that are relevant to competent interpersonal communication in general apply to conflict situations as well. Skills are developed through practice; the more we use a skill, the more we sharpen it.

A partial list of common behavioral skills is presented in Box 2-2. Our goal is not to depict all the possible interpersonal communication skills. We simply want to refer to commonly cited behaviors that are positively associated with interpersonal competence.

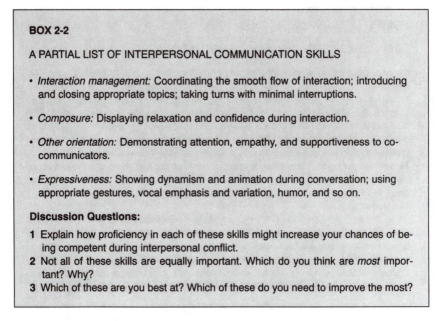

BOX 2-2

A PARTIAL LIST OF INTERPERSONAL COMMUNICATION SKILLS

- *Interaction management:* Coordinating the smooth flow of interaction; introducing and closing appropriate topics; taking turns with minimal interruptions.

- *Composure:* Displaying relaxation and confidence during interaction.

- *Other orientation:* Demonstrating attention, empathy, and supportiveness to co-communicators.

- *Expressiveness:* Showing dynamism and animation during conversation; using appropriate gestures, vocal emphasis and variation, humor, and so on.

Discussion Questions:

1 Explain how proficiency in each of these skills might increase your chances of being competent during interpersonal conflict.
2 Not all of these skills are equally important. Which do you think are *most* important? Why?
3 Which of these are you best at? Which of these do you need to improve the most?

AN EXPLANATORY MODEL OF INTERPERSONAL CONFLICT

Figure 2-2 offers a model of the key components of interpersonal conflict. The model forecasts the features we will examine more closely in subsequent chapters. If you come to understand these components and how they interrelate, you will acquire the type of knowledge that can help you competently manage your own episodes of interpersonal conflict.

Distal Context

The model begins with what is called the *distal context* for conflict. "Distal" refers to the fact that these factors are somewhat removed from any specific conflict interaction. Such factors are "background" characteristics that exist prior to the initiation of a conflict episode. Distal context is carried into interaction by communicators. Conflict parties are generally influenced in subtle and indirect, yet very important, ways, by the distal context.

One important factor of distal context is culture. As we'll see in Chapter 7, when conflict parties are from different cultures, certain challenges emerge. Different cultures may emphasize the importance of different rules, or place value on different goals. More important, perhaps, are the cultural differences in how people tend to manage conflict, and in what they see as competent.

| CONFLICT EPISODE | | | | |
Distal context $\longrightarrow$	Proximal context $\longrightarrow$	Conflict interaction $\longrightarrow$	Proximal outcomes $\longrightarrow$	Distal outcomes
Culture	Goals	Message tactics	Competence	Relational development
Individual dispositions	Rules	Strategies	Satisfaction	Mental growth
Relationship history and definition	Emotions	Patterns	Emotions	Physical health
Prior conflict outcomes	Attributions		Attributions	Cultural rules
Knowledge and skill				

FIGURE 2-2
A MODEL OF INTERPERSONAL CONFLICT.

Individual dispositions also affect the course of conflict. In various locations throughout the book we will discuss how personality traits and sex differences influence conflict management practices. For example, argumentative individuals may show more competitiveness during conflict. Individuals who are shy may tend to avoid conflict more often. Do you think that men and women tend to manage conflicts differently? Do we judge the same conflict behaviors exhibited by men and women to be equally competent? Or do we expect that what is competent for men is different from what is competent for women? In Chapter 4 we will review the evidence on this issue.

The relational environment in which conflict occurs is part of the distal context. If you are happy in a current relationship, for example, you are less inclined to blame your partner for conflict and you are more willing to give your partner the benefit of the doubt (Bradbury & Fincham, 1990). If you are satisfied and committed to a relationship, you generally want to keep the relationship and this desire is reflected in the way you manage conflict. In other words, your generally positive sentiments about the relationship have a halo effect on conflict in the relationship. On the other hand, if your relational climate is negative, you will be more likely to entertain negative perceptions about your partner during conflict, and you will be more inclined to show negative behaviors.

Prior successes and failures in managing conflict, as well as knowledge and skill, predipose conflict behavior. For example, if Jane knows that Scott, who is otherwise a reasonable person, becomes irrational and abusive when he is drunk, then Jane will avoid confronting Scott when he is drunk.

Proximal Context

Proximal context pertains to the perceptual environment that is immediately attached to a specific conflict episode. We have already indicated that goals and rules are important to assessment of the competence of conflict behavior. In any given conflict episode, each person formulates and prioritizes his or her goals. Perceptions of the rules that are relevant in a specific episode will constrain how the goals are pursued.

In addition, emotions and attributions set the tone of a conflict episode and can alter the path of conflict interaction. *Emotions* pertain to experienced arousal and the labeling of that arousal. We will consider emotions that are frequently associated with conflict, such as anger, contempt, and guilt. If you feel angry during a conflict, for example, you are more likely to be defensive and conflict is more likely to escalate.

Attributions are people's explanations of behavior in terms of causality and responsibility. For example, behavior may be attributed to contextual circumstances ("She must be under a lot of stress") or to personality ("He's a jerk"). As we will consider in Chapter 5, these interpretations have considerable influence on the course of conflict interaction (Sillars, 1980a). Similarly, whether you blame the other person or take some or all of the blame yourself will affect your basic approach to managing a conflict.

Conflict Interaction

Conflict interaction constitutes the focal *process* of a conflict episode. Conflicts are recognized, expressed, and managed through communication. In the following chapter, we will describe various types and patterns of communicative behavior, both verbal and nonverbal. Communication behavior during a conflict is influenced indirectly by the distal context, and more directly by the proximal context. Proximal context not only precedes conflict communication, but also evolves with it. Recall, for example, that goals can emerge during a conflict. Similarly, emotions and attributions can be formulated during a conflict episode and can change dynamically. Thus, communication during a conflict episode both affects and is influenced by ongoing emotions and attributions.

Proximal Outcomes

Each episode of conflict has immediate consequences—some of which are intended, and some of which are inadvertent. These immediate results are called *proximal outcomes* in the model. Proximal outcomes evolve during a conflict episode and immediately after an episode of conflict interaction has ended. For example, we can assess productivity following conflict, including determining what goals were accomplished and what progress was made in addressing the conflict issues.

As we indicated already, judgments of communication competence, made during or after conflict, are very important in influencing relational outcomes. These cognitive judgments are accompanied by feelings associated with the conflict interaction. When we perceive that conflict is handled competently, we tend to feel satisfied with the communication. If we achieve our goals and if our partner has behaved appropriately, we experience some communication satisfaction. Communication satisfaction can be considered the affective side of competence judgments. Satisfaction and perceptions of competence go hand in hand. Each tends to foster the other.

Distal Outcomes

Whereas proximal outcomes are immediate to the conflict episode, *distal outcomes* are somewhat removed and delayed. Latent effects from conflict can emerge over time, such as personal growth and the development of cultural rules. An important distal outcome of conflict that we mentioned earlier is the long-term growth and development (or deterioration) of the interpersonal relationship. Conflict interactions gradually influence such relational characteristics as trust, intimacy, and relational satisfaction. The more important and the more intense the conflict episode, the greater the effects on the relationship. As we illustrated previously, these relational effects are determined, in part, by the interpretations placed on conflict behavior. In other words, the proximal outcomes mediate how communication behaviors affect eventual relational consequences.

Both proximal and distal outcomes from a current conflict become part of the distal context for the next conflict between the same parties. If, for instance, Ed trusts Jack less because of the way Jack has handled conflict in the past, then Ed's attributions are likely to be more suspicious and his communication more cautious the next time Ed and Jack engage in conflict. The model in Figure 2-2 recognizes that the current course of a conflict (and therefore its eventual consequences) is influenced by the outcomes of past conflict.

SUMMARY

In this chapter we introduced some of the key concepts that are important for understanding interpersonal conflict. We suggested that judgments of communication competence are central to conflict processes. Communicators assess competence with respect to the dual criteria of effectiveness and

BOX 2-3

PHONE CALLS AT 1 A.M.: A CASE STUDY

Judy had just earned her M.A. degree when she met Derrick. They both were admissions counselors for colleges—she at a university in the Rockies and he at an eastern college. They happened to meet at a conference in Miami, Florida. Although the rest of the country was cold that December weekend, Judy and Derrick drank fruit cocktails and swam in the warm ocean.

Judy believed she had met the perfect man. He was handsome, intelligent, witty, and (most of all) appeared sincere. Derrick was immediately drawn to Judy for many of the same reasons. They planned for a reunion in six weeks.

After they returned to their respective universities, Judy and Derrick talked on the phone for hours, and they E-mailed each other at least three times a day. Their desire to see each other was intense, but they couldn't afford a jet-set commuter relationship. They had to settle for visits every month or two, and phone calls every day.

One problem they had to negotiate was *when* they would talk to each other. Derrick did not want to talk after 11 P.M. eastern time (9 P.M. mountain time), which was when Judy missed Derrick the most, especially on weekends. After 11 P.M., Derrick would go to sleep. The few times that Judy did call after 11 P.M., Derrick showed his displeasure.

At first, Judy did not feel justified in calling late at night. But after a few visits, and after they agreed they would date only each other, Judy wanted to be able to reach Derrick when she needed to. After all, she thought, what good are relationships if you can't even have a "phone date" on Saturday night. So she began calling after 11 P.M. eastern time. After a few nights, Derrick would not even answer the phone; he simply turned on the answering machine and turned down the volume. This upset Judy and made her worry even more. She pleaded with Derrick to be more accessible.

Derrick agreed that he would not turn on the answering machine, and Judy agreed she would not call unless she really needed to. But Judy did not last long. She began calling routinely after 11 again, which angered Derrick. He saw Judy as an insecure woman who had no business being in a long-distance relationship.

One night, after a lengthy conversation with Judy, Derrick turned on his answering machine, but he didn't turn down the volume. About 1 A.M., the phone rang. Derrick woke up angry and frustrated. He could hear Judy's voice in the night, pleading with him to "please pick up, please." He did and shouted, "What the hell do you WANT from me?" Judy answered meekly, "I just want to connect with you before I go to sleep." Derrick couldn't believe it: "Look, this is it—I can't take this anymore. You don't listen to reason and I can't meet your childish needs. Don't bother calling me ever again!" Then he hung up.

This interaction sent Judy over the edge. She dialed Derrick's number several more times that night, always getting the same message: "Hi. This is Derrick. At the tone . . ."). All she wanted to do was assure him that she would "be good" from now on and not call at all hours. She desperately wanted to talk with him, but he would not answer. So she pleaded with the answering machine to understand her, to give her another chance, to comfort her.

Discussion Questions:

1 What were Judy's goals in this conflict? What were Derrick's goals?
2 What is the conflict really about?
3 How did Derrick's emotions and attributions about Judy influence his behavior?
4 How did Judy's emotions and attributions about Derrick influence her behavior?
5 Other than prior conflict outcomes, what elements of the distal context do you surmise had an effect in this conflict?
6 Was Derrick competent? Was Judy? Explain.

appropriateness. These criteria are grounded in individuals' goals and shared rules. The tension between being effective and being appropriate is particularly acute in interpersonal conflict; sometimes it is the primary source of conflict.

We identified three personal characteristics that, when combined, enhance your chances of being seen as competent in any given episode of conflict. These are knowledge, motivation, and skill. Perhaps the most important skill is the ability to adapt behavior to contextual circumstances.

Finally, we presented an explanatory model of interpersonal conflict. This model contains five classes of variables involved in understanding conflict processes and outcomes: distal context, proximal context, conflict interaction, proximal outcomes, and distal outcomes. These variables, and their important interrelationships, will be explored in greater detail in the chapters that follow.

DISCUSSION QUESTIONS

1 In this chapter we presented the hypothetical example of Ron and Kathy, a salesman and his supervisor. Suppose Ron and Kathy have a work-related conflict; for example, they disagree about the performance appraisal that Ron receives from Kathy. If Ron and Kathy are also living together, how do you suppose their close relationship might affect the way they communicate during the work conflict? How might their personal relationship affect the competence judgments they make about each other? In what ways can the work-related conflict affect their personal relationship outside of work? Is it possible for people like Ron or Kathy to keep conflict at work and conflict at home completely separate?

2 The fact that we have multiple goals operating simultaneously during conflict complicates things. Do our own self-presentation goals ever run contrary to our instrumental goals? If so, how? Do our relational goals ever conflict with our instrumental or self-presentation goals? If so, how do these conflicting goals affect the conflict we have with another person?

3 What rules about managing conflict do you strongly endorse? Why do you endorse those rules? Where did they come from?

4 Usually we have the self-presentation goals of wanting to appear fair, firm, credible, intelligent, and so on, when we manage conflict with others. Describe conflict situations in which it might be desirable to give the impression that you are (a) weak, helpless, hurt; (b) hostile, intimidating, angry; (c) indifferent; (d) naive, unaware.

3

CONFLICT MESSAGES

Communication is central to all interpersonal conflicts. Interaction with others both generates conflict and provides the means to manage conflicts. Interaction between people creates the opportunity for conflict between them. That is, partners infer that they are in conflict by observing each other's symbolic behavior. Likewise, our intention to express anxiety, frustration, desire, resentment, anger, and so forth with the other person is made known through communication. When we confront conflict issues, they become explicit in the exchange of messages. Conversely, we can attempt to avoid disagreement by maneuvering around sensitive issues by carefully controlling what we do and don't say.

    The communication of conflict takes on many different forms. It can be a calm and rational discussion; a subtle, nagging, unspoken tension; or an explosive, rancorous, knock-down drag-out fight. In addition, as we discuss later, conflicts involve *patterns* of communication in which people might reciprocate or otherwise perpetuate a sequence of messages for a time.

In this chapter we consider the concrete manner in which people communicate during their interpersonal conflicts. The sections that follow describe the communicative behaviors of conflict interactions.

THE TOPICAL CONTENT OF CONFLICT INTERACTIONS

One way to think about the content of conflict interactions is to consider the issues that provide the focus of disagreement. When you experience conflict with others, what is it about? Are conflict messages to be taken at face value, or do they reflect a deeper emotional need?

We first addressed this aspect of conflict in Chapter 1. Recall that different levels of conflict represent different issues of disagreement. The three levels we discussed were conflicts about specific behaviors, conflicts regarding relational rules, and conflicts relating to personality (Braiker & Kelley, 1979). In addition, we can have meta-conflict—that is, conflict about how we manage conflict. When you accuse me of fighting unfairly because I pout and withdraw from constructively talking through our disagreements, you are identifying a disagreement about the manner in which we resolve disagreements. If I complain that we can't resolve our differences as long as you keep yelling and cursing at me, I'm complaining about your way of handling our conflict.

Specific topics of conflict are limitless. Almost any behavior we engage in, for example, can be seen by another as annoying or deficient or belligerent to some degree. But the most common conflicts relate to the type of relationship shared by communicators. The most frequent conflicts of marital partners, for example, concern disagreements about sex, money, communication (or lack thereof), household chores, raising children, in-laws, jealousy, annoying habits, how to spend leisure time, and so forth (Gottman, 1979; Mead et al., 1990). Ex-spouses who continue to interact disagree about such things as differing expectations about child custody, visitation rights and rules, child support, lingering resentment toward the partner for the failed marriage, and interference by one partner in the other partner's life (Hobart, 1991). Of course, not all conflict occurs within marital (or otherwise "romantic") involvements. Box 3-1 discusses the most commonly mentioned topics of conflict among platonic friends—friends who sustain a friendship without sexual activities.

Recent research suggests that satisfaction in relationships is associated with the frequency with which relational partners experience conflict in particular content areas. Kurdek (1994) asked partners from more than 200 gay, lesbian, and heterosexual couples to indicate how frequently they argued about each of twenty issues. On the basis of analysis that discerned the way in which different conflict issues clustered together, Kurdek derived six general areas of conflict. These areas included:

1 Power (for example, overcriticism, lack of equality)
2 Social issues (for example, politics, personal values)
3 Personal flaws (for example, drinking/smoking, driving style)
4 Distrust (for example, previous lovers, lying)
5 Intimacy (for example, sex, lack of affection)
6 Personal distance (for example, job or school commitments, frequent physical absence)

Kurdek found that partners' relational satisfaction (measured at the same time as the reports of frequent conflict) was negatively associated with the frequency of arguing in areas of power and intimacy specifically. When Kurdek followed up one year later by measuring satisfaction in these couples again, he found that the reported frequency of arguing about power issues was associated with a decrease in relational satisfaction over the one-year period.

BOX 3-1

FRIENDLY FIRE: CONFLICT ISSUES AMONG FRIENDS

Dr. Wendy Samter (University of Delaware) and her colleagues asked more than 500 college students to describe their most recent conflict with a close, platonic friend. The researchers analyzed the descriptions and identified the most common general sources of disagreement.

The most common issue dealt with *violating a friendship rule*. Examples included the failure of a friend to fulfill a friendship obligation and improper interference with the autonomy of a friend's behavior. Obligations reflected common rules of friendship, such as keeping promises, repaying debts, being fair and equitable, being considerate and respectful, being supportive, being loyal, and respecting privacy.

The second most common source of friendship conflict was about *sharing activities*. For example, one friend reported:

> We were watching TV. I wanted to watch the Eagles game, and she didn't, so we started arguing but eventually I won, so I watched the game.

The third most common source of conflict for friends pertained to disagreement about *sharing space and possessions*. These conflicts largely involved borrowing personal items and negotiating cohabitation. One example was disagreement between roommates about whose turn it was to do the dishes.

Other typical topics of conflict included *disagreements about ideas* (for example, debating about politics), *rival relationships* (for example, two girlfriends spending less time together because one of them acquired a boyfriend), and *annoying behaviors* (for example, one friend complaining that the other procrastinates too much).

Source: From Samter, Cupach & Nathanson (1995).

These findings make intuitive sense, given the strong relational implications that attend issues of power and intimacy.

Conflict issues are important because they trigger disagreements and structure conflict interactions. It stands to reason that you need to understand what a disagreement is about if you are to manage it competently. But the topical features of conflict tell only part of the story—revealing the surface of disagreement. To understand the nature and course of disagreement more fully, you must dig beneath the surface and explore how conflicts are enacted through communication. We consider this important subject in the following section.

CONFLICT TACTICS, STRATEGIES, AND STYLES

Conflict Tactics

Interpersonal conflicts are exhibited in interactions between people, which are made up of specific individual actions enacted by each conflict participant. The most commonly studied, fundamental unit of communicative behavior in conflict is an individual's specific action at a specific moment in the interaction. These specific moves or actions are referred to as communication *tactics,* of which there is a great diversity. Conflict tactics, for example, might involve a careful formulation of argument to support our point of view, a request for information from our partner, a hint about what we want, an attempt to divert the topic to avoid confrontation, a joke to relieve tension, and so on. At any time people can select from a wide variety of tactics.

The diversity of potential behaviors makes it difficult to catalogue efficiently all the tactics that can be observed during conflict. Still, several researchers have carefully organized tactics and strategies (for example, Ting-Toomey, 1983a; Gottman, 1994; Weiss & Summers, 1983). One such scheme, developed by Alan Sillars (see Sillars & Wilmot, 1994), is presented in Box 3-2.

Dimensions of Conflict Communication

Categories of conflict tactics, such as those proposed by Sillars (see Box 3-2), attempt to group behaviors that are functionally similar. Each behavior by each person, represented by a thought unit or a speaking turn, represents a tactic that can be observed, classified, counted, and analyzed. Most conflict interactions contain dozens, even hundreds, of conflict tactics strung together. To make sense of the numerous behaviors exhibited during conflict, it is useful to examine features that distinguish the types of conflict tactics from one another.

Van de Vliert and Euwema (1994) identify two dimensions that are useful for distinguishing among conflict tactics: disagreeableness and activeness.

BOX 3-2

SILLARS'S CLASSIFICATION OF CONFLICT TACTICS

Denial and Equivocation

- *Direct denial:* Statements that deny a conflict is present.
- *Implicit denial:* Statements that imply denial by providing a rationale for a denial statement, although the denial is not explicit.
- *Evasive remarks:* Failure to acknowledge or deny the presence of a conflict following a statement or inquiry about the conflict by the partner.

Topic Management

- *Topic shifts:* Statements that terminate discussion of a conflict issue before all parties have expressed an opinion or before the discussion has reached a sense of completion.
- *Topic avoidance:* Statements that explicitly terminate discussion of a conflict issue before it has been fully discussed.

Noncommittal Remarks

- *Noncommittal statements:* Statements that neither affirm nor deny the presence of conflict and which are not evasive remarks or topic shifts.
- *Noncommittal questions:* Unfocused questions that rephrase questions given by the researcher and include conflict-irrelevant information.
- *Abstract remarks:* Abstract principles, generalizations, or hypothetical statements.
- *Procedural remarks:* Procedural statements that supplant discussion of conflict.

Irreverent Remarks

- *Friendly joking:* Joking or laughter that is not at the expense of the other person.

Analytic Remarks

- *Descriptive statements:* Nonevaluative statements about observable events related to conflict.
- *Disclosure statements:* Nonevaluative statements about events related to conflict which the partner cannot observe, such as thoughts, feelings, and intentions.
- *Qualifying statements:* Statements that explicitly qualify the nature and extent of the conflict.
- *Solicitation of disclosure:* Nonhostile questions about events related to conflict that cannot be observed.
- *Solicitation of criticism:* Nonhostile questions soliciting criticism of self.

Confrontational Remarks

- *Personal criticism:* Remarks that directly criticize the personal characteristics or behaviors of the partner.
- *Rejection:* Statements in response to the partner's previous statements that imply personal antagonism toward the partner, as well as disagreement.
- *Hostile imperatives:* Requests, demands, arguments, threats, or other prescriptive statements that implicitly blame the partner and seek change in the partner's behavior.

Continued

BOX 3-2 (Continued)

- *Hostile joking:* Joking, teasing, or sarcasm at the expense of the partner.
- *Hostile questions:* Directive or leading questions that fault the partner.
- *Presumptive remarks:* Statements that attribute thoughts, feelings, and so on to the partner that the partner does not acknowledge.
- *Denial of responsibility:* Statements that minimize or deny personal responsibility for the conflict.

Conciliatory Remarks

- *Supportive remarks:* Statements that refer to understanding, acceptance, support, and so on for the partner and shared interests.
- *Concessions:* Statements that express a willingness to change, show flexibility, make concessions, or consider mutually acceptable solutions to conflicts.
- *Acceptance of responsibility:* Statements that attribute responsibility for the conflict to self or to both parties.

Source: Adapted from Sillars (1986). Used by permission.

Disagreeableness pertains to how unpleasant and straining, rather than pleasant and relaxed, the conflict behavior is perceived to be. *Activeness* regards the extent to which conflict behavior is responsive and direct, rather than passive and indirect. Any particular tactic during a conflict can be judged as more or less disagreeable and more or less active.

Referring to the conflict tactics presented in Box 3-2, confrontational remarks (for example, hostile questions and personal criticism) would be perceived by most people as more disagreeable than conciliatory remarks (for example, concessions and supportive statements). Analytical remarks would probably fall somewhere in between confrontational and conciliatory remarks in terms of disagreeableness. With regard to activeness, confrontational and analytic remarks are relatively more direct and confrontational than are topic management and noncommittal remarks (Sillars & Wilmot, 1994).

In Chapter 6 we will discuss the idea that some conflict tactics are associated with constructive personal and relational outcomes, while other tactics are correlated with destructive outcomes. Remember, however, that the timing, frequency, sequencing, and patterning of tactics are much more powerful and meaningful than is the mere presence or absence of any single tactic.

Conflict Strategies

Another useful way for studying conflict communication is to examine how an individual combines tactics into a coherent game plan during a conflict episode. Such a game plan, or group of conflict tactics, is called a *strategy*. A conflict strategy presents the general approach that tactics specifically institute; that is, tactics are the communicative messages that represent how people are oriented toward each other. For example, you may decide that you have had enough of your roommate's piling her books and papers on the dining room table, so you confront her, but in a nice way. Your general strategy is to be agreeable and active. But when it comes to institute the strategy, imagine that you engage in the following tactics (identified in italics):

> Do you have a second to talk *(request)*? I promise this will only take a second *(polite clarification of imposition)*. It seems to me that the dining room table has been full for the past week, mostly with lots of papers and books that happen to be yours *(descriptive statement)*. I realize you have been busy with two jobs and school and all *(supportive remark)*. And I know that there are habits of mine that are annoying *(acceptance of responsibility)*. I wonder if you could put your papers and books in the study, because I get frustrated when I can't eat in the dining room and I don't feel like I can move your things around *(disclosure statement)*.

This example includes six tactics that actualize the general strategy of cooperation.

Conflict strategies efficiently describe your orientation to a conflict based on and instituted by tactics you employ. Researchers have shown consistently that conflict tactics can be organized into three general strategies: *integration* (working *with* other people), *distribution* (working *against* other people), and *avoidance* (working *away from* other people). Although the labels used by different researchers differ, these three strategic approaches to conflict have been observed in numerous studies (for example, Canary & Cupach, 1988; Putnam & Wilson, 1982; Ross & DeWine, 1988; Sillars et al., 1982).

The integrative conflict strategy reflects a cooperative confrontation: it is direct and nice. That is, the integrative strategy provides a generally agreeable and active approach to conflict. It follows from a desire to solve problems and to seek mutually acceptable solutions. Key to this strategy are tactics such as these:

1 Seeking and disclosing information
2 Making supportive comments and listening in a supportive manner
3 Mutually defining the problem
4 Seeking areas of commonality and agreement
5 Negotiating fair solutions

The integrative approach to conflict seeks to identify shared goals and promote the interests of both parties. The assumption is that there are creative solutions in which each person can be satisfied with the outcome. Some authors argue that compromise, in which conflict parties "split the difference," is not integrative, because both parties give up something to obtain what they desire (Filley, 1975). However, compromise can be considered integrative when goals are truly incompatible and collaboration fails to yield a mutually acceptable solution. Compromise also ensures equity when there is insufficient time to explore more creative alternatives.

The distributive conflict strategy is another active approach to conflict, but compared to the integrative strategy, it is at the opposite end of the agreeableness continuum. Distributive behavior is usually competitive, stemming from an attitude that one can gain or win only at the expense of another person. In belligerent forms of distribution, people don't care enough even to consider how a particular message might affect the other person. Regardless of its intensity, distributive conflict focuses on the individual rather than on the partner's or mutual needs. The distributive strategy includes tactics such as the following:

1 Threats, demands, and prescriptions
2 Coercion, hostility, and intimidation
3 Personal criticisms, put-downs, and ridicule
4 Defensiveness and hit-and-run tactics
5 Sarcasm and contempt

The avoidance conflict strategy is low in the activeness dimension, in contrast to integrative and distributive strategies. In fact, the objective in using avoidance might be to keep tensions buried. Still, avoidance can be either cooperative or competitive (Fitzpatrick, Fallis & Vance, 1982). That is, avoidance can be relatively agreeable or disagreeable, depending on the context and the manner in which it is performed. Some tactics of avoidance include (Canary, Cupach & Messman, 1995):

1 Withholding a complaint when confrontation is deemed to be too costly
2 Making irrelevant remarks to divert interaction from conflict to a non-threatening topic
3 Acquiescing to the requests or demands of another
4 Verbally denying that there is a conflict
5 Withdrawing from the interaction (for example, leaving the room)
6 Not voicing complaints for fear of retaliation (the "chilling effect")
(Cloven & Roloff, 1993)

Communicating Conflict Orientations Nonverbally

Competence at managing conflict requires the appropriate and effective use not only of verbal strategies and tactics, but also of nonverbal communication. How we communicate nonverbally can radically affect our relationships with others (Gottman, 1979). As with verbal strategies, nonverbal behaviors used during conflict reveal people's orientations toward each other in terms of their positive versus negative affect as well as their level of involvement (Sillars et al., 1982).

Communicating Positive versus Negative Affect   Nonverbal behaviors convey a sense of our evaluation of the conflict and the partner. Interaction partners are often quite sensitive to nonverbal cues during conflict. As you

might imagine, positive and negative affect can be expressed thr(
nonverbal messages. Here we highlight some of the more imp........

First, as you might expect, people respond negatively to their partners' negative evaluations of them. No one likes to be treated with spite or malice. According to Gottman (1994), two such messages convey disgust and contempt.
People convey *disgust* by making a face to indicate their illness at the partner
or the partner's behavior (as if to say, "You make me sick!"). The two most
common nonverbal indicators of disgust are wrinkling the nose (as if you smell
something) and raising the upper lip (that is, wrinkling the nose at the same
time as showing one's teeth) (Gottman, 1994). *Contempt* is conveyed by
rolling the eyes (as if to say, "What an idiot!") and by using the dimpler muscle (that is, moving one side of your mouth laterally, as if to say, "I doubt that").

Anger refers to the negative feelings we have from being frustrated by
someone who has committed an objectionable action (Clore et al., 1993; see
Chapter 5). Through their nonverbal behaviors, people communicate anger
both intentionally and unintentionally. People can show their anger intentionally by raising their voices, drawing closer to the partner in an intimidating
manner, and clenching their fists. People can also show anger without intend-
ing to—with a flushed face, clenched teeth, and (more among women than
men) tears (Cupach & Canary, 1995; Russell & Fehr, 1994). In addition, some
people feel overwhelmed by their own anger and thus retreat from it and try
to suppress it. Anger is a natural response to one's environment, and the appropriate expression of anger (for example, increased involvement) can lead
to positive outcomes (see Chapter 6). That is, if one can communicate one's
frustration without showing malice, anger can work to the benefit of both parties (Gottman & Krokoff, 1989). For example, increased volume and rate of
speaking indicate involvement and intensity, but these nonverbal behaviors do
not have to be used in a threatening manner.

Sillars and colleagues (1982) examined the extent to which integrative,
distributive, and avoidance conflict strategies corresponded with various nonverbal behaviors. Some of the more relevant findings include the following:

1 Speech productivity (the length of talking, number of words used, and
so on) was positively correlated with an integrative orientation but negatively
associated with an avoidance orientation.

2 Adaptors (fixing one's hair, fidgeting, and so on) were positively linked
to avoidance but negatively associated with integrative behaviors.

3 Eye glances (looking quickly at the partner and then elsewhere) were
positively associated with avoidance but negatively linked to integrative orientations. Conversely, eye gazes (focusing on the partner) were positively associated with integrative behaviors and negatively associated with avoidance
and distributive behaviors.

4 Speech rate (the speed at which one speaks) was correlated much more
positively to distributive tactics than to integrative tactics.

5 Response time was negatively correlated with integrative behavior, indicating that people with a cooperative orientation did not hesitate to exchange messages with each other.

These findings suggest that people convey an integrative approach nonverbally by focusing on the partner, speaking for longer periods of time, and not engaging in adaptors. Avoidance was linked to a lack of productivity and eye gaze, but was indicated in adaptors. Distributive tactics were associated with a higher speech rate but less productivity, indicating that some negative responses involve one-line "zingers" that are used in a "hit-and-run" fashion (Sillars et al., 1982).

Communicating Involvement   Nonverbal messages indicate emotional involvement in conflict. Newton and Burgoon (1990a) examined how people's nonverbal communication corresponds to their verbal messages during conflict interaction. These researchers examined how each of seventeen nonverbal behaviors correlated with verbal strategies and reported three major findings:

1 More active, intense, and involving nonverbal behaviors were linked to the distributive tactics of invalidating the other person, accusing the other, and asserting oneself. Such nonverbal behaviors included using animated gestures, shaking one's head, speaking in a loud or sharp voice, speaking quickly, and being fluent.

2 Content validation verbal tactics (or focusing on the content more than on the person) were associated with less active nonverbal behaviors. That is, content validation was accompanied by the nonverbal behaviors of being calm and relaxed, speaking in a mellow and slow voice, and using a lower and deeper pitch (versus the higher pitch one uses when excited).

3 Supporting the partner was associated with active nonverbal messages that indicated a genuine concern for the partner's experience. Such nonverbal behaviors included facing the other person directly, being facially expressive and animated, and showing one's involvement both physically and vocally (through use of back channels, for example).

Examining nonverbal responses as a reflection of positivity versus negativity and of involvement can lead to some interesting analyses. Newton and Burgoon (1990a), for example, found that showing cooperation and involvement was positively associated with assessments of being satisfied with the conflict and with the relationship. Some nonverbal behaviors exhibited during conflict reveal incompetence. For example, *whining* represents a negative but involved nonverbal response to conflict. As Gottman summarized, "Whining is heard as a high-pitched, fluid fluctuation of the voice, generally with one syllable stressed toward the end of the sentence. It reflects dissatisfaction in a very childish way. It often is characterized by a 'thin edge' to the voice and an irritating nasal quality" (1994, p. 27). Similarly, the tactic of *stonewalling,* or refusing to discuss the issue, is clearly communicated nonverbally. Stonewalling is conveyed by negative and uninvolved nonverbal behaviors such as inattentiveness or blank staring, crossed arms, and flat intonation when one does respond ("If you say so," said without intonation).

Nonverbal messages operate in communication generally (Burgoon, Buller & Woodall, 1989). In conflict interaction specifically, nonverbal behaviors combine with verbal communication strategies to reflect a person's orientation toward the conflict and the other party. As a rule, nonverbal messages that reflect involved and positive, or cooperative, orientations appear more

---

BOX 3-3

NEGATIVE AFFECT SAYS "INTERPRET THIS THE OPPOSITE WAY!"

Statements said with negative affect can mean the opposite of what they literally say (Gottman, 1979). For example, agreement said with negative affect typically indicates disagreement; a compliment said with negative affect can reveal ridicule; and mind reading—that is, indicating what you believe is on your partner's mind—with negative affect is often personal criticism.

Consider the following dialogue between a mother (Debby) and her teenage daughter (Megan). First imagine that positive or neutral nonverbals are used with each italicized word. Then imagine that the italicized words are expressed with negative emotion.

Debby: Megan, I'm going to the store. Do you need anything?

Megan: Yes, I *need* some new ballet slippers.

Debby: But I didn't *plan* to go to the dance studio—I said I was going to the *store.*

Megan: I *know,* but I thought you could *drive* by the dance studio on your way back.

Debby: Oh sure, I can do that. *Do you need anything else?*

Megan: If you're *sure* it wouldn't be too much trouble—I could *use* some nylons.

Debby: Megan, you *always* seem to be needing nylons. *How many pair have you bought in the past week alone?*

Megan: A couple, I guess. Well, *can you get them for me or not?*

Debby: If you promise to do something for me.

Megan: What is it?

Debby: Clean the dishes. *You did such a good job last time that I would appreciate your doing them again tonight!*

Megan: Yeah, *OK, no problem! I have plenty of time before dance class tonight!*

competent than do nonverbal messages that reveal an uninvolved and negative, or competitive, orientation.

Conflict Styles

Have you ever known someone who consistently seems to try to avoid conflict? Or do you know someone who always seems to try to strike a compromise and bargain for a fair middle ground? A general tendency to perform
certain behaviors repeatedly in different situations is referred to as a person's
communicative *style* (Conrad, 1991; Sternberg & Soriano, 1984; Sternberg &
Dobson, 1987).

Conflict styles reflect people's proclivity for using similar conflict tactics
in different contexts or with different people. For example, you may have a
characteristic style for how you handle conflict with coworkers and you may
show a similar and consistent style of handling conflict with your roommate.
Our conflict styles represent our habitual inclinations for handling disagreements; we use them without much thought.

A more cognitive view of conflict styles is based on the idea that your
method for handling conflict reflects two dimensions: (1) the extent to which
you wish to satisfy your own goals and (2) the extent to which you are willing to satisfy the other person's goals (Blake & Mouton, 1964, 1970; Kilmann
& Thomas, 1977; Rahim, 1983). Crossing these two dimensions results in five
different conflict styles, as depicted in Figure 3-1. Several researchers have

FIGURE 3-1
STYLES OF MANAGING INTERPERSONAL CONFLICT.
(Adapted from Hocker & Wilmot [1985] and Rahim [1983].)

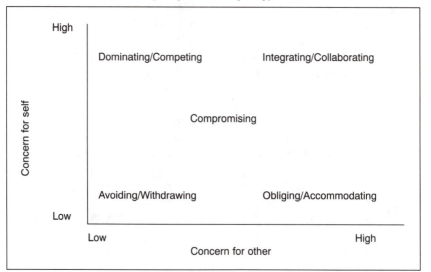

relied on this approach to defining conflict styles, although the labels for the styles differ from one author to another. The terms used here are drawn from Rahim (1983), who has constructed a self-report instrument to measure people's conflict style in the workplace. His measure has been successfully used in more informal contexts as well (Hammock et al., 1990; Utley, Richardson & Pilkington, 1989). The five styles are as follows:

1 *Integrating* (which is similar to the integration strategy discussed earlier) shows a high concern for both your own goals and the other person's goals. This style includes problem-solving communication, a desire to collaborate, and attempts at open exchange of relevant information.

2 *Avoiding* reflects of a low level of concern with both your own goals and the other person's goals. Conflict avoiders tend to withhold complaints, avert open discussion of conflictual issues, and withdraw from interactions involving conflict. Since avoidance is a passive approach to disagreements, it can be cooperative insofar as it permits the other person to get what they want. Avoidance can be competitive when it frustrates the other person's attempt to achieve goals.

3 *Dominating* is similar to the distributive strategy we identified previously. This style shows a high level of concern for one's own goals and a low level of concern for the other's goals and reflects competitive and power-oriented thoughts.

4 *Obliging* reflects a low level of concern for your own goals and a high level of concern for the other's goals. This style involves minimizing conflict by accommodating the needs of the other person and giving in to their wishes.

5 *Compromising* shows moderate and roughly equal concern for your own goals and the other person's goals. This style involves attempts to negotiate, to give and take, and to seek a middle ground.

These styles are related to the conflict strategies we discussed previously. Integrating and compromising styles are similar to the integrative strategy, although pushing for premature compromise could be considered a distributive strategy. Avoiding and obliging styles are similar to the avoidance strategy, and the dominating style resembles the distributive strategy. The difference is simply that a conflict strategy represents a general approach within a particular episode of conflict, whereas conflict style depicts tendencies and preferences for handling all conflict.

Although we all have preferable ways of managing our disagreements, we do not always behave accordingly. A supervisor, for example, may usually show an integrating style when managing conflict with subordinates. When faced with a specific instance of a noncompliant or belligerent subordinate, however, the supervisor may shift to a more coercive, distributive strategy (Conrad, 1991).

PATTERNS OF CONFLICT INTERACTION

Patterns of conflict behavior between partners offer insight above and beyond summary descriptions of each individual's behavior. Although examining the tactics of each individual is informative, observing patterns is useful for understanding the relationship between conflict participants. Parties to conflict influence one another's behavior, and this influence can be seen in conflict patterns.

Reciprocity

One of the most common conflict patterns is *reciprocity*. In a reciprocal pattern, one person's behavior mirrors the behavior exhibited by the other person; that is, a particular tactic by one person begets a similar tactic by the other person. If someone teases you, you tease back. You give someone a compliment, and it is met with a compliment that matches yours. Your insulting remark draws an insult from the insulted person. One partner's complaint results in the other partner's countercomplaint, as in this example:

Wife: Why must you make so much noise while I'm trying to talk on the phone?!

Husband: Well, if you didn't call someone every time I am just about ready to put dinner on the table, maybe I would be more considerate!

Reciprocal patterns of behavior are quite common in everyday interaction. They are heightened during episodes of conflict (Alberts, 1988; Pike & Sillars, 1985; Ting-Toomey, 1983a). Table 3-1 presents some of the common reciprocal patterns that have been detected by researchers.

As Table 3-1 shows, reciprocated behaviors can be either positive or negative. Conflicts escalate in intensity as chains of reciprocated negative behaviors build (Alberts & Driscoll, 1992; Ting-Toomey, 1983a) and negative feelings intensify. The participants feel more and more threatened and consequently respond with greater and greater defensiveness. The accumulating negative feelings are further inflamed by a tit-for-tat pattern in which each negative act stimulates a more negative response, which in turn increases the negativity of the response to the response, resulting in an ever-intensifying escalatory spiral. In short, reciprocation incites reciprocation.

Complementarity

Complementarity is the degree to which one person's communicative response relies on the partner's. Unlike reciprocity, however, complementarity reflects a pattern in which one response connects to a logically opposite type of response. For example, a confrontational remark followed by a conciliatory comment is a complementary pattern. One of the most common

TABLE 3-1
COMMON RECIPROCATION SEQUENCES

Pattern	Example
Negative reciprocation patterns	
Complaint-countercomplaint	*A:* Do you mind not smacking your food so loudly? *B:* Do you mind not being such a grouch all the time?
Proposal-counterproposal	*A:* Let's go to my family's for the holidays this year. *B:* Let's go to Florida and send everybody a card instead.
Disagreement-disagreement	*A:* I think Clinton has done a great job, given the Congress. *B:* No way! He's a coward and a liar! *A:* Yeah way! He did more in one year than Reagan and Bush did in twelve. *B:* No way! *A:* Yeah way! *B:* No.
Defensiveness-defensiveness (indifference)	*A:* I don't care what you think—this is my decision. *B:* I really don't care either.
Attack-counterattack (showing contempt)	*A:* You make me sick the way you kiss up to your sister like that. You look downright measly! *B:* Yeah, well that's some talk coming from the biggest kiss-ass of all time!
Metacommunication-metacommunication (said with negative feelings)	*A:* How can I talk when you won't listen? *B:* How can I listen when you won't talk?
Positive reciprocation patterns	
Validation (argument exchanges)	*A:* I think that we should not save any more money until the credit cards are paid off. It makes little sense to save at 10 percent when we owe at 15 percent. *B:* I agree with your point in general. I just want to have some more money in the bank for emergency situations.
Validation (contracting)	*A:* Let's go to my family's for the holidays this year. *B:* OK, I can do that, if you agree that we can go to Florida next year.
Convergence (joint arguments)	*A:* I think Clinton has done a great job, given the Congress he's had to work with. *B:* The New Right certainly has a different agenda from Clinton's. *A:* He accomplished more in two years than Reagan and Bush combined. *B:* He certainly has worked hard.

Continued

TABLE 3-1 (Continued)
COMMON RECIPROCATION SEQUENCES

Pattern	Example
Supportiveness-supportiveness	*A:* I want to have this baby, though I respect your wishes in the matter too. *B:* I appreciate that, and you should know that I respect what you want, whatever that is.
Cajoling	*A:* Ah, come on—admit it! You were flirting with her! *B:* I'll admit I was flirting if you admit you were flirting with her too! *(Both laugh.)*
Metacommunication-metacommunication (said with positive feelings)	*A:* I can't talk with you while you play that instrument. *B:* I know, it's hard to talk when someone seems distracted.

Sources: Adapted from Alberts (1988), Alexander (1973), Canary, Weger & Stafford (1991), Fitzpatrick (1988b), Gottman (1982), and Ting-Toomey (1983a).

complementary patterns in conflict interactions is the *demand-withdrawal* sequence (sometimes called the pursuit-retreat pattern). It goes something like this:

Wife: You haven't spoken two words since you got home. What's wrong?
Husband: Nothin'.
Wife: C'mon. I can read you like a book. I know when you're miffed about something. What is it?
Husband: I told you, nothing.
Wife: Are you mad that I invited the Parkers over for dinner without checking with you first? You told me the other day that we should try to do something with them this week.
Husband: No. I *told* you, nothing is *wrong*! *(Starts to read the newspaper.)*

As this above example illustrates, in the demand-withdrawal pattern, one person confronts a conflict issue while the other person avoids it.

Just as with negative reciprocal disagreements, extensive demand-withdraw patterns escalate the intensity of conflict and typically result in an unpleasant stalemate. Other common negative complementary patterns include *attack-defend* (one person's attack is met with self-defensive statements), *mind reading–disagreement* (one person's interpretation of the other's mood or motive is met with disagreement), and *control-obedience* (one person's unreasonable demands are met with immediate acquiescence).

BEWARE
OF
VICIOUS
CIRCLE

GKRRKK

Jennifer Berman

(Copyright© 1990 by
Jennifer Berman. Used by
permission of Jennifer Berman.)

Topical Continuity

Sillars and Wilmot (1994) contend that *topical continuity*—that is, the number of different issues raised during a conflict episode—constitutes an important feature of the structure of conflict interactions. Conflicts are sometimes simple in their topical structure; a single, specific issue of disagreement clearly dominates discussion. Often, however, conflicts expand to include multiple topics, and the issues of disagreement become complex and interrelated.

The discussion of substantive issues often reveals more general relational issues, which themselves become part of the conflict. If Taylor forgets to pick up her friend Lauren from work, as promised, the ensuing conflict discussion may overtly concern Taylor's "irresponsible" behavior. Beneath the surface, however, Lauren may be concerned about what Taylor's behavior means in terms of their friendship. Does it demonstrate a lack of respect for Lauren? Is it a sign that Taylor does not value the friendship? Does Taylor's behavior imply that the relationship is not fair and equitable?

As conflicts become more serious, they tend to involve more and more issues. For example, with greater levels of intensity and the corresponding defensiveness, people tend to introduce more complaints and reciprocations of them. Accordingly, people can become distracted by the introduction of a large number of issues, and they tend to drift from topic to topic, not resolving much of anything.

Intense and repeated conflict, however, often involves fundamental relational issues, even if they are not explicitly part of the conflict discussion. Hence, though some people might discuss many topics when the conflict escalates, other people might fixate on particular problems that are believed to be the "one" or "main" issue left unresolved (Sillars & Wilmot, 1994). For example, one might see all conflicts stemming from a transgression that occurred long ago, or from a lack of consideration, or from a lack of true affection. We discuss how conflict parties frame their particular conflict issues more in Chapter 5, when we discuss proximal effects on conflict behavior. The point here is that conflict tactics vary, and both jumping from topic to topic *and* reverting back to one topic do not appear to be competent ways of managing conflict.

Reacting to Negative Conflict Patterns

Accommodation can nullify negative escalating conflict. Rusbult and her colleagues define accommodation as "an individual's willingness, when a partner has engaged in a potentially destructive behavior, to (a) inhibit tendencies to react destructively in turn and (b) instead engage in constructive actions" (1991, p. 53). Recall that destructive actions are negative behaviors that undermine interpersonal relationships; constructive behaviors promote and maintain interpersonal relationships. Thus, accommodation helps break a chain of reciprocated negative behaviors. As we will discuss in Chapter 6, the willingness and ability to avoid or at least to counteract negative reciprocity is important in producing positive personal and relational outcomes.

Related to the idea of accommodation is the concept of *message variety* (Sillars & Wilmot, 1994). Patterns of conflict behavior show relatively more or less diversity in the structure of communication behaviors. Lockstep, highly reciprocal, highly predictable patterns of interaction tend to be constraining. As conflicts escalate in intensity, patterns tend to become more rigid, repetitive, and predictable.

Rigidity can perpetuate unproductive sequences of talk that fail to manage disagreement. On the other hand, flexibility in communication patterns affords the opportunity to counteract escalation and to compensate for accumulated negative actions and feelings. Research shows that satisfied married couples engage in negative acts, similar to their dissatisfied counterparts. However, satisfied couples (versus dissatisfied couples) stop negative cycles of interaction once they begin, allowing for constructive management of differences (Burman, Margolin & John, 1993; Gottman, 1994). We will elaborate on this and other factors associated with different conflict tactics and patterns in Chapter 4.

SUMMARY

Interpersonal conflicts are recognized, experienced, expressed, and ultimately managed through communication. Thus, understanding conflict messages becomes essential for understanding the processes and outcomes of conflict.

Conflict messages pertain more or less to sources of disagreement between people. Perhaps the most common source of disagreement is incompatible behavior. Unfair demands, rebuffs, insults, criticisms, and offensive or annoying behaviors are inevitable in human interaction, and they frequently instigate conflict (Peterson, 1983; Witteman, 1992). Just as common are disagreements about how shared relationships are to be defined. These conflicts revolve around such issues as who has more power, what level of intimacy is appropriate for the relationship, and what the privileges and obligations of each partner in a relationship are.

Conflict interactions are made up of many conflict tactics, the most fundamental unit of behavior. A conflict tactic is one message behavior by one person at one moment in time. Conflict tactics can be characterized and differentiated from one another according to two dimensions: (1) how relatively disagreeable the behavior is judged to be, and (2) how relatively active or passive the behavior is.

During an episode of conflict, tactics can be combined to represent one of three strategic orientations: integrative, distributive, or avoidant. General predispositions to behave in certain ways across episodes of conflict are represented by conflict styles.

Patterns of conflict interaction depict the mutual influence exerted by conflict participants. Reciprocity and complementarity patterns are the most common types observed. Extended chains of reciprocated negative behaviors and complementary patterns of demand-withdrawal typically are associated with conflict escalation. As we'll see in Chapter 6, they are also associated in a negative manner with relational satisfaction.

DISCUSSION QUESTIONS

1 Describe an instance in which you intentionally used the strategy of conflict avoidance. What did you do to avoid conflict? Why did you use the avoidance strategy? Do you think you were successful? Why or why not? Do you think the other person knew you were avoiding conflict? In general, when is the strategy of conflict avoidance desirable? What are the drawbacks of this strategy? When do you think you should avoid using an avoidance strategy?

2 If someone uses the avoidance strategy on you, how can you effectively confront them? How do you know for sure that they are avoiding you?

3 You might have gathered that using an integrative strategy should always be preferred over a distributive strategy. Can you think of instances in which a distributive strategy would be preferred over an integrative one?

4 Do you have a predominant conflict style? What is it? Why do you suppose you have that particular style? What do you think is good about that style? What are its drawbacks?

5 What style of conflict exhibited by other people gives you the most difficulty (that is, is most frustrating or annoying for you)? Why?

6 Examine Table 3-1. Can you think of other reciprocated patterns of negative or positive conflict behaviors?

7 Research indicates that women often confront men, and that men withdraw in the face of women who are confronting them. The exception to this rule occurs when the issue under discussion is the man's concern (that is, something the man wants the woman to change). How do you explain these findings? Do these run contrary to your understanding that men are supposed to be more assertive? If so, why?

4

BACKGROUND INFLUENCES ON INTERPERSONAL CONFLICT

CHAPTER OUTLINE

DISTAL INDIVIDUAL FACTORS THAT AFFECT
CONFLICT INTERACTION
    Argumentativeness
    The Tendency to Take Conflict Personally
    Locus of Control
    Sex and Gender Differences in Managing Conflict
DISTAL RELATIONAL FACTORS THAT AFFECT
CONFLICT INTERACTION
    Relational Development
    Relational Types: Blueprints for Close Relationships
    Dimensions of Developed Relationships
SUMMARY
DISCUSSION QUESTIONS

Students are often asked to discuss how they would behave in hypothetical interactions. Almost always, an astute student will note that how he or she might behave depends on the situation. Of course, this student is right. We don't behave the same way in all situations, and we adjust our responses to meet the behavioral requirements of the situation. In this chapter and the next, we present specific situational factors that affect how people respond in various conflict interactions.

Recall from Chapter 2 that distal factors contextualize conflict by referring to the background setting of the interaction episode. Many distal factors exist in conflict. In this chapter we discuss issues dealing with individual and relational distal factors. (Chapters 7 and 8 focus on intercultural and organizational issues.) *Individual* factors are salient predispositions that people have toward managing conflict, including differences due to sex. *Relational* factors include the character of the relationship (for example, the level of satisfaction and trust), relational development, and the type of relationship and its accompanying expectations. The particular factors that we discuss have been selected on the basis of research literature on the topic.

DISTAL INDIVIDUAL FACTORS THAT AFFECT CONFLICT INTERACTION

Some people seem to look for interpersonal trouble, or at least they don't go far out of their way to avoid it. Other people avoid conflict at all costs. In this section, we explore four salient individual factors that affect conflict interaction: argumentativeness, the tendency to take conflict personally, locus of control, and sex and gender differences.

Argumentativeness

Infante and Rancer (1982) defined *argumentativeness* as "a generally stable trait which prediposes the individual in communication situations to advocate positions on controversial issues and to attack verbally the positions which other people take on these issues" (1982, p. 72). There are two important features of this definition. First, argumentativeness refers to a predisposition to behave, not to actual behavior. Some people are more inclined than others to engage in verbal debate on controversial issues. Second, argumentativeness does not refer to attacks on a person's character. According to Infante and Wigley (1986), attacks on a person's character and sense of self-worth describe *aggressive* communication.

Research by Infante and colleagues (Infante et al., 1984; Infante & Wigley, 1986) suggests that highly argumentative people are seen as very competent at managing conflict situations, simply because they focus on the ideas under dispute and not on the flaws of the other person. In fact, this research provided evidence for a "skill deficiency model" of aggression, by showing that people who do not have the skill to engage others in analysis of ideas are more likely to resort to personal harm than do those who possess a proclivity for arguing ideas (Infante, Chandler & Rudd, 1989).

For example, Infante and colleagues (1984) had students with different levels of argumentativeness rate the extent to which they would use four different aggressive messages on a roommate who was thought to be either accommodating or obstinate (that is, would give in to a reasonable request or not). As predicted, highly argumentative people indicated that aggressive messages were unacceptable in either condition; people with moderate to low argumentativeness indicated increased preference for aggressive behaviors when the roommate was seen as obstinate. Apparently, the highly argumentative person's focus on ideas preempts a desire to resort to personal attacks.

Highly aggressive individuals, on the other hand, would readily attack the other person. For example, one study found that highly aggressive people are distinguished by the following behaviors: using verbal aggression to appear "tough," engaging in rational discussions that degenerate into fights, wanting to be mean to the partner (for whatever reason), and holding disdain for the partner (Infante et al., 1992). Infante and colleagues (1992) found that highly aggressive people were more likely than less aggressive people to attack the competence of the partner, attack the partner's personal background, attack the partner's physical appearance, tease the partner, ridicule the partner, swear at the partner, and nonverbally degrade the partner.

Why might people engage in aggressive behaviors rather than argument? Infante and Wigley offer four reasons that explain aggression:

1 *Frustration:* You see your goal as being deliberately blocked by the other person.

2 *Social learning:* You model the behavior of those who raised you or those who you admire.

3 *Psychopathology:* The person you are attacking represents in some way an unresolved pain or fear.

4 *Skill deficiency:* You lack the ability to communicate in an appropriate and effective manner.

Infante and colleagues have shown that a predisposition to argue about ideas is negatively associated with the use of aggressive behavior. Our goal throughout this book is to point out the productive ways to manage conflict, so that you see that you can manage conflict without attacking the other person maliciously.

The Tendency to Take Conflict Personally

The tendency to take conflict personally is the tendency of an individual to associate interpersonal conflicts with a negative emotional climate. Hample and Dallinger describe the person who takes conflict personally as feeling "threatened, anxious, damaged, devalued, insulted. . . ." "Face becomes an issue which overwhelms the substantive grounds of conflict. Self-defense is the first priority, and this leads to impulses to fight or flight, for competition or withdrawal" (1995, p. 306). Taking conflict personally leads to feeling pressured, to seeing conflict as competitive and as having a winner and a loser, and to becoming defensive in attitude and behavior.

Hample and Dallinger developed an instrument to measure the tendency to take conflict personally. Their work shows six specific aspects of this tendency:

1 Directly personalizing conflict, feeling hurt by it
2 Feeling persecuted
3 Experiencing a high degree of stress

4 Not believing that conflict can produce positive relational outcomes
5 Believing that conflict can lead to unfavorable relational outcomes
6 Disliking conflict interaction

Research by Hample and Dallinger (1995) found that the dimensions of the tendency to take conflict personally are associated with approaching or avoiding conflict in expected ways. Those who reported high scores on direct personalization of conflict, stress, and perceiving negative relational effects, also reported that they tended to avoid arguments. Those who reported that conflict produces positive relational consequences and who liked conflict tended to approach arguments with others. The tendency to take conflict personally and argumentativeness are similar concepts. Indeed, they may be two sides of the same coin. Argumentativeness represents your intention to approach or avoid argumentative situations; taking conflict personally reflects your emotional reaction to engaging in an argument.

Locus of Control

Locus of control is the expectation that you have for yourself to achieve certain outcomes (Lefcourt, 1982). For example, whether or not you do well in a class can be seen as the result of your own ability (for example, you have the intelligence required) and effort (for example, your grade depends on how much you study), or as the result of chance (for example, you guess correctly on exams) and whether the teacher rewards you (for example, the teacher is fair, is a "soft" grader).

An *internal* locus of control is the belief that your outcomes—both successes and failures—result from your own ability and effort. Accordingly, you see the "A" on the test and think, "Yes, I earned that one!" We refer to such people as "internals." An *external* locus of control is the belief that your outcomes are the result of chance, fate, or the actions of powerful others. From an external orientation, you might see the "A" on the test and think, "Whew—I was flat-out lucky" or "It was an easy test." Such people are known as "externals." People who vary in their control orientations—for example, they see their success as due to internal factors ("I earned that A") and their failures as arising from external factors ("That test wasn't fair")—are called "defensive externals."

As scholars have noted, people vary in their locus-of-control orientations depending on the domain of behavior (Brenders, 1987; Lefcourt, 1982). You might have an internal locus of control for making friends, for your own health, and for solving problems. At the same time you might have an external locus of control concerning political decisions (for example, who is elected president), economics (for example, balancing the budget), and your own personal achievements (for example, getting excellent grades).

Research has shown that locus of control specific to the domain of interpersonal relations affects how people manage conflict and solve their relational problems in general. For example, Miller and colleagues (1986) found that having an internal locus of control regarding marriage problems correlates positively with productive and positive discussion of problems. Those with an internal locus of control appear to try harder to succeed, using the problem-solving tools at their disposal. On the other hand, those with an external control orientation appear to give up easily and withdraw from the conversation or rely on forceful tactics to coerce the partner into complying (Goodstadt & Hjelle, 1973).

Canary, Cunningham, and Cody (1988) found that people have different locus-of-control orientations regarding conflict itself, as measured by the conflict locus of control (CLOC) scale. Consistent with previous research were the findings that internal CLOCs relied more on integrative, cooperative messages, whereas external CLOCs reported using more distributive, competitive messages and avoidance messages (see Chapter 3). Table 4-1 shows how conflict locus of control refers to both internal and external orientations. Items that represent both success and failure at obtaining favorable outcomes from conflict are presented as examples. As you examine Table 4-1, ask yourself whether you agree more with the internality items or the externality items. Our hope is that you balance external control orientations with internal control orientations, so that you can make a positive difference in the way you manage conflict. People who believe that they can control the outcomes of their conflicts tend to work harder to produce productive outcomes.

Sex and Gender Differences in Managing Conflict

Much has been written about sex and gender differences in communication behavior. Sex and gender reflect primary labels we use to understand people and their social interactions. As Cross and Markus pointed out, "People are socialized to consider gender a primary piece of information about a person, and gender knowledge significantly influences most subsequent interactions and thoughts about the person" (1993, p. 56). In this book, we refer to *sex* as the biological differences between men and women (and boys and girls), and we refer to *gender* as the social-psychological-cultural meanings attached to one's sex (although we know that variations on these definitions exist). If one's sex and gender affect interaction, in what ways might they affect conflict behavior? The answer to this question is more interesting than one might imagine at first glance.

First, consider that people develop schemas for interacting with men and women. That is, people develop blueprints for appropriate and effective behaviors in different settings (Pavitt & Haight, 1985). Such blueprints depend

TABLE 4-1
CONFLICT LOCUS OF CONTROL (CLOC) ORIENTATIONS

Perceived cause of outcome	Items concerning success	Items concerning failure
	Internality*	
Effort	I can work out almost any interpersonal problem if I try hard enough.	If I don't put forth much effort, I cannot resolve conflicts with others.
Ability	I have good communication skills that help me resolve my interpersonal problems successfully.	Conflicts turn out badly because the persons having the disagreement lack the ability to work things out.
	Externality*	
Chance	If I'm lucky, my conflicts turn out to my benefit.	How poorly my interpersonal problems are resolved is often due to chance.
Powerlessness	Conflicts are resolved to my benefit only if other persons are willing to resolve them	If my thoughts are not consistent with the other person's, I fail to get what I want.

*Internality = effort + ability; externality = chance + powerlessness.
Source: Adapted from Canary, Cunningham & Cody (1988, p. 434).

on expectations tied to people's roles. For example, you have different blueprints for how a teacher should behave, how a friend should behave, how a spouse should behave. We also have blueprints for how men and women should behave. In dealing with people we don't know, we must rely on the information at our disposal. Most often, we immediately notice the person's sex, and we rely on the gender expectations we have for that person's roles (Eagly, 1987).

Much of the time, people's expectations of roles are based on stereotypes of men and women. The stereotypical man is task-oriented, activity-oriented, assertive, and emotionally strong; the stereotypical woman is kind, relationally sensitive, and emotionally expressive (Deaux & Lewis, 1984). Eagly (1987) labels these two sets of stereotypical expectations as reflecting the view that men by and large are "instrumental," whereas women are "communal." According to these stereotypes, we would expect men to behave in very assertive and dominating ways during conflict, and we would expect women to be passive and cooperative (Bradley, 1980). Indeed, in most studies that assess conflict styles (see Chapter 3), men are reflected as assertive and even aggressive and women as passive and cooperative (Berryman-Fink & Brunner, 1987; for a review, see Gayle, Preiss & Allen, 1994).

To act in ways that reinforce sex role stereotypes appears quite reasonable when there is no other information available (Geis, 1993). Thus, we are often surprised when a woman acts in a hostile manner by rushing headlong into us, or when a large man apologizes with a tone of respect for bumping into us. As one might expect, when people we don't know negatively violate our expectations for behavior based on sex role stereotypes we might be offended at their lack of appropriateness (Bradley, 1980). But do such expectations exist when other information is available—as in close relationships?

In our recent exploration of the idea that sex stereotypes are consistently found in the conflict and anger research literature regarding close relationships (Cupach & Canary, 1995), we were surprised at what we found:

1 Most of the research on sex differences in close relationships finds more *similarity* than differences when it comes to self-reported *and* observed conflict behavior. On the basis of self-reports, Kelley and associates (1978) found that men and women in conflict engaged in more similar behaviors than dissimilar behaviors. On the basis of observation, Margolin and Wampold (1981) found that husbands and wives acted in a similar manner in about 75 percent of the types of behavior analyzed.

2 Of the differences that are discussed, men and women appear to act in ways *opposite* of what one would expect on the basis of stereotypes. Women are more assertive and at times aggressive, and men are more withdrawn and passive. Both sexes are equally likely to use cooperative behavior during conflict. For example, in the Margolin and Wampold (1981) study, husbands relied more on withdrawal (by not paying attention to the spouse) and avoidance (by offering excuses), but wives were more assertive in their use of complaints and criticisms of their husbands.

Following their review of the literature and report of several studies on the topic, Schaap, Buunk, and Kerkstra concluded, "All in all we think that self-report and observational research supports the following statements. Women tend to be more emotional and show more negative affect, while men are inclined to be more rational and withdrawn" (1988, p. 236). These authors also qualified these generalizations in terms of other background factors, such as relational satisfaction. In general, the data indicated that women, relative to men, are more assertive in conflict situations that are familiar to them (Falbo & Peplau, 1980; Putnam & Wilson, 1982).

3 Women tend to pursue the conflict topic, and men tend to withdraw. But these tendencies depend on the amount of equity in the relationship. The person who wants the relationship to change will confront the partner; the person who does not want the relationship to change will withdraw, regardless of sex. As Heavey, Layne, and Christensen point out, "It is reasonable to assume that the person who wants the change will express more negative affect simply in the process of elaborating their dissatisfaction" (1993, p. 26).

BOX 4-1

GENDER ROLES IN CONFLICT: A CASE STUDY

Tammy was a slight woman. Because she had been raised in the deep south, the lilting tone that lingered on her vowels made her speech sound different from "Yankee" talk. She was everything a southern lady should be and more.

Tom was a medium-build sailor. He had joined the merchant marines when he was twenty-one and had sailed around the world five times. He was not shy. In one of his stops in Savannah, Tom met Tammy and they began to date.

At first, everything went smoothly. Tammy was sometimes offended by Tom's crude manner, but she convinced him that she was worth changing for. After several weeks, Tom began to feel anxious whenever he and Tammy disagreed. He tried to change his manners, but they were never as polished as hers were.

Tammy: Tom, you act like a monkey on a greased stick. Please stop fidgeting.

Tom: Sorry. Pass the pepper.

Tammy: Had you listened more carefully to your mother, you would have said, "*Please* pass the pepper." What am I to do with you? (*She passes the pepper.*)

Tom: Sorry.

Tammy: What would you like to do after supper?

Tom: I don't care—whatever you want to do.

Tammy: Tom, since when do I look like a concierge at the Sheraton?

Tom: What?

Tammy: You know—"concierge"—do I look like an English teacher too?

Tom: Sorry.

Tammy: Soooo?

Tom: What?

Tammy: Sooo, what are we doing after supper—or are you feeble-minded as well?

(Tom stops eating and looks down.)

Tammy: Listen, Tom, I want you to wear the proverbial pants, but you must take control.

(Tom continues to look down. After a full minute, he decides to speak.)

Tom: Do you want any dessert?

Discussion Questions:

1 Do you find this dialogue offensive? Why or why not?
2 How does this dialogue compare with the interactions you have experienced or witnessed between men and women?

4 Women and men tend to report similar reactions to issues. For example, both women and men bristle at questions about their integrity. No one likes their self-worth questioned, especially when it comes to issues such as one's competence in a work role or role as a partner, lover, relative, or friend (Campbell & Muncer, 1987). As Frost and Averill concluded in their summary of the literature, "As far as the everyday experience of anger is concerned, men and women are far more similar than dissimilar" (1982, p. 297).

5 Women and men respond behaviorally in similar ways to anger, with one exception: Women tend to use tears more than men do as a response to anger (Frost & Averill, 1982). Men sometimes (usually mistakenly) think tears are a sign of weakness and capitulation. However, men should realize that tears probably should be taken as a sign of anger.

6 Any sex differences that have been found are largely wiped out by more immediate influences on conflict behavior. Such influences include the issue under discussion (for example, who seeks change), the partner's immediately preceding behavior (for example, whether the partner was nasty or nice), and other proximal influences. (Chapter 5 examines proximal influences in more detail.)

In order to summarize the extensive research on sex differences in conflict, we propose the following principle, which we term the "principle of ignorance":

Lacking any information besides the person's biological sex, people tend to behave in conventional, stereotypical ways with regard to managing conflict.

However, once we get to know someone better—and it may not take long— we change our blueprints for interaction, which leads to the "principle of familiarity":

In familiar situations, women and men behave opposite of what we might expect when assuming the principle of ignorance.

DISTAL RELATIONAL FACTORS THAT AFFECT CONFLICT INTERACTION

Interpersonal conflict requires two people. Accordingly, we should examine the development and nature of the relationship that emerges between two people (in addition to the individual differences we have been discussing). The remainder of this chapter focuses on relational factors that have a distal effect on conflict interaction.

Relational Development

The first relational factor that has an important distal effect on conflict is development. Two alternative senses of relational development are apparent in the research: (1) how the relationship has increased in intimacy (that is, how personal knowledge of the partner has grown), and (2) how the relationship changes over the life span.

Trajectories for Intimacy   As Braiker and Kelley (1979) noted, increases in intimacy mean increases in conflict. The reason is that closer involvements entail more interdependence, and increased interdependence requires more coordination to do things, more knowledge of the other, and more opportunities for conflict to emerge. However, "intimacy" means many things (Perlman & Fehr, 1987), and research on critical events indicates that there is more than one type of intimate relationship.

Huston and colleagues (1981) reported two studies that examined in retrospect how romantic relationships increase in intimacy, from the acquaintance stage to marriage. In both studies, these authors found three types of relationships. In *accelerated* relationships, couples became very committed to each other quickly. Within three months, on the average, these couples were more than 75 percent sure they wanted to marry. In *prolonged* relationships, on the other hand, couples refrained from commitment. These couples were less sure about each other (a 75 percent commitment to marriage took about eighteen months to two years). An important defining feature of the prolonged relationship is that the couple engages in more conflict than do other types of couples. Their lack of commitment may either lead to conflict or result from the conflict. Finally, couples in *intermediate* relationships, as the name implies, reach a high commitment stage in a period between the accelerated and prolonged types. These couples are 75 percent sure of marriage between six and nine months after the beginning of the relationship. The intermediate couples had the smoothest progression to commitment; that is, they had the lowest score on an index of turbulence (the ratio of decreases in commitment divided by the total number of significant turning points). Both intermediate and prolonged couples reported a higher level of love than did accelerated couples.

No doubt there are variations on each of these types of relationships, and you have probably experienced different relationships that varied in intensity and intimacy. This research implies that there is not just one correct way to develop a relationship and its corresponding pattern of conflict. Some relationships run smoothly and partners reach consensus early; others are roller-coaster rides that entail more conflict. These alternative developmental patterns provide a background context for how conflict should be managed.

Social Penetration   Altman and Taylor (1973) posited social penetration theory to explain how people come to know each other over time. Altman and Taylor likened increases in intimacy to peeling away different sections and layers of an onion to arrive at the core. These authors presented four stages whereby people theoretically get to know each other more intimately. In brief, the stages are as follows:

1 *Orientation:* Communication is based largely on social convention.

2 *Exploratory affect exchange:* Intimacy on a number of topics begins to increase.

3 *Affective exchange:* Intimacy increases both in intensity and in the number of topics explored.

4 *Stable exchange:* Communication is free and spontaneous, and the partner's personality core is penetrated.

According to Altman and Taylor, as a relationship progresses through these stages, communication between partners involves a greater number of topics, more unique symbols only the other person knows, greater efficiency, more spontaneous working together, more openness, and more evaluation. In other words, people in close relationships gradually obtain much information about each other. They see each other frequently and in different situations. During conflict, these observations provide information that is used to assess the seriousness of the conflict, the intensity of the partner's responses, and what is appropriate and effective communication. According to social penetration theory, then, as relationships develop, partners have more information to "use" during conflict, experience more areas for evaluating each other, and possess a wider variety of conflict tactics they can use on each other (see also Fitzpatrick & Winke, 1979).

Relational Development over the Life Span   Just as people change over their lifetimes, so does their communication behavior (Nussbaum, 1989). It is no wonder, then, that people's manner of managing conflict is affected by life-span issues. Sillars and Wilmot (1989) carefully reviewed how life-span changes affect conflict interaction. Some of the intriguing points they raise include the following.

Many younger couples interact in a way that reflects an "adaptation to the rapid pulse of family life in the early stages" (Sillars & Wilmot, 1989, p. 230). Young couples must learn how to live with each other, how to respond to declines in relational satisfaction, and how to negotiate parental roles (if they have children). Perhaps in sync with these many rapid changes, young couples engage in dynamic conflict behaviors that are confronting, analytical, and sometimes funny.

As people slide through middle age, they turn to other issues. As Sillars and Wilmot put it, "Whereas young couples struggle to achieve a comfortable balance between individual autonomy and interdependence, midlife couples are more likely to have found equilibrium, with interdependence occurring in many ways that the couple cannot articulate" (1989, p. 237). People's conflict behavior tends to reflect this sense of midlife arrival (assuming that no

BOX 4-2

FATAL ATTRACTIONS

Have you ever been "turned off" by some feature of your partner that was initially attractive to you? Was her arrogance once seen as self-worth? Was his annoying laughter once seen as cute? If so, then you are not alone, according to a study published by Diane Felmlee (1995), a sociologist at the University of California at Davis.

Fatal attractions, according to Felmlee, are those social qualities that draw us to someone but over time become repulsive. In this study, about 30 percent of the respondents reported that some initial attractions turned fatal (that is, were disliked later). Dr. Felmlee suggests three reasons for these fatal attractions:

1 We are attracted to features in other people that we do not possess, but over time the lack of similarity takes its toll. For example, you might find someone interesting because she reads so much literature. Later, however, you tire of spending all your time in the library.
2 We are attracted to features that really stand out—which may mean that the person has a particular feature in extreme. For example, you might like someone who takes a stand and is always honest about his feelings. But after a while you find this blunt honesty to be boring and dogmatic.
3 We are attracted to features that may not be conducive to a long-term association. For example, you might be attracted to someone because she is really sociable and knows how to party. After a few months you find her to be flirtatious and untrustworthy.

What are some typical fatal attractions? College students reported the following as especially deadly (Felmlee, 1995, pp. 302–303):

1 *Fun.* Yes, that's right. Being perceived as fun had some drawbacks. For example, one respondent noted that she was attracted to a man because she could have fun with him; over time, however, she saw his fun-loving nature as immaturity. In another example a woman who was attracted to a man's humor now only finds him silly.
2 *Caring.* One person cited the partner's deep interest in her as an initial attraction but later was turned off by his deep possessive nature.
3 *Competent.* Someone who is competent is seen as effective and able to achieve instrumental goals. In one example of a fatal attraction involving this characteristic, a man was attracted to a woman's intelligence and confidence, later to be turned off by her "ego."
4 *Physically attractive.* One man listed as many as ten physical features that drew him to his partner, then objected that their relationship was based primarily on physical characteristics.
5 *Exciting.* Some people's initial attraction to excitement transformed into perceptions of the partner being irresponsible or too different.
6 *Easygoing.* For example, originally you might have liked someone because he was not "anal" about time, but now you're annoyed because he's never on time for a date.
7 *Different.* Being different over the long haul bothered more people than not. Thus, expanding your horizons may not be the best reason for going out with someone.

Discussion Questions:

1 Why do fatal attractions occur, based on your experience or observation of others?
2 Are fatal attractions avoidable, or must we get to know someone before they become clear?

separation is occurring): Conflict tends to be more carefully and analytically articulated.

During later years, people report higher levels of relational satisfaction and interdependence. However, older couples' interactions are by and large constrained, especially in comparison to younger couples' interaction. During conflict, this sense of high interdependence and accommodation appears in the form of reduced confrontation and analyses of relational issues. Many older couples are quite passive in their conflict interactions, although some are case studies of "conflict habituated" types—always bickering.

Relational Types: Blueprints for Close Relationships

Recall that romantic relationships develop in different ways: accelerated, prolonged, and intermediate. Likewise, there is no single model for established relationships. According to Fitzpatrick (1988a), there are several different types of marriages, each with a preferred mode of managing conflict.

On the basis of years of research, Fitzpatrick (1988a) identified three "pure" marital types: traditionals, separates, and independents. *Traditionals* are marked by their adherence to "traditional" values (for example, the woman taking the husband's last name, the man performing the breadwinning roles, the woman cleaning the house). *Separates* (as their name implies) prefer to live in the same house but in different rooms. In other words, they are detached from each other emotionally and informationally. *Independents* seek partners who might help them achieve their own personal goals, and they do not adhere to traditional values. As Fitzpatrick and others have shown, the model one has for marriage dramatically affects the kinds of conflict that emerge.

Traditionals have conflicts, but these are reserved for important issues and entail cooperative sequences (Fitzpatrick, 1988b). This cooperation may result from mutual adoption of traditional roles. For example, there is no disagreement about who will cook and clean, because it is assumed that the woman will. Research on division of labor (Berk, 1985) verifies that traditional expectations about household performance often remain intact even if the woman works in a full-time job. Separates avoid conflict, simply because they do not want to share ideas or feelings. One study found that separates sometimes actively constrain their partners' behavior (Witteman & Fitzpatrick, 1986). However, the research suggests largely that separates prefer to avoid conflict altogether and never enter the discussion. Independents, who get miffed if the partner somehow deters them from their goals, prefer to engage the partner than to refrain from conflict (Fitzpatrick, 1988a). Fitzpatrick summarized one set of findings in the following manner:

> The Traditionals attempt to confront their conflicts with one another and do so with less negativity than do the other couples. Independents do not respond well to a

spouse's attempt to avoid discussing serious difficulties and confront them when they attempt to withdraw. At the act level, Separates show contentious behavior toward the spouse but appear to withdraw immediately from the discussion if the spouse contests their statements. (1988b, p. 250)

According to Fitzpatrick (1988a), people have different relational models, or schemas. Schemas work like blueprints, so relational schemas outline how relationships should be built. Unfortunately, people often do not realize that there are different models and thus presume that others should follow the same model that they follow. Fitzpatrick's (1988a) summary of research indicated that almost half of martial partners do *not* share in the partner's blueprint; that is, they have different models of relating. As Fitzpatrick documented, these "mixed" types have the least relational satisfaction and the most problems.

In sum, a relationship develops in two senses: (1) People develop associations by getting to know each other, and (2) these associations change over the life span. Of course, these findings are qualified by the fact that there are different kinds of relationships.

Dimensions of Developed Relationships

How would you respond if you believed that one of your friends was trying to steal your boyfriend or girlfriend? Your response would depend on the nature of the relationship, including how satisfied you are, how much you trust your friend and your partner, whether you cooperate or compete with each other, and how committed you are to each other. These features represent aspects of developed relationships. Specifically, relational satisfaction, trust, control, mutuality, and commitment provide a relational context that both defines the nature of the relationship and affects how people manage conflict.

Relational Satisfaction   Much research on marriage and the family has focused on whether conflict behavior corresponds to the extent of satisfaction couples claim. This research as a whole reflects one simple principle: Conflict both reflects and affects relational satisfaction more dramatically than does any other type of interaction.

Gottman (1994), for example, having reviewed the literature on marital satisfaction and conflict observational studies, offered two conclusions that distinguish satisfied from dissatisfied couples. First, *satisfied couples engage in more constructive conflict behavior relative to destructive conflict behavior.* Gottman reported the ratio of positive to negative conflict behavior in discussions between partners in a satisfied couple as 5:1. In other words, for each negative conflict behavior, the satisfied couple would enact five positive behaviors.

BOX 4-3

SAME NEIGHBORHOOD, DIFFERENT WORLDS: A CASE STUDY

Mark and Cleo were raised next door to each other, though you could swear they came from different countries. Like his parents, Mark was very traditional. He believed that women were the "fairer" sex who should be taken care of and who in turn should provide a warm and nurturing home. Cleo, on the other hand, was raised in a home where the mother and father both worked full-time. Cleo learned that with careful planning and hard work she could make her mark on the world.

Simply because they ran into each other often, Mark and Cleo became engaged. Mark had visions of coming home to Cleo and a hot meal. Cleo had visions of Mark's sharing equally in all the tasks they faced. They both realized they had differences but hoped that the differences would pass in time. Of course, they didn't.

After the honeymoon, Mark was displeased that Cleo remained at her job at the counseling center. It wasn't a good job; besides, she was ignoring her "real" duties at home and didn't keep regular hours. Cleo, on the other hand, was totally nonplussed by Mark, mainly for one reason: He never helped around the house. If anyone was going to have a hot meal, she would have to cook it. (Mark's involvement in cooking resided entirely in barbecuing hamburgers.) The dishes would stack up for days. Mark would watch ESPN and wonder when Cleo was going to come home. At times they had it out, and their conflicts went something like this:

Cleo: (from the kitchen) I can't get at anything in here!

Mark: (from the TV room) Why *is* the kitchen such a mess?

Cleo: Search me! When was the last time you did the dishes?

Mark: Me? Why should I do the dishes? I work long hours at work.

Cleo: Oh yeah? And *I* don't work? You really don't value my job, do you?

Mark: What? Of course I do! But how long are you going to stay there? I thought we were going to start a family.

Cleo: Well, so did I. But I can't do everything by myself. You are *so* inconsiderate!

Mark: What . . . what have I done? I do all that anyone can expect from me!

Cleo: What do you mean? You never, ever help me around here.

Mark: Now you're exaggerating—I cooked last week!

Cleo: You think that's fair?

Mark: Look, I do what I have to—and you should do the same.

After a day of sulking, one of them would clean the kitchen, make breakfast, and promise to start again "with a more positive attitude."

Discussion Questions:

1 What are the chances that Mark and Cleo will resolve this conflict to *both* parties' satisfaction?

2 Do you know people who appear to have different relationship blueprints?

In dissatisfied couple discussions, however, the ratio is 1:1; for every negative statement only one positive statement is offered. According to Gottman, satisfied couples more effectively balance their conflict interactions. For example, Noller and colleagues (1994) found that satisfied couples were much less likely than dissatisfied couples to engage in coercion, manipulation, or threats.

Second, Gottman (1994) reported that *satisfied couples (in contrast to dissatisfied couples) do not reciprocate negative emotion.* In the typical satisfied relationship, when a partner said something negative, the other person would avoid exchanging the insult, complaint, or show of anger. In the typical dissatisfied relationship, couples would often engage in exchanges of negative statements that would last several turns. For example, Ting-Toomey (1983a) found that dissatisfied couples engaged in reciprocation patterns of attack-defend and attack-attack messages, whereas highly satisfied couples did not engage in these patterns when such behaviors emerged. Instead, satisfied couples reciprocated confirming or other integrative messages (see Chapter 3). In Chapter 5, we show how the partner's behavior and escalation of emotion act as immediate, proximal factors that affect behavior. For now, we want to stress that the reciprocation of negative conflict appears to reflect an unhappy relationship, and it adversely affects the relationship.

Trust   Trust is the degree to which you are willing to make yourself vulnerable to someone. Most people require that the person they trust be both benevolent and honest; that is, the person must care about your welfare and mean what he or she says (Larzelere & Huston, 1980). Research indicates that trusting a person has a distal effect on managing conflict (Canary & Cupach, 1988). We are more likely to act in a cooperative manner with those we trust than with those whose intentions we doubt or whose words have proved unreliable.

Cloven and Roloff (1993) have argued that people experience a "chilling effect" due in part to a lack of trust in the partner. People who feel powerless and who are afraid of their partner will not raise their concerns. Of course, we can imagine how withholding information from the partner would increase one's sense of powerlessness and perhaps lead to the partner's engaging in forceful behaviors. One implication of this research is that one should feel a sense of relief when one's partner feels comfortable enough to present his or her complaints—if they are presented in a cooperative manner.

Control Mutuality   According to Morton, Alexander, and Altman (1976), every "viable" relationship requires that partners agree on who has rightful influence power. If parties cannot agree who has the right to lead, whether it be one person or both persons, then the relationship lacks control mutuality. For example, if a mother and her seventeen-year-old son do not agree that the mother has the right to discipline the son (for example, to "ground" the son, to prohibit his use of the family car, or to require him to do housework), the lack of mutuality on the control issue can lead to many difficult conflicts between them (Morton, Alexander & Altman, 1976).

Kelley (1979) has argued that control issues concern both outcomes regarding goals (or what he called "fate control") and how parties go about living their daily lives ("behavioral control"). Kelley also noted that relational partners differ in their mutual fate and mutual behavioral control: Some people are very cooperative in how they define who influences whom in terms of goals and everyday actions, whereas other people are very unilateral in their controlling behaviors. In general, people dislike unilaterally defined relationships—with one partner using threat, intimidation, ridicule, and the like to get their way (Falbo & Peplau, 1980). Instead, productive conflict behavior has been positively associated with the extent that both parties agree on who has control over whom and in which areas that control may exist (Canary & Cupach, 1988).

Commitment Another relational feature relevant to conflict is commitment. Commitment is the extent to which one wants to remain in the relationship indefinitely. Commitment serves two important relationship functions. First, it protects the relationship from outside forces (Lund, 1985). Second, it motivates couples to behave in constructive ways to manage relationship problems.

Rusbult and colleagues (Rusbult, 1987; Rusbult, Johnson & Morrow, 1986; Rusbult, Drigotas & Verette, 1994) have argued that one's commitment to the relationship determines how cooperative one is in responding to relational problems. They have presented four primary responses, which are based on active-versus-passive and destructive-versus-constructive dimensions. The responses are exit, voice, loyalty, and neglect (Figure 4-1).

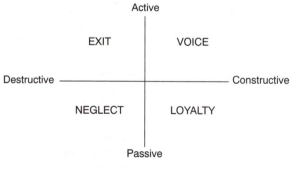

FIGURE 4-1
EXIT, VOICE, LOYALTY, AND NEGLECT RESPONSES.
(From Rusbult [1987]) Used by permission.

Exit represents an active, but destructive, tendency to hurt the relationship through such behaviors as threatening to leave the partner, shouting, and abusing the partner. *Voice* is an active, constructive response to improve the relationship by talking things out. *Loyalty* presents a passive, though constructive way to manage relational problems. Loyalty can be seen in people's willingness to wait and see in order to accommodate the partner. Finally, *neglect* behaviors—avoiding the partner, ignoring the partner, and the like— reflect a desire to see the relationship deteriorate. As Rusbult, Drigotas, and Verette (1994) summarized, commitment is *macromotive;* that is, commitment promotes the use of voice and loyalty and is negatively associated with the use of exit and neglect.

SUMMARY

In this chapter, we examined several distal influences on conflict interaction that have been explored recently in the research and provide background to how conflicts unfold. We stressed both individual and relational factors that contextualize conflict interaction.

People have different personalities, and some personal traits appear to affect conflict management behavior. Two of the more salient individual factors are the tendency of people to approach or avoid disagreements (that is, variations in argumentativeness) and the tendency of people to believe that conflict outcomes depend on their own ability and effort (or internality) *or* on chance, fate, or powerful others (or externality). Those who would rather deal with disagreement and believe they can bring about positive outcomes are more likely to enjoy positive, productive conflicts. Those who avoid arguments or who see their conflict outcomes as outside of their personal control are more likely to enact avoidance or distributive conflict behaviors, which in turn tend to bring about perceptions of incompetence and few productive outcomes (see Chapter 6).

Much has been said regarding sex differences, though the research points to more similarities than differences when one considers the factors that predict conflict behaviors. In social relationships, we can reliably predict that people behave in stereotypic fashion. However, in close, personal relationships where people have lots of information about their partner, sex roles may reverse themselves, and women often take control of discussing issues under dispute.

The development, type, and character of one's relationship also set the stage for conflict. Relationships that are characterized by high satisfaction, trust, control mutuality, commitment, and intimacy provide a rich background and appear to promote direct and cooperative conflict. As we have suggested, researchers know relatively little about how adult friends or parents and their adult children manage their conflicts. Nevertheless, we can speculate that the baseline information gained from increased intimacy would provide a distal context for understanding these conflict interactions as well.

DISCUSSION QUESTIONS

1 Have you ever known someone who was dogmatic—that is, someone who disagreed about an issue even though he or she clearly was wrong? Is it possible to be argumentative and not dogmatic?

2 Should people believe that they have control over their conflict outcomes? Why or why not? In addressing this question, offer examples of people who might blame others for the conflict and of people who tend to take responsibility for conflicts.

3 Do you think that men and women are fundamentally similar or different? Does a person's biological sex affect his or her conflict behaviors in close relationships? Do you think that people with traditional ideologies hold on to sex role stereotypes more than do those with nontraditional beliefs?

4 We have argued that satisfaction, trust, control mutuality, and commitment define the nature of the relational context. Can you think of other factors that might be just as important to how couples manage conflict? Do these characteristics apply universally to all relationship forms, including friendships and relationships with relatives?

5 Have you ever been really jealous in a relationship, or have you known of someone who has been very jealous in a particular relationship? What might explain that jealousy? Do you think if the relational features we discussed were all positive that the jealousy would disappear, or is jealousy more an individual trait?

6 What type of marriage do you imagine you might someday have—traditional, independent, separate, or mixed (a combination)? Why? Do you expect your partner to share your blueprint of marriage? Why or why not?

5

PROXIMAL INFLUENCES: SPONTANEOUS REACTIONS TO CONFLICT

CHAPTER OUTLINE

ANGER AND ANGERLIKE RESPONSES
  Anger
  Emotions Associated with Anger

INITIAL REACTIONS TO THE CONFLICT SITUATION
  Physiological Reactions
  Temporary Response Modes
  Scripts

HIGHER-ORDERED THOUGHTS
  Attributions about Causes of Conflict
  Expectations for Achieving Goals

THE DYAD AS A SYSTEM THAT AFFECTS EACH
PERSON'S BEHAVIOR
  System Properties
  System Dysfunctions

SUMMARY

DISCUSSION QUESTIONS

People are sometimes amazed by the way they respond to a conflict. Normally rational and self-controlled persons can become highly emotional perpetrators of conflict escalation, and aggressive people at times behave timidly. Such unpredictable responses cannot be adequately explained by background relational and personality factors alone. In addition, we must examine influences on behavior that come into play immediately before and during conflict. Before we begin that examination, we present two observations that guide this chapter.

First, the unexpected emergence of conflict requires immediate, spontaneous reactions. By "reactions" we mean thoughts and emotions as well as behaviors. Rarely do people plan conflicts in advance, though people may well benefit from planning to discuss problems at established times and places (Bach & Wyden, 1968). Conflict surprises people arising most frequently while individuals are involved in an activity besides talking, such as balancing the checkbook, driving through heavy traffic, or making dinner (Sillars & Weisberg, 1987). This surprise feature of conflict can compel people to feel as though they are unwitting parties or even victims of a situation thrust upon them.

Second, as Chapter 3 indicated, conflict interaction involves the behavior of both people. In other words, both parties create a *system* through their patterns of interaction. Over time, partners have a hard time interacting in ways that do not maintain the system. Accordingly, we should stress at the outset that although we focus on individual factors, two people, at least, experience these processes and jointly define, by their interaction, how the conflict episode evolves.

Discussing proximal influences on conflict helps us become more aware of the processes of conflict interaction. In this chapter we discuss several proximal factors that occur almost at the same time. (Because they are almost simultaneous, we argue no causal order among them.) First, we discuss initial emotional responses to conflict. The role of anger and associated experiences are stressed. Next, we discuss people's *modi operandi* for the initial processing of conflicts, including physiological reactions and scripts that guide the expression of anger. A discussion of higher-ordered thoughts that affect behavior, including people's attributions, expectations, and goals, follows. We conclude by discussing how relational systems constrain individuals' conflict behavior.

ANGER AND ANGERLIKE RESPONSES

Anger

Anger is a natural and fundamental coping response to negative events in one's social environment (Berkowitz, 1993). Unfortunately, people who cannot adequately express anger or who overexpress anger suffer many physical ailments (e.g., hypertension, heart disease) (Siegman, 1994) and devastating social effects (Tavris, 1984). As a rule, conflict is a negative event and often yields angerlike responses. To understand how we might respond to conflict, we need to understand how people in general experience and express anger.

Causes of Anger   Researchers have uncovered many causes of anger (Cupach & Canary, 1995), ranging from specific behaviors of others (for example, hurling insults) to the view that anger is a fundamental orientation to your world (for example, as a coping mechanism). Table 5-1 suggests some causes and subcategories of anger. In general, anger is triggered by the perception that another person frustrates you from achieving an important goal, questions an aspect of your integrity, or engages in some other reprehensible behavior.

TABLE 5-1
CAUSES OF ANGER

Cause	Sample subcategories	Examples
Identity management	Integrity threat	A classmate questions your ability to read.
	Condescension	A coworker acts superior and talks down to you.
	Insult	An acquaintance makes fun of your new dress, attributing the choice to bad genes.
	Blame/reproach	You are accused of being self-centered because you did not buy a wedding present for an acquaintance.
Aggression	Physical threat/harm	Your roommate threatens to punch you out if you don't leave the apartment.
	Sexual aggression	Someone you don't like keeps trying to seduce you.
	Verbal abuse	Your stepfather constantly intimidates you with threats, swearing, and demeaning comments.
Frustration	Goal interference	Your roommate watches TV all the time, making it hard to study.
	Expectation violation	Your daughter comes home for a short visit and never spends any time with you. Instead she visits with all her friends.
	Thwarting of plans	Someone calls you an hour before a date and cancels, without a good reason.
	Impotence	You cannot convince the video store clerk that you returned the video on time, so you must pay a fine.
Lack of fairness	Inequity	Your brother expects you to call him all the time, though he never calls you.
	Blameworthiness	Your friend gets drunk and picks a fight with your new neighbor.
	Hurt feelings	Someone has just left your best friend for another person.

Continued

TABLE 5-1 (Continued)
CAUSES OF ANGER

Cause	Sample subcategories	Examples
Incompetence due to ignorance	ncompetent others	The service station attendants cannot find out what is wrong with your car, and they've had it for a week.
	Thoughtless actions	You receive the same present from your brother that you gave him last year.
Incompetence due to egocentric motives	Self-centeredness	Your friend turns every topic to something that interests him.
	Opinionatedness	A classmate offers an opinion on every topic discussed in class.
Relationship threat	Jealousy	You are extremely jealous in a particular relationship.
	Unfaithfulness	You discover you have good reason to be jealous, since your partner admitted being unfaithful most of last year.
Predispositions	Predisposition due to experiences	Someone who was raised in an abusive home tends to display aggressive behavior.
	Predisposition due to drug dependence	A friend of yours acts edgy when he can't get a drink, and he gets aggressive when he does drink.
General learned reaction	Coping processes	An acquaintance gets angry at the slightest change of the weather.
	Response to aversion	You become angry whenever you experience negative feelings.

Source: Adapted from Canary, Spitzberg, and Semic (in press).

Types of Anger   Clore and colleagues have specified types of anger by delineating what people focus on when experiencing anger: Angerlike emotions can be separated in terms of (1) whether someone's action is blamworthy, and (2) whether the consequences of the other's action are undesirable (Clore et al., 1993). Imagine that your roommate has borrowed your car and is supposed to return it by 1 P.M., but doesn't arrive until 2 P.M. Your roommate's behavior may be irresponsible but does not cause any serious consequences. However, if you had a job interview across town at 2 P.M., then you probably would be more upset, given the negative consequences of that person's behavior (a job opportunity probably lost). Combining assessments of blameworthiness and consequences suggests some likely emtional reactions, four of which are angerlike responses: frustration, reproach, anger, and resentment (see Table 5-2). We will elaborate on this analysis briefly.

TABLE 5-2

TYPES OF ANGER AND RELATED EMOTIONS

Blameworthiness of other's actions	Outcomes for self		Outcomes for other	
	Negative	Positive	Negative	Positive
Blameworthy	"Pure" anger	Relief	Gloating	Resentment
Not blameworthy	Frustration	Joy	Pity	Pride

Source: Adapted from Clore and colleagues (1993).

First, you would feel *frustration* if you experienced a negative outcome that wasn't necessarily linked to a reproachable behavior. For example, performers sometimes become ill and can't perform, which is frustrating for ticket holders. Frustrating anger is experienced in feelings such as displeasure, sadness, and even grief.

Reproach might be your response if the action of another person was blameworthy but did not have a negative consequence for you. For example, assume that you catch a fellow classmate obviously cheating on a major exam. If the instructor does not grade on a curve, then the cheater's score will not affect yours. You may thus feel reproachment anger toward this person—that is, anger in terms of contempt, indignation, and disdain, but not personal distress.

"Pure" *anger* arises from both a negative outcome and blameworthy behavior. Restating the examples already given, if you discovered that the rock star faked an illness for publicity reasons or if your grade was lowered because of someone else's cheating (and raising the curve), you would experience pure anger; that is, you feel exasperated, offended, indignant, and perhaps outraged.

Finally, *resentment* arises when the outcomes for someone else are positive, but undeserved. For example, you might know someone who unjustly gets ahead in this world for no good reason, perhaps because of how they look or who they know. You may feel resentment anger in terms of envy or jealousy.

Categorizing anger into types helps reveal alternative responses when the outcomes for you are positive or for the other person are negative. For example, Table 5-2 indicates that if you were rewarded despite the reproachable behavior of others, you would experience *relief* (for example, you got the job even though your roommate did not return your car on time). Likewise, you might feel like *gloating* over someone who acted in a reproachable manner and who experienced a negative outcome (for example, a cheater who failed the test). And you might be *proud* of someone who obtained a positive outcome by acting in a just manner (for example, a relative who was promoted because of hard work).

Emotions Associated with Anger

People can feel anger in conjunction with other kinds of negative, aversive feelings. Berkowitz (1993) showed that people act aggressively when they experience sadness or pain. For example, in two studies women were either subjected to pain (by having a hand kept in very cold water) or not subjected to pain (by having a hand kept in room-temperature water). In one study the women were then asked to evaluate another person's ideas and to reward or punish the other person. The women whose hands were in cold water gave out fewer rewards and more punishments than the women whose hands were in room-temperature water. There was no apparent anger-provoking event—only pain. In a second study, women exposed to pain recalled more conflict interactions with their boyfriends than did those who were not exposed to pain (Berkowitz, 1993).

Why should pain and sadness bring about angerlike responses? Berkowitz (1993) observed that "any given emotional state is best regarded as an associative network in which specific types of feelings, physiological reactions, motor responses, and thoughts and memories are all interconnected" (1993, p. 9). Thus, almost any negative arousal can elicit angry responses. Environmental factors such as heat, pollution, foul odors, and cigarette smoke (Berkowitz, 1993) can cause aggression simply because negative experiences are associated with the expression of anger. Living in a polluted, crowded city during hot summer months sets the emotional stage for aggressive responses. In short, people tend to become angry more easily as their comfort level decreases and might lash out at a partner, regardless of any anger-provoking behavior on the part of the partner.

A related and important emotional predictor of how people manage conflict is *stress*. Among undergraduate students, stress has been associated with physical aggression toward one's partner (Makepeace, 1983). When people undergo pressure to meet deadlines and they are highly motivated to meet those deadlines, obstacles or distractions can trigger indifference to others' needs, as well as angerlike responses (Darley & Batson, 1973; Zillmann, 1990). Recall the roommate who returned your car late when you needed to get to a job interview. Not only would you be angry at your friend, but you would be anxious and primed for anger by the stress of running late. So, you might act in anger at other drivers in front of you who simply obey the speed limit: You might tailgate, honk your horn, and curse at them. These drivers do nothing reprehensible; they just happen to be in the way. People who chronically experience stress are handicapped in terms of meeting deadlines and in their emotional reactions to others.

Angerlike responses are not the only types of reactions to conflict. People also respond to negative experiences with *fear.* Berkowitz (1993), for example, argued that in aversive or threatening situations, people seek to escape or avoid the issue confronting them. Alternatively, people may respond to their fear in an angry manner, trying to regain control of the situation (Hocker & Wilmot, 1995). They may rely on defensive behaviors that evaluate the other, control communication, show indifference, dominate the partner, and the like (Gibb, 1961). Accordingly, people who are afraid and who choose not to use integrative behaviors may *act as if they are angry.*

BOX 5-1

PLANNING A ROMANTIC EVENING: A CASE STUDY

Jack was looking forward to Saturday evening with Jill. He was going to prepare Jill's favorite dish, Cajun chicken. He bought the groceries and planned to clean his apartment. It was going to be a romantic night.

Jill was supposed to arrive at 7 P.M., and Jack was still busy cleaning when the doorbell rang at 6:45. Jill had come early to see if Jack wanted any help.

"No, I don't want you to do anything. I'm running a bit behind though, so please have a seat and make yourself comfortable. I'll be right with you."

Jill sat in the living room and turned on the TV.

Jack finished cleaning about a half hour later and realized that he had forgotten to buy the red peppers. "Honey, I need to get something. Just keep relaxing—I'll be right back." On his way home, Jack thought to get some dessert, so he went to a bakery to get the chocolate cream pie that Jill liked so much. Jack returned a little after 8 P.M., and in need of a shower.

Jill looked at him with hungry eyes. "Are you *sure* there isn't anything I can do, like wash the vegetables?"

"No, no—*please* let me do this for you," Jack pleaded. He put away the groceries, grabbed a quick shower, and dressed. About fifteen minutes later, Jack returned to the kitchen and informed Jill that he was making Cajun chicken with "dirty" rice.

Jill was getting very hungry by now, but she remained very polite and even supportive. "Sounds great!" she said. She came into the kitchen and noticed that the chicken had a lot of fat on it. "Honey, would you mind if I trimmed the fat off the chicken?"

Jack felt the screws tighten a bit. "You don't want fat on your chicken? OK . . . fine! I'll trim the fat—you just get out of here and let me handle this!"

Discouraged, Jill returned to the living room. She could hear cupboard doors slamming and pots banging and occasional cursing. It was almost 9 P.M.

Then Jack had another setback. He had begun the vegetables too far ahead of the chicken, which he was still trimming, and the rice wouldn't be ready for another fifteen minutes. Jack threw the chicken in with the vegetables and hurriedly began setting the table. A couple minutes later, he returned to the kitchen and decided that the vegetables were getting too cooked and that everything needed to be served immediately. He called to Jill, "Dinner is served!"

Continued

BOX 5-1 (Continued)

Jill sat down at the table, though she knew that Jack hadn't cooked the chicken more than a few minutes. "Honey, this smells great. But how long did you cook the chicken?"

"Long enough," Jack replied flatly. He was still feeling frazzled and just wanted to get on with the damn dinner.

"I don't mean to complain, but you know that we can die if this isn't properly cooked," Jill informed him.

Jack replied curtly, "We won't die, I promise. Let's just eat."

Jill was not convinced. "Do you mind if I cook it a few minutes longer?"

Jack was offended. "Of course I mind! I spend all day preparing this evening for you and unless it's done *your* way you don't want any! OK . . . fine. Go ahead and finish the cooking. *I'll* go watch some TV!"

Jill was offended at the implication that she was lazy. "Look, I offered to help! I knew you were having trouble in here!"

Jack felt that his competence was being directly attacked. He retorted, "No, that's not the issue. The issue is that everything must be done *Jill*'s way or not at all!"

Jill shot back, "I wish I had a video camera! The issue is *not* things being done my way. The issue is whether the chicken is safe for us to eat! *I* don't want to die from salmonella poisoning!" Just then, the timer buzzer went off, indicating that the rice was ready.

Both Jack and Jill were disappointed; "romantic" was not a term either of them would use to describe that evening. The vegetables were soggy and the chicken was cold. Dessert would have to keep for another time.

Discussion Questions:

1 What emotions or experiences were associated with Jack's anger? With Jill's anger?

2 How might Jack or Jill have shown more grace under pressure?

Negative emotions of many forms provide a proximal context for conflict. Hence, although you may do nothing that is sufficient in and of itself to cause a conflict, your partner's negative emotional state may trigger his or her angry response (and vice versa).

INITIAL REACTIONS TO THE CONFLICT SITUATION

Physiological Reactions

One of the most intriguing features of one's immediate response to conflict is physiological reaction. Research indicates that people respond with excitation to discussions of problems. Gottman and Levenson summarized people's physiological responses in this way:

> Within the autonomic nervous system (ANS), the classic "flight-fight" . . . pattern is well known, consisting of such changes as increases in cardiac rate and cardiac contractility, sweating, deepened breathing, redirection of blood flow toward large skeletal muscles, and release of catecholamines (i.e., epinephrine and norepinephrine) from the adrenal medulla. (1988, p. 189)

In other words, when faced with a problematic situation (including stressful conflicts), your body responds to the brain's "fight" or "flee" signals to increase your energy. You experience this instinctive response by feeling your heart pounding, by sweating, and by being flushed and alert. At first you are startled (typified by a blink, a gasp, shoulders hunched); then you quickly focus on the situation as your heart pumps greater amounts of blood (Gottman, 1994).

Once people are aroused physiologically, they require time to return to a normal state—that is, for the arousal to dissipate. For most people, this takes a few minutes, or the time it would take to cool off after a workout (as the heart settles from about a hundred beats per minute to about seventy-five beats per minute) (Gottman, 1994). However, interpersonal conflicts often involve more than one point of arousal. When people exchange messages—particularly negative messages—they also exchange stimuli that prevent physiological recovery. Zillmann summarized people's physiological reactions to interpersonal conflict accordingly:

> Escalating conflict can be conceptualized as a sequence of provocations, each triggering an excitatory reaction that materializes quickly and that dissipates slowly. As a second sympathetic reaction occurs before the first has dissipated, the second reaction combines with the tail end of the first. As a third reaction occurs before the second and first reactions have dissipated, this third reaction combines with the tail ends of both earlier reactions. In general, the excitatory reaction to provocation late in the escalation process rides the tails of all earlier reactions. (1990, p. 192)

Because of this buildup of negative arousal, people experience excitation at levels that appear to be an overreaction to the initial cause of the conflict ("I don't know why you get so angry when I only want to talk with you!"). In addition, Zillmann showed that too much excitation prevents people from thinking clearly and efficiently about the issue under discussion—a state Gottman (1994) called "flooding."

During conflict men, compared to women, appear to experience more physiological flooding that takes longer to dissipate; that is, men show stronger signs of negative physiological arousal for longer periods and tend to be more aware of their body's "fight" versus "flight" orientation (Levenson, Carstensen & Gottman, 1994). Gottman (1994) explained this sex difference as stemming from the fact that men are not accustomed to exploring relational issues, since most of their childhood time involved sports and games, instead of playing house and similar relationship-oriented activities. Accordingly, men want to "flee" conflict situations because of their negative arousal, whereas women tend to ignore their physiological reactions in order to confront the relational problem. However, recall that, if they feel inequitably treated, both men and women confront their partners. The point is that people can moderate their physiological arousal with higher-ordered thoughts, an issue we explore a bit later.

Temporary Response Modes

Besides having physiological reactions, people develop initial appraisals and response modes to react to the conflict situation. *Temporary response modes* are immediate cognitive reactions that occur during the particular conflict episode and that are not necessarily linked to one's general personality (Frijda, Kuipers & Schure, 1989; Zillmann, 1988). For example, one morning you may feel strong and self-confident—willing to confront anyone who gets in your way—whereas usually you feel physically weak or too distracted to assert yourself.

These response tendencies may lead to *action readiness plans,* or your inclination to use different forms of interaction behavior (Frijda et al., 1989). Such plans may also be based on one's state of health, familiarity with the social situation, whether the company is friendly or hostile, and cues given from the partner (Schacter & Singer, 1962). Box 5-2 shows how emotional cues from one person can affect the behavior of another.

Response tendencies may translate into one or more of three response modes in a given encounter: *moving toward, moving against,* and *moving away* from others (Davitz, 1969). That is, you might be inclined in a given situation to respond in a cooperative, competitive, or avoidant manner. For example, if you experience "Monday blues," you might feel inclined to avoid others until the caffeine kicks in at 10 A.M., after which time you become mostly competitive. But on Tuesday, you feel ready to work with others and maintain a cooperative response mode all day. Many people refer to response modes as "moods." The term "response mode," however, emphasizes a mental state of readiness to implement different strategies.

Scripts

Recall from Chapter 4 that people have blueprints to outline their relationships. Similarly, people have scripts for how conflicts should progress and for how they should handle anger when they experience it. As Russell and Fehr

BOX 5-2

EMOTIONS ARE CONTAGIOUS

In the early 1960s, an important study showed that people intepret their own emotions on the basis of the behavior of the other person (Schacter & Singer, 1962). Schacter and Singer held that people attempt to label their emotions given the information available to them. If people do not have a reasonable explanation for their emotions, they rely on situational cues—including the other person's behavior.

Schacter and Singer observed participants' reactions and survey responses regarding a fictional new vitamin, Superoxin. Superoxin was actually epinephrine, which causes feelings of excitation—mild increases in heart rate, blood pressure, muscle and cerebral blood flow, blood sugar, lactic acid, and breathing rate. Following the injection of the epinephrine, participants (who were male students) experienced different experimental conditions.

The first condition concerned the explanation for their physical reactions to Superoxin. Participants were informed in one of three ways: (1) They were accurately told about the physical symptoms they would experience because of Superoxin; (2) they were misinformed about their reaction to Superoxin (for example, that their feet would feel numb, though they never did); or (3) they were told nothing about physical changes.

The second condition involved another person's behavior. Once the physician had left the room, a confederate (someone who the experimenter has trained to behave a particular way) was brought in. The participant was told that the confederate was, like him, participating in the study. The participant did not know that the confederate had been told to act in a joyous and euphoric way *or* in an angry manner. Euphoric behaviors included playing "basketball" with crumpled paper and playing with a hula hoop. Angry behaviors were complaining about the experiment and showing increasing rage at the study.

The authors hypothesized that the confederate's behavior would affect participants' emotion and behavior, but only when participants lacked a reasonable explanation for their emotions. And that is exactly what Schacter and Singer found.

Participants who were informed accurately about their physical reactions to the epinephrine were not affected by the behavior of the other person in the experiment. Participants who were ignorant of the causes for their physical symptoms relied much more on the behavior of the confederate to understand their own emotions. These participants mirrored the behavior of the confederate. Those in the euphoria condition acted significantly more joyous, and those in the angry condition acted significantly angrier. Of course, those in the euphoria and anger conditions in reality had the same physiological reactions. The only difference between groups was in the behavior of the partner, the confederate.

Discussion Questions:

1 Have you ever had such an experience?
2 Have you ever not known you were in a conflict until someone else indicated that a disagreement was taking place, or vice versa?
3 How is it possible to diffuse an angry situation, knowing that other people rely on you to discover their own feelings?

observed, "To know the concept of anger is to know a script (to be able to simulate a scenario) in which prototypical antecedents, feelings, expressions, behaviors, physiological changes, and consequences are laid out in a causal and temporal sequence" (1994, p. 202).

A typical anger script among college students appears to have three general acts. In Act 1, social actors see themselves as *reactors* to negative events that somehow violate their rights, expectations, and the like (Shafer et al., 1987). In other words, people identify a cause for their anger (see Table 5-1). This act could be titled "The Scene of the Crime."

In Act 2 of the anger script, the participants react negatively. Shafer and colleagues (1987) reported several alternative scripted reactions that people have to anger: (1) various kinds of verbal attacks, yelling, and complaining; (2) physical attack threats, such as clenched fists and threatening nonverbals, and physical attacks on objects (breaking things); (3) nonverbal ways of showing protest and anger, including slamming doors, stomping around, frowning, and being flushed; (4) feelings of anxiety and discomfort, which may be revealed in crying; (5) internal escape responses, including brooding and focusing on one's anger; and (6) avoidance, by suppressing one's outrage or defining one's feelings of anger as inappropriate. The second act could be titled "The Hero Confronts the Villain."

Act 3 shows how people recover from their anger. Like the previous acts, Act 3 has alternative scenes that conclude the play: (1) The participants realize that if the anger continues, one or both parties and the relationship will certainly be hurt. In this version, the parties attempt reconciliation by taking a moment to collect themselves, "making up," and reaffirming each other. (2) One or both parties decide that the best way to reduce tension requires further distance or time apart. (3) Neither party knows how to manage conflicts productively, so they enact the script of aggression. Here, violence is seen as the preferred mode for reducing anger and rectifying the partner's reproachable behavior. Each of these versions of Act 3 could be titled "The Aftermath."

Let's focus on the script alternatives in Act 2. Note that the second act has no productive behaviors associated with it, simply because people typically do not see productive behavior as part of their anger script (Shafer et al., 1987). However, other scholars have questioned whether the behaviors in Act 2 portray the various ways that people manage their anger (e.g., Clore & Ortony, 1991). There is no doubt that people follow other scripts besides the anger script for managing problems, since people report more self-control in real situations than they might expect of themselves in a typical anger script (Fitness & Fletcher, 1993). Nevertheless, the research on anger scripts is important, because people probably rely on them to enact their roles during conflict. The educational task, then, is to identify any scripts you rely on when managing conflict, including the anger scripts we have mentioned here.

HIGHER-ORDERED THOUGHTS

In addition to your first inclinations to respond, you can rely on higher-ordered thoughts, or thoughts that involve central memory processing. Such thoughts permit one to gain self-control (Feshbach, 1986).

However, people who have cognitive deficits have difficulty using self-controlling thoughts. For example, intoxicated individuals cannot prepare rational responses, do not clearly process their partners' cues, and do not attend diligently to social expectations for behavior (Zillmann, 1990). Likewise, people who take in high levels of caffeine (more than two cups of coffee or 36 ounces of cola) may be too excited to think clearly, whereas people using marijuana may feel entirely unmotivated to work at solving problems interpersonally (Lubbit & Russett, 1984). In addition, people who become overly excited or "flooded" by the conflict find it very difficult to reappraise the situation in rational terms (Zillmann, 1988). It may be better for either or both parties to avoid the conflict discussion until people with cognitive deficits can re-collect themselves (Tavris, 1984).

Nevertheless, most people in most situations can use two kinds of higher-ordered thoughts directly relevant to conflict interactions: the attributions you have about the cause of the conflict and the assessments of probable outcomes of your behavior (Berkowitz, 1993). We wish to point out our use of the word "can," which implies that people have the ability to think before acting.

Attributions about Causes of Conflict

Attribution Dimensions   *Attributions* are explanations that people have for the causes of social events (see Chapter 2). Several dimensions characterize people's explanations for conflict situations. The dimensions most important to conflict appear to be globality, stability, locus, intent, selfishness, and blameworthiness (Fincham, Bradbury & Scott, 1990). *Globality* refers to whether the cause of the event is seen as specific to the situation or as something that explains many situations. *Stability* concerns whether the cause occurs reliably over time; stable causes last a long time and unstable causes apply only for a while. *Locus* refers to where the problem lies, whether internal or external to the person and/or relationship. *Intent* concerns whether the cause indicates a conscious decision for the event. *Selfishness* refers to whether the cause suggests a person's motive as self-serving. Finally, *blameworthiness* is responsibility for a failure (in contrast to *praiseworthiness,* which is responsibility for a success). For example, using the attribution "immature" to describe a thirty-year-old man can explain various events and behaviors (globality) over a long period of time (stability) that are also internal to the partner (locus) and reflect a selfish, blameworthy motive. The attribution "depressed" is also global, but it implies less stability, little intent, and no selfish or blameworthy motivation.

Which attribution dimension most directly affects conflict behavior is not altogether clear, because these dimensions overlap when discussing a single attribution. But research suggests that people who see the causes of conflict as global, stable, internal, and selfishly motivated have dissatisfying and turbulent relationships (Fincham, Bradbury & Scott, 1990; Vangelisti, 1994). People who view the cause of their conflict as reflecting global, stable, internal, and selfish dimensions are more likely than those who do not make these attributions to engage in negative behavior and less likely to experience positive relational outcomes. For example, in a study of roommates, Sillars (1980a) found that those who viewed the cause of conflict as stable and internal to the partner were more likely than others to engage in distributive conflict behavior (for example, threats, sarcasm). Ironically, since *both partners can simultaneously make attributions,* both persons simultaneously may view the cause of conflict as the partner's fault.

People who accept some responsibility for a conflict tend to respond in a positive manner—for example, by focusing on what they can do to remedy the situation. In addition, people who refrain from generalizing from the conflict interaction itself to broader issues and who explain their partners' behavior in unstable, external, and unselfish terms are less likely to use distributive, negative behaviors.

People might generalize from the conflict behaviors themselves to assess relational issues (Gottman, 1994). For example, you might attribute the cause of your partner's negative behavior to thoughtlessness. From there you might generalize that you are unhappy in the relationship because you cannot be satisfied with an inconsiderate person.

Attribution Biases   People not only vary in their attribution dimensions, but they also have biases. One of the most important biases is the *actor-observer bias*—that is, the tendency to link the partner's behavior to the partner's internal dispositions ("She didn't return my phone call because she is *rude*") while linking our own behavior to external factors ("I couldn't return his phone call because I was *very busy* with clients"). Because of actor-observer bias, we quickly attribute motives to others (but not as quickly to ourselves) *during* conflict because we can see their physical features and expressions, but we cannot see our own physical expressions of dismay, disapproval, and the like (Storms, 1973).

The actor-observer bias can be seen in everyday events. For example, Steve Spurrier, head football coach of the University of Florida Gators, was asked in a CNN interview (December 23, 1995) about a photograph of him on the cover of *Sports Illustrated,* which showed Spurrier with an angry look on his face. Coach Spurrier said that he had simply been responding to a referee's bad call. However, the CNN interviewer, Bob Lorenz, said the photo indicated that Spurrier was "excited" about the game of football. Spurrier then shrugged his shoulders at this explanation. Who was correct? The answer is both and neither. Both parties are biased, and these biases reflect the information available to them: Spurrier could explain his behavior as being caused by the specific call that prompted his reaction, whereas the interviewer had only Spurrier's behavior (as captured on film) to make an attribution. We discuss attributions as outcomes of conflict more fully in Chapter 6.

A second attribution bias—the *activity bias*—is the tendency to make quicker attributions for extraordinary behavior (than for ordinary, normative behavior). Because people expect others to treat them with general respect and positiveness, people more readily notice behaviors that are less positive, such as avoidance and negative messages (Canary & Spitzberg, 1990). This is the reason that people cannot simply "balance" a negative comment with a positive one (Gottman, 1994); people are more sensitive to others' violating the norm of cooperation. If you recall some of your recent conversations, you probably will recall a higher proportion of negative behaviors, because these are more salient to you. In a conflict episode, negative or blatantly avoidant messages will stand out because they are unexpected (along with other unexpected behaviors).

Expectations for Achieving Goals

Expectations you have for achieving goals affect your choice of conflict strategies. Expectations can be categorized according to the kinds of goals that people seek. This classification of expectation types helps us understand the kinds of higher-ordered thoughts that individuals engage in before acting. After discussing the nature of expectations, we will examine specific interaction goals.

Expectations   By "expectations" we mean the likelihood that acting in a particular way will bring about particular consequences (Sillars, 1980b). Since many consequences represent positive as well as negative outcomes, researchers often assess the perceived value of the consequences (Eagly & Chaiken, 1993). Such expectations, sometimes called *expectancy-value* assessments, can be represented by a simple mathematical formula:

behavior = likelihood of consequences $\times$ value of consequences

You may calculate this formula so often that it has become almost automatic. Every day you decide the likelihood that cooperating with, competing against, or avoiding others will bring about desired consequences and prevent undesired consequences.

The more important the conflict consequences are to you, the more careful you become in your calculations. For example, imagine that a teaching assistant (TA) appears to grade papers using subjective impressions, and he gives you lower grades than you usually earn. When going over the most recent assignment, the TA states simply that he "did not care for your word choice." If you needed an A in the class to qualify for graduate school, you might give a lot more thought to your response than if you just wanted to pass the course. Should you confront the TA and, if that doesn't work, complain to the department chair? Should you present your honest feelings of surprise and show how you fulfilled the assignment? Or should you act likeable and thank the TA for his honesty? If you needed only to pass, there would be little need to think about your response, and you probably would turn your attention to something else more important to you. But if you needed an A, you would carefully consider your response. You might even brood about the event all day, reconstruct the TA's weak answer, and rehearse a carefully crafted reply ("I'll show *him* word choice!").

Instrumental, Relational, and Self-Presentation Goals   No one calculates expectations for consequences in a social vacuum. According to theory and research, people have three types of general goals they pursue on a routine basis: instrumental, relational, and self-presentation (Canary & Cody, 1994; Clark & Delia, 1979; Newton & Burgoon, 1990a). These goals help clarify the kinds of consequences that you seek. (Instrumental, relational, and self-preservation goals were introduced in the discussion under "Effectiveness" in Chapter 2.)

Instrumental goals are objectives for personal advancement. As such, these goals are often concerned with obtaining resources or favors (Roloff & Janiszewski, 1989), and they are task-related. For example, you may need someone to take notes for you, to loan you money to cover a bill, or to babysit your kids so that you can study without distractions. In the United States, instrumental goals appear to be a primary concern (see Chapter 7); that is, people often approach others for their own personal gain in order to accomplish a task.

Relational goals are objectives to develop, maintain, or de-escalate relationships (for example, as professional associations, as friendships, as uncommitted romantic interludes). The goal of maintaining a close relationship exerts a powerful influence on your choices of communication strategies to influence another person to obtain an instrumental goal (Sillars, 1980b). On the other hand, if your partner in conflict is a stranger or an acquaintance, your concern for the relationship diminishes in the face of your instrumental objectives (unless, of course, you anticipate seeing this person again and routinely). In addition, when two people disagree about the nature of their relationship, relational goals in conflict can preoccupy the minds of communicators (for example, one person wants to remain friends, whereas the other person wants to terminate the relationship completely).

Self-presentation goals focus on how you want to be seen. Your public image is important to you for many reasons, including the fact that you present your own understanding of who you are in your self-presentation messages. People typically want to be seen as competent and likable (so they smile and make witty comments), although sometimes people want to be seen as weak (to achieve help) or dangerous (so that people respect them) (Canary & Cody, 1994). When a person's presentation of self is questioned, confrontation likely follows. Indeed, some scholars hold that self-presentation goals are most important in anger-provoking situations (Ting-Toomey, 1988; see also Table 5-1).

All three goals operate to some degree during conflict discussions. When you disagree with your supervisor, for example, you want to fulfill an instrumental goal, such as obtaining a particular work schedule or pay raise. You also want to maintain a positive and appropriate work association (relationship goal), and you want to be seen as responsible and fair (self-presentation goal).

To the extent that these three goals remain in operation during conflict, you and your interaction partner may not agree on the issue at stake. Recall the subjective TA. You enter his office to obtain an instrumental objective (grade change); however, the TA may view this confrontation as your doubting his authority over you (a relationship issue) and his ability to grade fairly (a self-presentation and identity issue). So, he responds abruptly by claiming that he did not like your word choice and, not only that, did not make your work a priority, given other "more important obligations." You then would likely become offended at the relational level ("he doesn't care enough about me to read my work") and self-presentation level ("he thinks I'm stupid"), forgetting for the moment your instrumental goal (the grade change—why you went to see the TA in the first place).

Tracking which goal motivates which conflict behavior can be difficult for several reasons (Sillars & Weisberg, 1987). First, goals change before, during, and after conflict (Hocker & Wilmot, 1995). For example, a person might initially want to obtain information ("I need to ask why I got this grade, so I can improve next time"), be questioned about his or her motives ("Are you trying to show me up?"), and then realize a new goal at stake ("I better show that I am sincere"). After the event, the person may recall a different version of the goal to others ("I just wanted to state my opinion about the assignment"). People are also more likely than their partners to claim they were effective at obtaining their goals during the conflict (Canary & Spitzberg, 1990). These behaviors suggest that people modify their recollection of the event to fit their self-concept (for example, as someone who is competent and successful at influencing others). Second, people do not always have a clear understanding of their goals or of when their goals have been achieved. Some goals are abstract and distal ("I want to be seen as nice so we can stay on good terms"); other goals are concrete and immediate ("I want to respond by seeking areas of commonality and compromise. Maybe then he will change my grade from a C to a B"). Of course, the clearer you are to yourself about what you want, the more likely you will obtain what you want. Similarly, the clearer you are about your interpersonal goals, the clearer you will be about your success at obtaining them.

Expectancy Value and Goals   In our experience, people roughly calculate expectancy value in terms of their goals. That is, before people enact conflict strategies, they assess the likelihood that those strategies will achieve their salient instrumental, relational, and self-presentation goals. Research indicates that, in the United States, communicators usually value primarily their instrumental goals; relational and self-presentation goals are secondary (Dillard, Segrin & Harden, 1989; Sillars, 1980b). In our earlier example, if the instrumental goal to earn a higher grade outweighs relational or self-presentation goals, you might discuss the issue with the TA in a clear manner, becoming more assertive if the initial attempts at achieving the goal have failed ("If you don't raise my grade, I'm taking my case to the department chair").

People shift focus from instrumental goals to other goals in two important ways. First, people seek their instrumental goals within the context of other goals, and these other goals constrain how people pursue their instrumental goals (Dillard et al., 1988). For example, you would not simply be clear with the TA about your desire for a higher grade; you would also likely be careful to show respect (to verify your relationship and to maintain the image of a "nice" person). Second, and perhaps more critically, conflict often escalates not because of the instrumental goal in question, but because the people involved feel that their public identities are at stake. Thus, the focus of conflict shifts to self-presentation issues (Schönbach, 1990). At times you may have felt that someone who disagreed with you did so to increase his or her public image at the expense of yours. For example, men who want to appear strong cannot easily back down from an argument (or they risk the perception of being weak), and the conflict topic itself becomes less relevant than who acts more "manly." Or you may have heard someone explain her rude behavior with the cliché, "It's not the issue, but the principle of the thing that matters." A closer look reveals that the "principle" in question most often concerns the person's self-presentation goal.

In sum, before people respond, they assess the causes of conflict in terms of attributions based on the information directly in front of them and in terms of how particular communicative behaviors would likely work to achieve their goals. Although people may often seek instrumental goals, their relational and self-presentation goals should not be underestimated.

THE DYAD AS A SYSTEM THAT AFFECTS EACH PERSON'S BEHAVIOR

Emotions are contagious. One person's feelings tend to bring about similar emotions in the other person. In our view, *emotional contagion* is the product of people interacting with each other. That is, your "catching" someone else's emotions during a conflict episode depends on the verbal and nonverbal behaviors of the other person. Consider the following three observations:

1 In several studies, the most powerful predictor of one's conflict behavior was the partner's immediately preceding behavior. For example, Burggraf and Sillars (1987) found that the partner's preceding behavior predicted one's own behavior and "swamped" any influences due to biological sex.

2 People often engage in patterns of interaction that they do *not* want to use. For example, Pearce and Conklin (1979) found that people engage in "unwanted repeated patterns" of behavior. Pearce and Conklin showed that these patterns are unpredictable in part because rules defining these episodes are difficult to define.

3 Dissatisfied couples are "stuck" in rigid patterns of negative affect, whereas satisfied couples more quickly get out of negative patterns when they do occur (see Chapter 4).

From a systems view, conflict (like all other forms of interaction) requires not only that we take into account the individual's internal wiring, but that we focus on how the *dyad* interacts over time (Fisher, 1978). Pragmatically, the individual's thoughts, emotions, and motives may even be irrelevant to understanding the individual's behavior (Watzlawick, Beavin & Jackson, 1967). In other words, interaction itself matters more than thoughts and plans for interaction.

System Properties

One of the steps in becoming an adult is realizing that interpersonal conflicts are the product of a dyadic system and not only the result of one person's violation of another's rights (Selman, 1980). To understand how people interact in conflict, we should examine properties of this dyadic system (Hocker & Wilmot, 1995, p. 139).

First, human relationships are open living systems. By "open" we mean that external sources of information affect the relationship. For example, Bandura (1973) stressed that people learn aggressive behavior not only from experience, but also from observing and then modeling examples in their family, subculture, and media. Accordingly, external sources of information affect the dyad when each person models others' responses to conflict. Moreover, the influences from the external world continue. For example, observing how your sister and her husband communicate during conflict can affect your proclivity for managing conflict a particular way ("Ridicule is not cool"). A "living system" refers to any living and organized entity with a subsystem, including individuals, groups, subcultures, and nations (Miller & Miller, 1992). In this light, a relationship contains two individuals as subsystems and is itself a subsystem of a larger group (for example, friends, family network) or organization.

Second, human relationships seek *equifinality* (or stable variation) through interaction. In other words, people maintain their relationship and adjust to their environment through communication. Robin and Foster (1989), for example, argued that families are "homeostatic systems," and that biological changes to children undergoing adolescence disrupt the system. Accordingly, parents increase their control to compensate for the adolescents' increased demands for personal independence. A similar concept, *equilibrium,* which applies to closed systems, refers to the stability of a system (without adjustment to its environment). A converse concept is *entropy,* or the total decay of the system. Entropy is characterized by random behavior. People in open systems seek to retain order by adjusting to the external influences, thereby preventing or postponing entropy.

Third, subsystems are interdependent in a way that makes obsolete any ideas of cause and effect. In a relational system, both parties affect each other simultaneously. Selman (1980) has shown that a critical step in an individual's personal development is coming to an understanding of conflict as one way that systems must be adjusted instead of one's rightful response (effect) to an anger-provoking event (cause). In addition, disagreement about how to "punctuate" behaviors in terms of who caused what and who is responding to whom lies "at the root of countless relationship struggles" (Watzlawick, Beavin & Jackson, 1967, p. 56).

Finally, human relationships are characterized by *nonsummativity,* the idea that the whole is greater than the sum of its parts. One cannot dismantle the relationship and discover its "meaningfulness" in the personalities of the two people. The relationship requires both parties and is composed of the connections between them.

System Dysfunctions

Human relationship systems can be dysfunctional in several ways. We discuss three widely recognized system dysfunctions.

Transactional Redundancy In systems characterized by transactional redundancy, there is little behavioral variation (Millar & Rogers, 1987). For example, people in dissatisfied relationships engage in negative reciprocations for long periods of time. People can also quickly agree with each other, not allowing partners to present their reasons for believing the way they do; avoid each other; or be so vigilant about maintaining a positive tone that any conflict appears extraordinary and "unnatural." People in these systems appear to be caught *inside* their patterns of interaction.

People can also be caught *between* patterns of interaction. That is, dyadic systems may have a routine that exists across episodes (Sillars & Wilmot, 1994). A couple might have the same fight pattern; for example, jealous couples who cannot get over a transgression may reenact a conflict they've had before, conclude it the same way, and then start again a few weeks later. Or a couple may have a pattern in which they have a "big fight" on Tuesday, do not see each other until the weekend, make up by Sunday, and fight again on the next Tuesday.

Dyadic partners may not realize that behaviors are being constrained by the system they themselves perpetuate. Members of the system understand their role relationships to each other by the very action of the system. Behaving as expected lends credence to the behavior and perpetuates the system, making it even more difficult to change. Such affirmation is given despite how undesirable the behavior may be to the partners. In fact, partners can prevent deviations from the system pattern by negatively sanctioning the deviations (Shimanoff, 1980). People outside the system often can see how rigid this interaction is and may attempt to offer advice ("Just avoid getting into a competitive shouting match when you're both stressed"). However, chronic transaction redundancy makes it difficult for parties to adjust readily to new information.

Subsystem Breakdown Most people realize that our bodies are composed of complex subsystems that are interdependent such that a breakdown in one subsystem threatens the entire organism. For example, if we do not exercise our muscular subsystem, our respiratory and cardiovascular subsystems become inefficient. In personal relationship breakdowns, one person becomes inefficient, ineffective, or otherwise unable to function as a healthy individual (for example, that person develops physical illness, chronic depression, or drug dependence) (Miller & Miller, 1992). How can the breakdown of individuals reflect a system problem? Several situations come to mind: Verbal and physical abuse may harm one of the parties, avoidance may cause one party to feel isolated, or couples may treat each other unfairly such that one person suffers while the other benefits from the inequity. An example of the last point illustrates subsystem breakdown.

Hochschild (1989) reported that some women attempt to fulfill roles both as career women and as traditional housewives; that is, they work fifty hours a week and remain responsible for cooking, cleaning, and caring for children. Many of these women collapse under the strain of too many obligations (also called *role strain*), and they must choose one system over the other (career or family). Hochschild concluded that such role strain results from marriage systems that are *transitional*—that is, a system in which both partners agree that the woman has the right to do whatever she wants as long as she fulfills her obligations at home. This means, of course, that the man does none of the traditionally female chores. Hochschild reported two other, more personally rewarding, couple systems: *traditional,* in which the woman works only at home and does all of the household chores; and *egalitarian,* in which the man accepts the changing roles of women and does his share of the household chores.

Exceeding Roles   Partners may exceed their roles in the relationship to the detriment of both parties and the system. Nervous uncles who advise their sisters about raising nieces and nephews, friends who repeatedly set up other friends on blind dates, and coworkers who desire romantic relationships with colleagues illustrate how the primary relational function might suffer when people act in ways that exceed their roles.

One of the most critical findings regarding this system dysfunction concerns children who intervene in their parents' conflicts (Robin & Foster, 1989; Stafford & Bayer, 1993). Such interventions include giving less affection, less obedience, and more disruptive behavior to the parent who the child perceives as having shown less love to the spouse. In addition, the child may assume a parental function by giving one parent more support than his or her marriage partner does. This *parentification* of the child may give the child a sense of power in the short term, which would be witnessed in one-sided coalitions during conflict, with one spouse and the "parentified" child fighting against the other spouse (Stafford & Bayer, 1993).

Systems have an immediate and ongoing impact on people's interaction behavior. Once established, rigid systems are difficult to change, and couples in such systems may have a difficult time adjusting to new information from external sources. Although people outside the system may clearly see how the system is dysfunctional and provide advice, it can be difficult to follow others' advice for how we should act within our own relationship systems.

SUMMARY

This chapter has described various kinds of proximal influences on conflict behavior. In our view, each of these factors can be salient in any conflict situation. Therefore, it is important for the student to know the various kinds of spontaneous reactions that he or she might have to conflict. These factors act in combination, directly affecting our conflict behavior choices:

1 Anger-provoking events *and* other aversive emotions (such as depression) can bring on angerlike responses.

2 Physiological reactions and initial cognitions point to preferred responses.

3 Higher-ordered thoughts consider causes for conflicts and consequences of behavior in terms of desired goals.

4 The relational system constrains behavior.

We stop short of presenting these factors as a causal progression for two reasons. First, we believe that these events happen so quickly that they all represent features of the same transactional process. Second, because people are reflective, they might consider the latter points before getting angry; that is, anger-provoking actions can be a product of attributions about the partner's behavior. People can recollect and "stew" over an event that occurred a long time ago, making themselves angrier and angrier at the different attributions they construct for the event.

Higher-ordered cognitions can moderate initial reactions, such as "fight" or "flight" physiological reactions and response readiness modes, assuming that the reactions do not flood the individual and that the person has the mental capacity to deliberate the causes and appropriate response alternatives to maximize his or her goals. One's personal system of ethics undoubtedly guides higher-ordered thoughts about how to respond to conflict. We'll elaborate on this in Chapter 11. Here we want to underscore that people are ultimately responsible for their own behavior, and that our selection of key scientific factors does not excuse individuals from making sound and promotive choices for action. We believe that knowing the processes we are prone to as humans allows us to be more circumspect and competent in our conflict interactions.

The discussion of goals suggests that people assess the extent to which particular conflict strategies will yield positive outcomes in terms of obtaining their primary (instrumental) goal; then they modify their plans on the basis of how much damage the strategy might do to relational and self-presentation goals. Of course, people may operate with other priorities: considering self-presentation goals first and then other goals ("Whether or not I am right, I must look good to others"), or considering the relational consequences of behaving a particular way and then thinking about instrumental objectives won or lost ("I don't care if he wins this argument, I don't want him to be upset with me"). The priorities one places on goals are a personal decision, but regardless of such preferences, the resulting conflict behavior reflects those goals.

Finally, seeing that you are part of a system may help you pause for a moment to determine how the system needs to be changed, perhaps by a concerted effort to negotiate functions that allow both parties to function as individuals. Systems that do not reflect each person's values may require a closer look and modification to reach a more satisfactory steady state. In the next chapter, we discuss selected consequences of the conflict behaviors we have seen in this chapter.

DISCUSSION QUESTIONS

1 Examine Table 5-1. On the basis of your experience, rank the top two or three causes of anger. (Recall that some researchers emphasize that anger stems from one cause more than others.) Why did you rank the anger causes the way you did? Compare your ranking to someone else's in class.

2 Recall experiences you have had with the emotions listed in Table 5-2 in response to another person's reproachable behavior. Discuss how the person's behavior was reproachable and how you responded in terms of both your feelings and your actions. Do you think that Table 5-2 provides an insightful way of looking at the emotional context of conflict? Offer reasons for your assessment.

3 If you had to write a short play entitled "A Day in the Life of My Family's Conflict," how would it read? Discuss the major parts of the script (the acts) and the roles of your family members in the play. What is your role? If you could revise the script so that you liked it better, what would you change?

4 Think about an ongoing problem you have had in a relationship, whether in a parent-child, sibling, friendship, or romantic involvement. Write down the cause for the problem. Discuss the kinds of attributions your cause implies: Is the cause global or specific? Stable or unstable? Internal or external? Selfishly or unselfishly motivated? Blameworthy or praiseworthy? What attributions do you think the other person is making? Discuss how both of you might be right *and* wrong in your explanations.

5 Examine the following scenarios. Discuss the kinds of goals being pursued and whether confronting the person or avoiding the person (for example, by changing the topic) would more likely lead to desired consequences. You may want to act out these situations in class.

   a You need your fourteen-year-old daughter to help clean the house for a family holiday party. Your daughter, whose only weekly chore is to clean her bedroom, gets upset and tells you she is unfairly treated.

   b Your brother is upset with you because he wants to borrow money that you simply do not have. He tells you that he doesn't believe you, and he takes it personally that you do not want to help him.

   c A coworker constantly likes to talk about herself. Whenever you relate a story, she seems to need to offer a better (and longer) one about herself. You tell her you got to work late because of the huge traffic problem. She replies, "That's nothing—I had to drive through much worse conditions this morning."

6 Do you believe that relational systems constrain behavior more powerfully than do individual response tendencies or attributions? Provide reasons for your view. If your instructor is willing, you might use this question to have a timed, in-class debate between two groups, each group representing one view (system versus individual).

6

CONFLICT OUTCOMES

CHAPTER OUTLINE

The model we presented in Chapter 2 (see Figure 2-2) showed two types of outcomes associated with interpersonal conflict, proximal and distal. Proximal outcomes are the immediate consequences of a conflict interaction, including the thoughts and feelings that occur during and shortly after a conflict interaction. We can usually describe how a conflict episode has affected us in the short term; that is, we usually know the proximal outcomes of a conflict.

Distal consequences are long-term effects of conflict. The management of conflict episodes that recur over time between two people can affect the durability and climate of their relationship, as well as their individual well-being. Proximal outcomes are salient because they occur in proximity to the conflict episode. Our awareness of distal consequences, in contrast, is somewhat dim because the effects are delayed and (usually) somewhat removed from specific occurrences of conflict. Proximal consequences can accumulate over time to produce distal consequences.

PROXIMAL CONSEQUENCES

Attributions

In Chapter 5 we described how attributions about behavior can directly shape the course of conflict. Actually, the connection between attributions and conflict behavior is reciprocal (Gottman, 1994). Attributions both precede and result from conflict actions. In fact, most research on attributions and communication is correlational, making it difficult to specify which of the two comes first.

Because the attributions you make are integral to your interpretation of a conflict situation, they influence how you behave during conflict. As we saw in Chapter 5, when you infer that the cause of another person's behavior is global, stable, and internal, and that the behavior is blameworthy, intentional, and selfishly motivated, you are more inclined to enact distributive conflict behaviors (Fincham & Bradbury, 1992; Sillars, 1980a, 1980b). At the same time, the likelihood of making these negative attributions is greater when the person you disagree with engages in distributive behaviors. Thus the association between negative attributions and distributive behavior during conflict is reciprocal. Negative attributions both engender and result from distributive behaviors.

As the intensity of conflict increases, attributions become more biased and more polarized (Sillars, 1981). With increasingly defensive behavior, conflict escalates and attributions regarding others become more rigidly negative and critical. Negative behavior leads to negative attributions, which create further negative behavior, which leads to more negative attributions, and so on.

In that the attributions we make contribute to our understanding of a conflict episode, they are cognitive outcomes. Depending on the intensity and importance of the conflict, these attributional outcomes may be relatively strong or weak, enduring or fleeting. Enduring attributional outcomes will likely surface automatically as proximal influences in the next episode of conflict between two parties. If at the end of a conflict discussion, Ken perceives Don's behavior as internally motivated and malevolent, Ken may anticipate that Don's behavior in their next conflict will be internal and malevolent. The attributions at Time 1 (a proximal outcome) emerge to "frame" the interpretation of later conflict at Time 2 (a proximal influence). Research indicates that as individuals become less satisfied in a relationship, attributions become more rigid and biased in a negative direction (Baucom, Sayers &

Duhe, 1989). Both positive and negative behaviors are interpreted in a skeptical way.

Emotions

The role of emotions in conflict runs parallel to the role of attributions. Emotions are as much consequence of as they are antecedent to a conflict episode. Emotions provide a context for performing and interpreting behavior. At the same time, the conflict behaviors enacted during an episode of conflict exert a potent influence on the nature and intensity of feelings.

The feelings we experience during and after a conflict are emotional consequences. A disagreement may cause you to feel anxiety, anger, hurt, frustration, relief, sadness, excitement, guilt, and many other emotions. The intensity, complexity, and duration of your feelings in the aftermath of a conflict episode depend (among other things) on the intensity and importance of the conflict and on the overall climate of your relationship. When the feelings endure, particularly if they are negative, they probably will emerge in subsequent conflicts as part of the proximal context.

One person's attributional and emotional outcomes stem, in part, from the behavior of the partner. At the same time, one's behavior stimulates the attributions and feelings held by the partner. The interdependent association between one person's thoughts and feelings and another person's behavior is depicted in Figure 6-1.

Suppose Jeff confronts Steve in a belligerent and blaming way. Steve is likely to see Jeff's behavior as unreasonable and perhaps irrational, and Steve will probably feel hurt, maybe a bit angry. These thoughts and feelings may lead Steve to respond to Jeff in a defensive and aggressive manner. Jeff may then interpret Steve's behavior as selfish, intentional, blameworthy, and internally caused, leading Jeff to become angry. Jeff's thoughts and feelings about Steve's behavior may lead Jeff to respond to Steve in an increasingly defensive and aggressive manner. And so it goes. A negative escalating spiral of conflict ensues, fueled by interlocking feelings and thoughts that lead to

FIGURE 6-1
THE INTERCONNECTEDNESS BETWEEN ONE PERSON'S BEHAVIOR AND
ANOTHER'S COGNITIONS AND EMOTIONS.

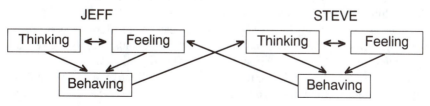

behaviors in one person, that in turn produce feelings and thoughts in the other person, which affect the other person's behavior, and so on.

Judgments of Competence

Although we are not always mindful of it, we make judgments about our own communication competence and the communication competence of others with whom we interact. In Chapter 2 we argued that assessments of competence are particularly relevant to conflict situations. It is reasonable to assume that the immediate outcomes of conflict are tied to the quality of communication.

Two essential criteria for assessing communication competence, as noted earlier, are *effectiveness* and *appropriateness.* Research consistently demonstrates that conflict communication strategies correlate with judgments of communication effectiveness and appropriateness, as well as overall perceptions of communication competence. In general, integrative conflict behaviors are seen as more effective, appropriate, and hence competent than distributive behaviors (Canary & Cupach, 1988; Canary & Spitzberg, 1987, 1989).

Effectiveness   Sometimes we initiate conflict when we have no clear goal or we are only dimly aware of a goal. We all create trivial disagreements simply because we are in a grumpy, disagreeable mood. We may simply need catharsis. Most of the time, however, the desire to achieve our own goals motivates us to initiate and to escalate conflict. In other words, people tend to fight for issues important to them, including their salient goals and values, more so than for trivial concerns (for example, about how many inches of snow fell last night).

Communication is judged to be effective when individuals fulfill their objectives and achieve their goals. If the outcome of an argument between Harry and Sally shows that Harry has won and Sally has lost, we might say that Harry was effective and Sally was ineffective. Since each person has multiple goals, however, the issue of effectiveness can be complicated. Harry may have been effective at achieving his instrumental goal with Sally (he got his way in an argument about how they should arrange the furniture in their apartment), but he may have been totally ineffective at promoting the desired impression that he is a fair and sensitive partner. Indeed, Harry may "win the battle" by getting his way in this instance but "lose the war" when Sally dumps him for another, more compatible partner.

Since goals can be transactive—that is, they can change during a conflict— the judgment of effectiveness may not always be obvious. Box 6-1 gives an example of being effective without fulfilling the original goal.

You occupy the best position to judge your own effectiveness. You implicitly and explicitly know what your goals are, both prospective and transactive,

---

BOX 6-1

EFFECTIVENESS TAKES INTO ACCOUNT ALL YOUR GOALS

June was an industrious and productive employee for eight years in the management information systems division of a large company. Frustrated with the manner in which policies were being implemented in her division, June complained to her supervisor. She wanted to change certain procedures.

During their discussion, June learned that some of her ideas were inconsistent with the company philosophy and were not likely to meet with the approval of higher management. June also discovered, however, that she could rotate into a different division of the company where she would be able to advance into a management position much more quickly than in her current division. June's supervisor, learning of June's dissatisfaction, was even willing to facilitate the transfer.

June's confrontation with her supervisor did not (at least in the short term) result in any policy changes. So June was ineffective if judged by her initial goal. But the exchange did alert June to desirable work opportunities of which she had been unaware. June actually got more out of the confrontation with her supervisor than she initially had imagined. Even though she had not anticipated the nature of the outcome of the discussion with her supervisor, she certainly felt effective.

June's supervisor thought that her own conflict management behavior was effective too. She knew that June was a committed employee who possessed management potential. She was happy to work out a deal to keep June happy, even though she disagreed with some of June's ideas about policy. June's manager felt that she had been successful in facilitating the career development of a valued employee, which was very good for the company (despite the fact that she was losing the employee to another division).

---

and therefore serve as the most educated judge of the extent to which you achieve your goals. To be communicatively competent, however, as we contended in Chapter 2, you must not only be effective; you must also be appropriate in the manner in which you pursue your goals.

Appropriateness Appropriate communication meets your expectations for what behavior fits a given situation. Just as goals are used to determine effectiveness, rules serve as our benchmarks for determining appropriateness. Rules indicate what behaviors should or should not be performed in various situations. Although you are in the best position to assess the effectiveness of your own behavior, the opinions of others are probably more relevant when it comes to judging your appropriateness.

Rules vary in their level of abstractness, or "crystallization" (Shimanoff, 1980). A rule of friendship, for example, might be that friends are loyal to one another. Individuals' ideas about what constitutes loyalty and what constitutes an act of disloyalty can be rather diverse, however. In comparison, the rule that you should not interrupt someone during conversation is more concrete and specific. Most people would agree on what constitutes an interruption (although they may disagree on how important the rule is).

The violation of rules is a source of interpersonal conflict. Violation of a serious rule, or repeated violation of important rules, can be grounds for the termination of a friendship or romantic relationship (Argyle & Henderson, 1984; Baxter, 1986).

Where do rules originate? We are all familiar with social rules of etiquette and politeness, though by no means do people enjoy consensus regarding these rules. Social rules are heavily influenced by our culture and operate most strongly in public settings or in communication with others in a nonintimate relationship. In more intimate relationships, partners determine for themselves the rules for appropriate behavior between them. That is, they develop their own rules regarding preferred or prohibited behaviors in the context of the relationship.

Unlike laws that officially stipulate regulations in writing, rules implicitly prescribe and proscribe behavior. We infer rules and take them for granted. In fact, we usually recognize a rule only after perceiving its violation and wishing to correct the transgression.

When one person directly accuses another of breaking a rule, conflict discussions often focus specifically on the nature of the rule and whether or not it was broken. Newell and Stutman call these discussions *social confrontation episodes* and identify six questions that communicators might address in such episodes (1988, p. 274):

1 Is the implied rule mutually accepted as legitimate?
2 Is this a special situation?
3 If invoked, is the superseding rule mutually accepted as legitimate?
4 Did the accused actually perform the behavior in question?
5 Does the behavior constitute a violation of the rule?
6 Does the accused accept responsibility for the behavior?

People who discuss these questions contribute to the establishment and clarification of rules. Communicators use such discussion to negotiate mutual acceptance of rules, as well as when those rules apply, what their exceptions are, and what they "mean."

Assessments of appropriateness in conflict behavior not only figure prominently in conflict discussions; they also represent proximal conflict outcomes. In other words, judgments of communication competence during conflict discussions are tied to the perceived appropriateness of conflict communication.

Among the rules that govern communication, some apply specifically to dealing with conflict. Table 6-1 illustrates some conflict rules common in marital relationships (Jones & Gallois, 1989). Of course, not all marital partners subscribe to these rules. Relational partners negotiate rules to fit their

TABLE 6-1
CONFLICT RULES COMMON IN MARITAL RELATIONSHIPS

Issue addressed by rule	Examples of rules
Consideration	Don't belittle, humiliate, or use character-degrading words about the other person. Don't dismiss the other person's issue as unimportant. Don't blame the other person unfairly or make unfair accusations.
Rationality	Don't get angry. Don't raise voice. Don't be aggressive or lose your temper.
Self-expression	Keep to the point; don't get involved in other issues. Get to the point quickly. Be honest and say what's on your mind.
Conflict resolution	Explore alternatives. Make joint decisions. Explain reasons for your point of view.
Positivity	Try to relieve the tension in arguments (e.g., make appropriate jokes, laugh together). Use receptive body language (e.g., open body position). Look at each other.

Source: Adapted from Jones and Gallois (1989).

particular relationship (Honeycutt, Woods & Fontenot, 1993). Some partners, for example, develop the norm of avoiding overt confrontation as much as possible. Others might share a rule that each person should honestly express anger during disagreements (which would weaken the "force" of rationality rules; see Table 6-1). Compatibility depends not so much on which rules each partner wishes to enforce, but on the extent to which partners share the rules. If June's boss (see Box 6-1) believed that complaints about policies should be offered in writing, June might never have learned about other advancement opportunities. But June and her boss shared the rules and therefore perceived the management of the conflict to be appropriate, as well as effective.

Communication Satisfaction

Judgments of communication effectiveness and appropriateness represent cognitive proximal outcomes associated with communication competence. Concurrently, perceived communication competence correlates with one's affective response of communication satisfaction. Competent communication leaves communicators feeling satisfied with the interaction (Spitzberg & Cupach, 1984; Spitzberg & Hecht, 1984).

Research shows that behaviors generally perceived to be competent are also associated with communication satisfaction. For example, your partner's use of integrative and supportive conflict behaviors is positively associated with your own communication satisfaction (Canary & Cupach, 1988; Canary & Spitzberg, 1987, 1990; Newton & Burgoon, 1990a) as well as with your satisfaction with the outcome of the conflict (Sillars, 1980a). Emotional validation and problem-solving facilitation by your partner are likewise positively associated with your satisfaction with the conflict interaction (Haefner, Notarius & Pellegrini, 1991). Moreover, responsiveness and lack of criticism positively affect satisfaction with the outcome of conflict discussions (Koren, Carlton & Shaw, 1980).

Face Threat and Restoration

One motivation that underlies all social interaction is the desire of communicators to have their identities confirmed. In other words, when you interact with others, there is a tacit agreement that you respect each other's face (Goffman, 1967). *Face* is the part of your identity that you present during interaction and expect will be accepted by others. Maintaining face is part of the ever-present self-presentation goal.

Normally, face maintenance, or the presentation and confirmation of self, is taken for granted. We assume others will accept who we are (that is, who we present ourselves as), and others assume we will support who they are. The idea is that we can at least show respect for each other as persons, whether or not we agree with each other's ideas or behaviors. We maintain our dignity by protecting our own face, and we show consideration when we protect the face of others. The ability to maintain face during interaction and to repair face successfully when it has been damaged is a fundamental attribute of appropriate communication and reflects communication competence (Cupach & Metts, 1994; Weinstein, 1969; Wiemann, 1977).

Conflict creates circumstances that are inherently face-threatening. First, when someone confronts you, they constrain your freedom by making you respond in some way to the issue, even if you prefer not to engage in conflict. Second, when someone disagrees with you or presents you with a complaint, you may take it as personal criticism. Disagreeing with your idea translates into an indirect disagreement with *you*. If the idea holds importance for you and if the person disagreeing is important to you, you may feel personally challenged. If someone complains about your behavior, you may feel that they disapprove of you. The experience of such disapproval threatens your face. Of course, the manner of complaining or disagreeing has much to do with the degree of face threat we perceive. If your roommate constructively complains that you have not pulled your weight in cleaning

TABLE 6-2
EXAMPLES OF EVENTS THAT THREATEN FACE

You can threaten your own face by:

Losing an argument
Losing your temper
Seeking forgiveness
Getting caught in a lie
Breaking a promise
Making a mistake
Looking foolish or inept
Being disloyal

You can threaten other people's face by:

Making personal criticisms
Making them feel stupid or incompetent
Insulting or ridiculing them
Invading their privacy
Blaming them for causing a problem
Pressuring them to do things they don't want to do
Devaluing your relationship with them
Being disloyal

---

up the apartment for an upcoming party, you might perceive the gripe as legitimate and not take it personally. However, if your roommate disdainfully refers to your "laziness" about cleaning up, you probably will feel unfairly attacked.

Third, when conflict escalates in intensity, people tend to become close-minded and defensive. Negative behaviors such as yelling, demanding, threatening, being rude and sarcastic, and making hurtful put-downs occur more frequently. Naturally, these behaviors can be employed intentionally to threaten face. Whether or not face threat is intended, however, as recipients we tend to perceive these negative behaviors as face-threatening. In general, belligerent, antagonistic, and defensive behaviors undermine the expression and perception of respect and lead to feelings of contempt. Just as some people enact face-threatening behaviors more than others (that is, they routinely try to bully and show disrespect), some people take disagreements personally, even when confronted gently and politely.

According to Goffman (1967), each of us is emotionally attached to our face, so when it is threatened we must defend it. When we lose face, we usually attempt to restore or repair the damage. Communication designed to prevent or counteract threats to face is called *facework* (Goffman, 1967; Tracy, 1990). We save face by couching potentially face-threatening behaviors in polite language (Brown & Levinson, 1987) and a respectful tone. If part of your performance appraisal includes criticism about the way you perform a certain task, your boss can minimize the face threat by praising your hard effort and by expressing understanding that you are new to the task.

We also save face by actively repairing damage done to it. If I insult you, I obviously have threatened your face. If I want to make up for the damage, I should sincerely apologize. If I am caught violating a mutually accepted rule, I should offer a credible explanation and promise not to repeat the inappropriate behavior. If we have a heated disagreement about what was said during a conversation a week ago, and it turns out I am wrong, I should admit it.

Saving face facilitates the management of conflict. Face threats complicate conflict and make the successful management of conflict more difficult. When someone threatens your face, you can interpret the threat very personally and respond defensively. Conflict gets bogged down and individuals become distracted when they feel compelled to defend their own face instead of discussing the substantive issue of disagreement. When people maintain face and when parties to conflict remedy face threats with facework, individuals feel less threatened and more efficiently attend to resolving substantive issues. Face saving also enables partners to handle future conflicts more effectively. Conflicts are less likely to turn into destructive negative cycles when individuals feel that they can disagree without the conflict becoming personal and attack-oriented.

Remember that face maintenance is a two-way street—a cooperative venture whereby each person depends on the other for face support. We must save each other's face if we are to save our own. If someone apologizes, he or she saves your face at the expense of their own. In turn, your graceful and ungrudging forgiveness saves your partner's face. If your partner admits to being wrong about a disputed fact, his or her admission helps save your face. In short, don't keep harping "I told you so" if you wish to save the face of a person who admits to being wrong.

Physical Health

Obviously, conflict can harm your physical health if it escalates into violence. But can heated discussions and verbally aggressive debates adversely affect your general physical well-being? We have no definitive answer to this question yet, but preliminary evidence suggests that some people may be affected physically by their conflict interactions.

As we saw in Chapter 5, an episode of conflict can be associated with anxiety and negative feelings such as anger, as well as physiological arousal. What are the consequences of the arousal that can accompany conflict—particularly, intense, escalated episodes of conflict? Research on the conflict interactions among newlyweds by Kiecolt-Glaser and colleagues (1993) showed that negative conflict behavior produced adverse effects on individuals' blood pressure and immune systems. The immune system changes were still apparent a full day after the conflict. Research also indicated that negative conflict may alter the levels of various hormones in the body (Malarkey et al., 1994). Clearly, there are potential proximal physical effects associated with conflict and its management.

The Cumulative Nature of Proximal Consequences

When negative behaviors become routine and repeated during conflict interactions with a certain individual, negative attributions and negative sentiments regarding that person may become habitual. The repeated and cumulative effect of proximal consequences can create proximal influences for future conflict episodes. These proximal influences may facilitate or undermine conflict management.

In Chapter 2 we cited research to support the idea that perceptions of competence *mediate* the connection between conflict communication and distal relational features. In other words, conflict communication eventually affects distal relational outcomes by first influencing proximal outcomes.

When your partner uses integrative conflict strategies, you tend to perceive your partner as communicatively competent and you feel satisfied with the conflict communication. These outcomes—your feeling of satisfaction and your judgment that your partner is competent—translate over time into constructive relational qualities such as trust, mutuality of control, intimacy, and relational satisfaction (Canary & Cupach, 1988; Canary & Spitzberg, 1987, 1990). Competent conflict management thus is constructive in the sense that it fosters relational growth and solidarity.

Similarly, when your partner uses distributive strategies, you tend to perceive the partner as being *less* communicatively competent and you feel less satisfied with the interaction. These negative proximal outcomes, in turn, undermine positive relational qualities over time.

Research on attributions in marital relationships supports the mediational role of episodic or proximal outcomes (Epstein, Pretzer & Fleming, 1987). The attributions that spouses make regarding each other's behavior act as filters through which behaviors eventually influence marital satisfaction. When negative conflict behaviors are perceived to be due to the partner's malicious intent, for example, relational satisfaction diminishes.

Attributions, emotions, and judgments of competence and satisfaction of individual episodes of conflict translate into longer-term consequences that are removed from any specific instance of conflict, but are nevertheless significant. These distal consequences are considered in the next section.

DISTAL CONSEQUENCES

Relational (Dis)Satisfaction and (In)Stability

Perhaps the most robust generalization in the conflict literature is that frequent negativity in conflicts destroys relationships (McGonagle, Kessler & Gotlib, 1993). In Chapter 4 we discussed some of the copious research that distinguishes distressed from nondistressed marital couples. The research consistently shows that, compared to satisfied couples, dissatisfied couples

1 Engage in negative behaviors more frequently (for example, threats, demands, coercion, hostility, criticisms, put-downs, defensiveness, sarcasm, and contempt) (Birchler & Webb, 1977; Gottman, 1979, 1994; Koren, Carlton & Shaw, 1980; Raush et al., 1974)

2 Rely on positive behaviors less frequently (for example, agreement, approval, and humor) (Gottman & Levenson, 1992; Raush et al., 1974)

3 Exhibit more frequent and lengthier patterns of negative reciprocation (for example, complain-complain, complain-defend, attack-attack, and defend-attack) (Alberts, 1988; Billings, 1979; Gottman, 1979; Margolin & Wampold, 1981; Ting-Toomey, 1983a)

4 Entertain negative attributions about the partner's behavior (for example, attribute behavior to global, internal, and stable causes or blame marital difficulties on partner's selfishly motivated behavior) (Baucom, Sayers & Duhe, 1989; Fincham, Beach & Nelson, 1987; Bradbury & Fincham, 1990)

In many of these studies it is difficult to separate causes and effects. Are unhappy couples more likely to engage in negative behaviors and thoughts because of their unhappiness, or do the negative behaviors and thoughts lead to unhappiness? The answer, of course, is both. Relational climate and behaviors reciprocally influence each other over time. Longitudinal research of married couples shows that negative behaviors during conflict discussions and negative attributions about a partner's behavior can predict subsequent dissatisfaction a year or more later (Fincham & Bradbury, 1987; Gottman & Krokoff, 1989). Moreover, the behaviors and cognitions that lead to dissatisfaction predict the likelihood of eventual marital separation and divorce (Gottman, 1994; McGonagle et al., 1993).

Although we can list many behaviors that can be considered negative, the extensive research on marital interactions by Gottman (1994) and his colleagues has identified four especially problematic types of behavior: criticism, contempt, defensiveness, and stonewalling. When enacted frequently in a relationship, these behaviors undermine the climate of the relationship and contribute to its demise. Hence, Gottman refers to these behaviors as the "Four Horsemen of the Apocalypse." These four negative behaviors form a negative cascade, with one leading to the next, in relationships that are on a destructive path. Criticisms can eventually lead to contempt, which produces defensiveness, which invites stonewalling.

Criticism is more than simple complaining. Rather than describing disagreeable behavior, criticism attacks the character or personality of an individual. This manner of complaining threatens the face of the recipient of the criticism. If Ray doesn't like Sarah's new green dress, he can criticize her poor taste or tell her she "looks lousy" in the dress. Sarah would likely take the complaint personally if Ray presented it in either of these ways. Alternatively, Ray could offer the less critical complaint that he prefers the red dress, or that he was really hoping she would wear the red dress tonight.

Contempt is the opposite of respect. Exhibiting contempt for another shows a blatant disregard for that person's face. Insults, put-downs, sarcasm, mockery, derision, and the like are examples of ways to show contempt.

As indicated in Chapter 5, *defensiveness* represents an attempt to protect oneself. You behave defensively when you feel victimized or unfairly attacked. People show defensiveness in various ways, including denying responsibility, making excuses, answering one complaint with another, and whining. Note the defensiveness of both Taylor and Joe in the following example. Each evades responsibility for the problem; each shows contempt, leading the other to be defensive.

Joe: You forgot to call up the Smiths to tell them we weren't coming for dinner. Now we look like real jerks! How can you be so irresponsible?

Taylor: You were supposed to call the Smiths, not me!

Joe: So you think that falsely blaming me gets you off the hook?

Taylor: You're the one doing the false blaming. We talked about this last week—it was your job to call.

Joe: I should have called, because I knew you would forget—like you always do.

Taylor: That's malarkey! *I* wouldn't forget something like that.

Joe: Liar.

Stonewalling occurs when one party completely withdraws during a conflict discussion. The stonewaller offers no feedback, just cold silence and lack of expression. Stonewallers often claim that their behavior represents a neutral state, but as Gottman (1994) says, stonewalling conveys distance, smugness, and disapproval.

All of us, on one occasion of conflict or another, probably have engaged in one or more of these behaviors. Even happy and stable marital couples sometimes engage in negative behaviors. These behaviors have the potential to corrode a relationship (1) when they become habitual—that is, they are more common than uncommon—and (2) when their occurrence is grossly disproportionate to positive behaviors. As Gottman's (1994) research demonstrates, a satisfied couple balances negative behaviors with positive ones, regardless of the couple's style of managing conflict. In satisfied couples, the ratio of positive to negative behaviors is roughly 5:1. In dissatisfied couples, this ratio is closer to 1:1.

Positive Consequences Are More Than Merely Avoiding Negative Consequences

Thus far in our discussion of distal consequences we have emphasized negative behaviors and patterns. But it would be misleading to conclude that competent conflict management merely forestalls negative distal outcomes. Constructive conflict management over time is constructive for the relationship. Just as incompetent conflict management leads to relational dissatisfaction and instability, competent conflict management promotes relational satisfaction and stability.

First, conflict serves as the impetus to solving problems. When conflict management is competent, problems are more clearly identified and more often resolved, which prevents smaller disagreements from turning into larger, more serious disputes. Since problems are resolved more often than not, you feel happier.

Second, conflict energizes relationships. Boredom and predictability in the extreme can destabilize intimate bonds. Conflict affords stimulation and challenge, thereby producing needed novelty and vitality for relational patterns.

Third, being able to overcome disagreements produces a feeling of mutual accomplishment and strengthens the connections between relational partners. The mutuality of the process and the positivity of the outcomes associated with competent conflict management foster interpersonal solidarity.

Finally, conflict offers opportunities for personal exploration, understanding, and growth. According to Deutsch, "Conflict is often part of the process of testing and assessing oneself and, as such, may be highly enjoyable as one experiences the pleasure of the full and active use of one's capacities" (1973, p. 9). Thus, competent conflict contributes to an individual's mental hygiene, which is likely to facilitate one's competence as a relational partner.

Physical Health

Earlier we cited evidence that physiological arousal accompanying disagreement can produce health-related physical changes immediately following the conflict episode. Research also demonstrates that these proximal physical effects accumulate to produce more serious distal physical effects. For example, ongoing anger is associated with ailments ranging from acne and warts to ulcers, hypertension, and heart disease (Holt, 1970; Siegman, 1994). Extended negative conflict takes its physical toll over time, in subtle, creeping ways, just as it takes its mental toll. Chronic negative conflict behaviors gradually lead to rigid and negative attributions about one's partner, negative feelings about the relationship, and more negative behaviors. The effects of negative thoughts and behaviors accumulate to erode the relationship, although the extent of the physical damage depends on the individual.

SUMMARY

Conflict has many potential consequences. In this chaper we discussed some of the more important ones. Some of the same factors that affect how we conduct ourselves during conflict, namely attributions and emotions, also emerge as proximal conflict outcomes. Not surprisingly, positive feelings and relationship-enhancing attributions are more likely (1) when the relationship in which the conflict takes place is congenial and satisfying, and (2) when conflict is managed with integrative strategies.

The attributions we make and the feelings we have during and after a conflict are interesting in their own right. They take on greater significance when we realize that they mediate the association between conflict behavior and relational outcomes. Our attributions and feelings operate as interpretive filters that subtly translate the effects of individual conflicts on the overall relationship over time.

Similarly, judgments of communication competence influence the connection of conflict behaviors to relational qualities. Communication satisfaction and successful facework are two proximal outcomes associated with communication competence. Effective communication leads to satisfaction, and appropriate communication entails mutual face saving.

In discussing distal outcomes, we noted that conflict episodes can have cumulative effects on the relationship and on physical health. We do not wish to leave the impression that the connection of conflict to distal outcomes is only negative. Integrative conflict management can be relationship-enhancing, personally rewarding, good for your mental hygiene, and stress-reducing. Relational bonds are strengthened when conflict is competently managed. Interestingly, married couples who have the greatest number of serious disagreements report the highest levels of *avoidance* of conflict discussion (McGonagle, Kessler & Gotlib, 1993). Routine avoidance of serious disagreements is just as problematic as overly aggressive confrontation. Competent conflict engagement is constructive and highly positive in its consequences.

DISCUSSION QUESTIONS

1 Recall an incident in which you violated a rule and were called upon to account for your behavior. What kind of excuse did you offer? What did you say? Did you give the true reason for breaking the rule, or did you withhold the real reason and

provide an excuse that was more "acceptable"? What kind of attributions do you think others made about you on the basis of your excuse? How would their attributions be different if you gave a different excuse? Explain.

2 We are sometimes unaware that our behavior influences our own feelings as much as it influences the behavior of someone else. During conflict, what behaviors of your own contribute to your feelings of anger? guilt? hurt?

3 Why are you in a better position than other people to judge the effectiveness of your own conflict communication? Why are you not in the best position to judge the appropriateness of your own conflict behavior?

4 Think about how a friend or acquaintance usually manages conflict. Does this person follow the general rules of consideration, rationality, self-expression, conflict resolution (problem solving), and positivity? Do you two share other rules that may supersede these rules? What are they?

5 What is the connection between saving your own face and saving the face of the person with whom you disagree? When does saving your own face threaten the other person's face? How does saving the other person's face threaten your own? How do you reconcile a situation in which saving your own face seems to conflict with saving the other person's face? Whose face takes precedence? Why? Does threatening another's face ever simultaneously threaten your own face? Give an example.

INTRODUCTION TO
CONTRIBUTED CHAPTERS

Chapters 7 through 10 examine processes of interpersonal conflict in specific types of interaction settings. These chapters are written by well-respected scholars who possess knowledge and professional experience specific to these contexts. Each chapter extends and applies the competence-based approach to conflict.

In Chapter 7 Dr. Stella Ting-Toomey discusses the nature of conflict between individuals who come from different cultures. We learn that differences in expectations that are based on cultural differences can radically affect how we communicate and assess other people's communication.

Drs. Michael Papa and Wendy Papa discuss organizational communication in Chapter 8. They describe conflict in the organizational setting by employing a fascinating case study and some real-life illustrations of organizational conflict. The authors describe three phases that characterize competent conflict management. In addition, Papa and Papa examine organizational conflicts in various settings: interpersonal, bargaining and negotiation, conflict between groups, and conflict between organizations.

In Chapter 9 Dr. Brian Spitzberg presents provocative and enlightening research on violence in intimate relationships. Dr. Spitzberg's analysis causes us to question some long-standing assumptions about how violence functions in close relationships.

In Chapter 10 Drs. Claudia Hale and Amy Thieme draw on their professional experience as mediators to demonstrate the intricacies of conflicts mediated by a third party. They apply principles of competence to both disputants and mediators. The result is a clear and coherent account of the rules and resources that mediators can employ to manage conflict effectively and appropriately.

Each of these four chapters illustrates that the unique facets of a conflict affect the course of conflict interaction. Nevertheless, across all interpersonal settings, principles of competent communication provide insight about the successful management of conflict.

7

INTERCULTURAL CONFLICT COMPETENCE

Dr. Stella Ting-Toomey is professor of speech communication at California State University, Fullerton. Dr. Ting-Toomey earned her Ph.D. at the University of Washington. One of the top international experts in intercultural communication, she has written or edited several books and numerous journal articles and book chapters. Dr. Ting-Toomey's writings have focused on facework negotiation, ethnic identity, and cross-cultural conflict.

CHAPTER OUTLINE

A CULTURAL VARIABILITY PERSPECTIVE
    Individualism/Collectivism
    Self-Concept
    Low/High-Context Communication
FACTORS IN INTERCULTURAL CONFLICT
    Conflict Assumptions
    Conflict Rhythms
    Conflict Norms
    Conflict Styles
    Ethnocentric Lenses
COMPETENCE IN INTERCULTURAL CONFLICT
    Criteria for Conflict Competence
    Knowledge, Motivation, and Skill in Intercultural Conflict
SUMMARY
DISCUSSION QUESTIONS

Intercultural miscommunication and misattributions often underscore intercultural conflict. Individuals from contrasting cultural communities bring with them different value assumptions, expectations, verbal and nonverbal habits, and interaction scripts that influence the conflict process. Intercultural conflict is defined as the *perceived incompatibility of values, norms, processes, or goals between a minimum of two cultural parties over identity, relational, and/or substantive issues.* Intercultural conflict often starts off with different expectations concerning appropriate or inappropriate behavior in an interaction episode. Violations of expectation, in turn, often influence the effectiveness of how members of two cultures negotiate their interests or goals in the interaction. If inappropriate or ineffective negotiation behavior continues, the miscommunication can very easily spiral into a complex, polarized conflict. The following dialogue between two intercultural strangers trying to get acquainted in the Los Angeles International Airport lobby illustrates this type of conflict.

Example 1

Mr. Gass (a young, enthusiastic Euro-American businessman, shaking hands with Mr. Lim vigorously): Welcome to L.A., Mr. Lim. Nice meeting you, finally. My name is William Gass. Just call me Bill. Here is my business card. [*Bill forwards the card with his right hand.*]

Mr. Lim (an elderly Korean businessman): Nice meeting you, Mr. Gass. I'm Peter Pyong Gap Lim. Here is my business card. [*Mr. Lim forwards his card with both hands.*]

Mr. Gass: Please, call me Bill. I hope we'll be doing a lot of business together here in L.A.

Mr. Lim: Yes, I hope so too.

Mr. Gass (glancing quickly at Mr. Lim's card): Pyong Gap, I'll give you a call tomorrow after you get some rest in your hotel. Maybe we can have lunch together.

Mr. Lim (with a polite smile): Yes, maybe, Mr. Gass. Please call me tomorrow. I will await your phone call.

When members of different cultures greet one another in an initial encounter, they often draw on their own cultural scripts to guide their behavior. In Example 1, Mr. Gass is very pleased with the initial encounter with Mr. Lim. He is especially pleased that he called Mr. Lim "Pyong Gap"—his client's Korean name rather than his American name. Mr. Gass feels that he has succeeded in building an informal, symmetrical relationship with Mr. Lim by addressing him on a first-name basis and paying attention to his Korean ethnicity. Mr. Gass believes that they will be able to work well together, since Mr. Lim departed with a smile and a firm handshake.

Mr. Lim, on the other hand, is very uncertain about the initial meeting with Mr. Gass. First, Mr. Lim feels uncomfortable that Mr. Gass forwarded his business card using only one hand. In the Korean culture, a business card represents the face, or public self-image, of an individual. It should always be treated with proper respect and dignity. Mr. Gass should have forwarded his card with both hands and received Mr. Lim's business card with both hands. Second, Mr. Gass should have taken the time to read and admire Mr. Lim's card carefully before putting it away in his wallet. Third, Mr. Lim was uncomfortable and insulted when Mr. Gass addressed him by his Korean name. He would have preferred that Mr. Gass address him more formally as "Mr. Lim"; after all, Mr. Lim is the client and is much older than Mr. Gass.

As an older Korean businessman, Mr. Lim would like to see more asymmetrical deference and respect from Mr. Gass. If Mr. Gass insists on being informal, he should at least address Mr. Lim as "Peter" rather than "Pyong Gap," since Mr. Lim created his western name "Peter" just for the sake of informal interaction in American business transactions. Mr. Lim smiled because he was embarrassed by Mr. Gass's imposed intimacy. His smile was to cover his own embarrassment for the "face loss" incurred in the first few minutes of the initial encounter.

Both Mr. Gass and Mr. Lim have been conditioned by their own cultural norms or standards to behave in a certain way. While Mr. Lim is already anticipating difficulty in working with this "overbearing" American, Mr. Gass has no idea that he has offended his client in so many ways in the first few minutes of interaction. Although no explicit, interpersonal disagreement took place in Example 1, the seeds of potential disagreement or perceived incompatibility were sown. If similar miscommunication between Mr. Gass and Mr. Lim becomes a pattern in subsequent interactions, Mr. Gass may not be able to secure the business contracts he wants from Mr. Lim. Even though both Mr. Gass and Mr. Lim attempted to be sensitive to each other's cultural background, their effort created a cultural chasm.

Not all intercultural conflicts are caused by miscommunication or misunderstanding. Some intercultural conflicts arise because of deep-seated hatred, centuries of antagonism, and clear understanding. However, most everyday intercultural conflicts that we encounter can be traced to cultural miscommunication or ignorance. As cultural beings, we are socialized or "programmed" by the values and norms of our culture to think and behave in certain ways. Our family, peer groups, educational institutions, mass media system, political system, and religious institutions are some of the forces that shape and mold our cultural and personal values. Our learned values and norms are, in turn, expressed through the way we communicate.

The study of intercultural conflict in contemporary U.S. society is especially critical today for several reasons. First, in the United States, immigrants (many of whom are non-English speakers), members of minority groups, and women represent more than 50 percent of the present workforce. Second, by the year 2000, 85 percent of the *entering* workforce in the United States will be new immigrants, minority group members, and females (Loden & Rosener, 1991). Third, four out of every five new jobs in the United States at present are generated as a direct result of foreign trade (Lustig & Koester, 1993). As the global economy becomes an everyday reality in most societies, we will inevitably encounter people who are culturally different in diverse workplace and social environments. Learning to manage such differences, especially in intercultural conflicts, can bring about alternative perspectives and multiple solutions to an existing problem. Competence in intercultural conflict means managing cultural differences appropriately, effectively, and adaptively.

This chapter examines some of the cultural background factors (that is, distal context) that influence face-to-face intercultural conflict. The chapter is developed in three sections: First, the cultural variability perspective of individualism/collectivism, in conjunction with self-concept and low/high-context communication, is presented; second, some underlying factors that contribute to intercultural conflict are identified; third, a competence-based approach to intercultural conflict management is discussed.

A CULTURAL VARIABILITY PERSPECTIVE

Culture refers to a group-level construct that embodies a distinctive system of traditions, beliefs, values, norms, rituals, symbols, and meanings that is shared by a majority of interacting individuals in a community. Simply put, culture refers to a patterned way of living by a group of interacting individuals who share similar sets of beliefs, values, and behaviors. A complex frame of reference influences our thought patterns, our feelings, and our everyday functioning. In order to understand differences and similarities in the assumptions and behaviors in conflict across cultures, we need a perspective or framework to explain in depth why and how cultures are different or similar.

Although there are many potential dimensions in which cultures differ, one dimension that receives consistent attention from intercultural researchers around the world is *individualism/collectivism*. Individualism/collectivism explains group-level differences between cultures. Research in different regions of the world indicates that individualism/collectivism is particularly relevant to explaining conflict interactions across various cultures (Leung, 1987, 1988; Ting-Toomey et al., 1991; Triandis, 1995). A value-based dimension such as individualism/collectivism, can provide us with a more in-depth understanding of why members of two contrasting cultures (for example, American and Korean cultures) approach conflict differently. In addition to this dimension are the dimensions of self-concept and low/high-context communication. The former explains individual-level approaches to conflict; the latter explains cultural differences in conflict style.

As a whole, a cultural variability perspective emphasizes the following three dimensions: individualism/collectivism, self-concept, and low/high-context communication. These three dimensions influence the values we hold in approaching or avoiding conflict, the way we attribute meanings to conflict events, and the way we communicate in specific conflict episodes.

Individualism/Collectivism

Individualism refers to the broad value tendencies of people in a culture to emphasize individual identity over group identity, individual rights over group obligations, and individual achievements over group concerns. In contrast, *collectivism* refers to the broad value tendencies of people in a culture to emphasize group identity over individual identity, group obligations over individual rights, and group-oriented concerns over individual wants and desires (Hofstede, 1980, 1991; Triandis, 1995). Individualism is expressed in interpersonal conflict through the strong assertion of personal opinions, the revealing of personal emotions, and personal accountability for any conflict problem or mistake. Collectivism is manifested in interpersonal conflict through the representation of collective opinions or ideas, the restraint of personal emotional expressions, and group accountability, if possible, for the conflict problem. The following dialogue between a supervisor (a Jewish American) and a supervisee (a recent Chinese immigrant) at an international firm in New York City illustrates the individualism/collectivism dimension of intercultural conflict.

Example 2

Ms. Shapiro (the supervisor): David, is the new computer procedure working yet?

Mr. Chang (the supervisee): There were some minor problems.

Ms. Shapiro: How soon will it be ready?

Mr. Chang: It's hard to tell, Ms. Shapiro. We need to look into it more carefully.

Ms. Shapiro (impatiently): Whose idea was this new procedure, anyway?

Mr. Chang (with apologetic smile): Well . . . we'll definitely be more careful next time. We've learned from this lesson.

Ms. Shapiro (decisively): It came from Derrick Wong's division, didn't it?

Mr. Chang (hesitantly): Well . . . many people worked on this project, Ms. Shapiro. It's hard to say . . .

Ms. Shapiro (frustrated): All right, just give me a definite time line for when the procedure can be up and running. I've got to run to the next meeting. I don't have time to waste.

In Example 2, Ms. Shapiro is operating from an "I-oriented" mode of conflict behavior, Mr. Chang from a "we-oriented" mode. Ms. Shapiro expects two pieces of information from her line of questioning—namely, who is responsible for the problem and when Mr. Chang can fix the problem. However, Mr. Chang appears "fuzzy" on both issues. Because of his Chinese group-oriented perspective, Mr. Chang feels uneasy singling out a culprit for the computer mistake. From his attribution process, Mr. Chang perceives that many people have contributed to the oversight. In addition, since he perceives the project as a team effort, he has to consult the opinion of the entire group before he can offer his supervisor a feasible time line.

Ms. Shapiro, on the other hand, feels the need to confront Mr. Chang for more information and a specific time line because she wants to uncover the "truth." She is eager to identify a particular person or a name with the mistake so that she can reward the good workers and sanction the bad ones. From her attribution process, Ms. Shapiro desires to be an effective supervisor, and she wants to deal with the problematic situation equitably and fairly. She does not want to blame the entire work team for one person's mistake.

To preserve the appearance of group harmony or group "face" (that is, social self-image), Mr. Chang feels he has answered Ms. Shapiro appropriately and perhaps even effectively. On the other hand, Ms. Shapiro walks away from the conflict frustrated because she perceives Mr. Chang's response as neither effective nor appropriate. She feels "betrayed" by Mr. Chang because he has not leveled with her openly and honestly. Communication openness and honesty are two qualities that Ms. Shapiro prizes deeply. In brief, both Mr. Chang and Ms. Shapiro have been "programmed" by their cultural beliefs and values to think and act in a certain manner. However, both remain unconscious of the underlying value assumptions (such as individualism and collectivism) that drive their behavior.

In research on intercultural communication, the British, French, German, Scandinavian, Swiss, Australian, Canadian, and U.S. cultures have been identified consistently as high in individualistic value tendencies (Hofstede, 1980, 1991). Comparatively, strong empirical evidence suggests that many Asian, southeast Asian, Mediterranean, Latino, Middle Eastern, and African cultures can be identified clearly as group-based cultures (Gudykunst & Ting-Toomey, 1988; Hofstede, 1980, 1991; Kim et al., 1994; Triandis, 1994, 1995). Different degrees and forms of individualism and collectivism (see, for example, Triandis, 1995) exist in different cultures.

Nevertheless, we can also find "both individualistic and collectivistic elements in *all* of these countries, in different combinations" (Triandis, 1995, p. 2). In addition, considerable differences within cultures have been uncovered in many pluralistic societies. For example, within a pluralistic society such as Canada or the United States, different ethnic communities can display distinctive individualistic and group-oriented value tendencies. Cultural miscommunication and conflicts often arise because of our ignorance of different value priorities and modes of behavior in different cultures. Moving beyond the general discussion of culture-level differences, we can examine individual-level differences within and across cultures.

Self-Concept

An alternative way to understand individualism and collectivism focuses on how individuals within a culture conceptualize the sense of self. Markus and Kitayama (1991) argue that the placement of self-concept in our culture profoundly influences our communication with others. Individuals with a strong sense of *independent self* tend to see themselves as autonomous, self-reliant, unencumbered agents of change, and as rational choice makers. Individuals with a strong sense of *interdependent self* tend to see themselves as group-bound, role-based, interconnected, obligatory agents, and as harmony seekers. Both types of self-concept exist within a culture. Overall, however, whereas independent concepts of self are more common in individualistic cultures, interdependent concepts of self are more common in collectivistic cultures.

The following dialogue takes place between a Japanese American (with a strong sense of independent self), Ms. Sueda, and a Japanese national (with a strong sense of interdependent self), Mr. Ota. Ms. Sueda is the representative of the accounting department of a joint-venture U.S.-Japan firm. Mr. Ota is the representative of the marketing department based in Tokyo. The dialogue takes place in a staff meeting (with Japanese and American staff members) in Tokyo.

Example 3

Ms. Sueda (enthusiastically): Since we're all here today in the meeting, I would like to discuss with you my opinion on the renewed contract with the Fuji advertising firm. But before I do that, Ota-san, what do you think of the Fuji firm?

Mr. Ota (taken by surprise): Ms. Sueda, what about the Fuji firm?

Ms. Sueda: Ota-san, I don't think they are working out for us. I don't think they are being aggressive enough in pushing our springwater products. I seriously think we should switch to a new firm. Their ads did not seem to have any impact on generating new sales for us.

Mr. Ota: [*Long silent pauses*] . . . Ms. Sueda, have you discussed this with others in our department?

Ms. Sueda (looking around): Not really. That's why I'm sounding you out right now.

Mr. Ota: Well . . . it is a good idea to get as many people's opinions as possible on this important decision. Why don't we wait?

Ms. Sueda (impatiently): But I'm really not satisfied with Fuji's "soft-sell" approach on our products. If you have any opinion, now is a good time to speak up. So what do you think?

Mr. Ota: Um . . . We really have to give this some more thought. . . . After all, we've cultivated a good relationship with the people in the Fuji firm. . . . Maybe I'll check around with other people in the department after the meeting to ask their inputs.

Ms. Sueda: Well, all your department people are here in this room. Why don't we ask them right now? Okabe-san, what do you think?

Mr. Okabe (taken by surprise): Well . . . [*a long pause*] . . . We should spend more time thinking together.

Ms. Sueda (very frustrated): All right, everyone, wasted time is wasted effort. Ota-san, back to you. What do you really think?

Mr. Ota (glancing around the room and sensing tension): Well . . . [*a very long pause*] . . . I really couldn't say right now. . . . It takes time to make such an important decision.

While Ms. Sueda is direct in her approach to dealing with a problematic issue, Mr. Ota is cautious. Coming from an interdependent-self perspective, Mr. Ota perceives major problems in changing from an old advertising firm to a new one. It takes time to cultivate reliable, reciprocal social ties in Japan. It will take a long time for him and his staff to nurture network relations with a new firm. In addition, Mr. Ota resents the fact that he is being singled out so suddenly by Ms. Sueda for his personal opinion in a group setting. Her action causes him to "lose face" in front of his colleagues because he is underprepared to answer. Mr. Ota wishes that Ms. Sueda had consulted with him before the staff meeting. He does not want to state his opinion in the public setting for fear that his opinion goes against the opinion of other members of his group. Also, in front of other staff members (which include both Americans and Japanese), Mr. Ota does not want to raise all the issues openly with Ms. Sueda, because that may cause her to "lose face" (for example, the issue that "soft-sell" advertising works better in Japan than "hard-sell" advertising), and appear incompetent.

If Ms. Sueda had listened attentively to both the verbal and nonverbal nuances conveyed by Mr. Ota, she would have realized that Mr. Ota's answer to her initial question was a "no-maybe" response. By remarking that "we've cultivated a good relationship with the people in the Fuji firm," Mr. Ota is implicitly saying, "No, but let's talk about this issue later, maybe privately, and maybe we can work something out."

Ms. Sueda, on the other hand, perceives herself as being a very consultative colleague. Coming from an independent-self perspective, Ms. Sueda expects everyone else in the room to speak up openly and freely. In soliciting everyone's input in the open-door staff meeting, she views herself as very respectful of staff members working in this joint-venture operation. By asking Mr. Ota's opinion, Ms. Sueda thinks she is being "face-sensitive" to Mr. Ota's status as head of the marketing department in Tokyo. She is baffled and frustrated by Mr. Ota's hesitant pauses and effusive style of speech. She has started to think that maybe her Japanese colleagues do not like to work with a woman, especially a *sansei* (third-generation) Japanese-American woman from the United States.

Independent-self people tend to make sense of their environment through autonomous-self lenses; interdependent-self people tend to make sense of their surroundings through group-bound–self lenses. Independent-self individuals tend to worry about whether they present their individualistic self credibly and competently in front of others. Interdependent-self individuals tend to be more reflective of what others think of their projected face image in the context of in-group/out-group relations (which are discussed later in the section on *Conflict Norms*). Finally, while independent-self individuals tend to practice direct verbal communication, expressing their own thoughts and feelings, interdependent-self individuals tend to practice responsive communication, anticipating the thoughts and feelings of the other person. Direct verbal communication is a low-context way of communicating; responsive communication is a high-context way of communicating (Hall, 1976, 1983).

Low/High-Context Communication

According to Hall (1976), human interaction can be divided into low-context and high-context communication systems. Low-context communication emphasizes expressing intention or meaning through explicit verbal messages. High-context communication emphasizes conveying intention or meaning through the context (for example, social roles, positions) and the nonverbal channels (for example, pauses, silence, tone of voice) of the verbal message. In general, low-context communication refers to communiation patterns of direct verbal mode, straight talk, nonverbal immediacy, and sender-oriented value. In low-context communication, the speaker is expected to construct a clear, persuasive message that the listener can decode easily. In contrast, high-context communication refers to communication patterns of indirect verbal mode, ambiguous talk, nonverbal subtleties, and interpreter-sensitive value (Ting-Toomey, 1985). In high-context communication, the listener or interpreter of the message is expected to read "between the lines," to infer accurately the implicit intent of the verbal message, and to observe the nonverbal nuances and subtleties that accompany the verbal message. High-context communication emphasizes the importance of multilayered contexts (for example, historical context, social norms, roles, situational and relational contexts) that frame the interaction. The following dispute between two Euro-American neighbors illustrates a low-context communication style.

Example 4

Jane (knocks on her neighbor's open window): Excuse me, it is eleven o'clock already and your high-pitched opera singing is really disturbing my sleep. Please stop your gargling noises immediately! I have an important job interview tomorrow morning, and I want to get a good night's sleep. I really need this job to pay my rent!!

Diane (resentfully): Well, this is the only time I can rehearse my opera!! I've an important audition coming up tomorrow. You're not the only one who is starving, you know. I also need to pay my rent. Stop being so self-centered!!

Jane (frustrated): I really think you're being very unreasonable. If you don't stop your singing right now I'm going to file a complaint with the apartment manager and he could evict you.

Diane (sarcastically): OK, be my guest. . . . Do whatever you want. I'm going to sing as I please.

In contrast, the following dialogue between two Japanese housewives illustrates the high-context communication style (Naotsuka et al., 1981, p. 70).

Example 5

Mrs. A: Your daughter has started taking piano lessons, hasn't she? I envy you, because you can be proud of her talent. You must be looking forward to her future as a pianist. I'm really impressed by her enthusiasm—every day, she practices so hard, for hours and hours, until late at night.

Mrs. B: Oh, no, not at all. She is just a beginner. We don't know her future yet. We hadn't realized that you could hear her playing. I'm so sorry you have been disturbed by her noise.

In Example 4, Jane and Diane spell out everything in their mind with no restraints. Their exchange is direct, to the point, disclosing, and full of face-threatening verbal messages. Although this dialogue represents unproductive conflict, Jane and Diane could make their dialogue more productive by identifying common interests (such as urgency of job search and rent payment) and constructive options (such as closing windows or practicing in another room). They could use the strengths of low-context, explicit talk in dealing with the conflict issue openly and nonevaluatively.

In Example 5, Mrs. A has not directly expressed her concern over the piano noise with Mrs. B, because she wants to preserve face and her relationship with Mrs. B. Rather, Mrs. A uses only indirect hints and nonverbal signals to get her point across. However, Mrs. B correctly reads between the lines of Mrs. A's verbal message and apologizes appropriately and effectively before any real conflict bubbles to the surface. In high-context conflict situations, even minor disagreement is perceived as a major face-threatening situation if the face, or social self-image, of the conflict parties is not upheld or preserved. From the high-context communication viewpoint, minor disagreement can easily turn into a major conflict if face-threatening and face-saving issues are not dealt with strategically, appropriately, and effectively.

If Mrs. A were the neighbor of Diane in Example 4, Diane might not be able to read between the lines of Mrs. A's verbal message. Diane might not even realize that a conflict is already simmering between her and Mrs. A. Diane might take Mrs. A's verbal message literally, inferring it as a compliment and thus might sing even louder. While Mrs. A and Mrs. B learn and practice the high-context interaction scripts in Japanese society, Jane and Diane tend to use the low-context communication styles more often than high-context styles in the United States.

As Barnlund, in commenting on the communication style differences between Japanese and Americans, observes:

> Conflict is far less common in Japanese society for a number of reasons. First, the emphasis on the group instead of the individual reduces interpersonal friction. Second, an elaborate set of standards emphasizes "obligations" over "rights," what one owes to others rather than deserves for oneself. Third, the value attached to harmony cultivates skill in the use of ambiguity, circumlocution, euphemism, and silence in blunting incipient disputes. The ability to assimilate differences, to engineer consensus, is valued above a talent for argument. (1989, p. 39)

Individualism and independent-self concept in the United States promote the need for verbal self-assertion, and verbal self-assertion often promotes individual differences and competitions. In contrast, collectivism and interdependent-self concept in Japan promotes the need for verbal circumspection, and verbal circumspection often promotes face preservation and relational harmony.

To summarize, while independent-self individualists engage in low-context styles of conflict management, interdependent-self collectivists engage in high-context styles of conflict negotiation. Overall, the cultural variability dimensions of individualism/collectivism, independent/interdependent-self concept, and low/high-context communication patterns help guide us toward a general understanding of conflict between members of individualistic and collectivistic cultures.

FACTORS IN INTERCULTURAL CONFLICT

Drawing from the key ideas of a cultural variability perspective, this section identifies the underlying factors that create intercultural frictions and conflicts between individualists and collectivists. These factors include differences in conflict assumptions, conflict rhythms, conflict norms, conflict styles, and ethnocentric lenses.

Conflict Assumptions

The values of individualism versus collectivism, and how these values are linked to individual self-concepts and low/high-context communication patterns, affect our assumptions about conflict. Cultural assumptions about conflict color our attitudes, expectations, and behaviors in the conflict episode. Different cultural assumptions toward conflict are one factor contributing to intercultural miscommunication and conflict.

For individualists, the resolution of interpersonal conflict follows an outcome-oriented model. For collectivists, however, the management of interpersonal conflict follows a process-oriented model. An *outcome-oriented model* emphasizes the importance of asserting individual interests in the conflict situation and moving rapidly toward the phase of reaching tangible outcomes or goals. A *process-oriented model* emphasizes the importance of managing mutual or group face interests in the conflict process before discussing tangible outcomes or goals. "Face," in this context, refers to upholding a claimed sense of positive public image in any social interaction (Ting-Toomey, 1994a). From the collectivistic perspective, face is not about what one thinks of oneself, but about what others think of one's worth, especially within the in-group/out-group context.

For individualists, effective conflict negotiation means settling the conflict problem openly and working out a set of functional conflict solutions conjointly. Effective conflict resolution behavior (for example, emphasizing the importance of addressing incompatible goals or outcomes) is *relatively* more important than appropriate facework behavior. For collectivists, on the other hand, appropriate conflict management means the subtle negotiation of in-group/out-group face-related issues—pride, honor, dignity, insult, shame, disgrace, humility, trust, mistrust, respect, and prestige—in a given conflict episode. Appropriate facework moves and countermoves are critical before tangible conflict outcomes or goals can be addressed.

In commenting on face issues in collectivistic cultures, Cohen observes, "For the representatives of interdependent cultures the experience of international negotiation is fraught with considerations of face. The very structure of the situation, in which competing parties pit their wills and skills against each other, is uncongenial to societies that see social harmony, not confrontation, as the desired state of affairs" (1991, p. 132).

To summarize, independent-self individualists tend to operate from the following outcome-oriented conflict assumptions:

1 Conflict is perceived as being closely related to the goals or outcomes that are salient to the respective individual conflict parties in a given conflict situation.

2 Communication during conflict is viewed as dissatisfying when the conflict parties are not willing to deal with the conflict openly and honestly.

3 Communication during conflict is viewed as satisfying when the conflict parties are willing to confront the conflict issues openly and share their feelings honestly (that is, assertively but not aggressively).

4 Conflict is perceived as unproductive when no tangible outcome or plan of action is reached or developed.

5 Conflict is perceived as productive when tangible solutions are reached and objective criteria are met.

6 Effective and appropriate management of conflict means that individual goals are addressed and differences are dealt with openly, honestly, and properly in relation to timing and situational context.

Interdependent-self collectivists follow the conflict assumptions of a process-oriented model:

1 Conflict is weighed against the threat to face that is incurred in the conflict negotiation process and is interpreted in the webs of in-group/out-group relationships.

2 Communication during conflict is perceived as threatening when the conflict parties push for a discussion of substantive issues before properly managing face-related issues.

3 Communication during conflict is viewed as satisfying when the conflict parties engage in *mutual* face-saving and face-giving behavior and attend to both verbal and nonverbal signals.

4 Conflict processes and outcomes are perceived as unproductive when face issues are not addressed and relational or group feelings are not attended to properly.

5 Conflict processes and outcomes are defined as productive when both conflict parties can claim that they have "won" with respect to both face-related and substantive issues.

6 Appropriate and effective management of conflict means that the faces of both conflict parties are saved or even upgraded in the interaction, and the parties have dealt with the conflict episode strategically in conjunction with substantive gains or losses.

Thus, while individualists are concerned with resolving conflict problems, collectivists are concerned with the dynamic issues of in-group/out-group face. These implicit conflict assumptions are superimposed on the rhythms and pacing of intercultural conflict resolution.

Conflict Rhythms

The consciousness of conflict management rhythms varies along the individualism/collectivism divide. Differences in conflict rhythms are the second factor contributing to intercultural conflict between individualists and collectivists. Individualistic values tend to foster *monochronic-time rhythms,* and collectivistic value tendencies tend to cultivate *polychronic-time rhythms.*

As Hall and Hall explain: "In monochronic cultures, time is experienced and used in a linear way—comparable to a road . . . M-time [monochronic time] is divided quite naturally into segments; it is scheduled and compartmentalized, making it possible for a person to concentrate on one thing at a time. In a monochronic system, the schedule may take on priority above all else and be treated as sacred and unalterable" (1987, p. 16). Hall and Hall identified Germany, Scandinavia, Switzerland, and the United States as prime M-time examples. In contrast, they note: "Polychronic (P-time) systems are the antithesis of M-time systems. P-time is characterized by the simultaneous occurrence of many things and by a great involvement with people. There is also more emphasis on completing human transactions than on holding schedules. . . . P-time is experienced as much less tangible than M-time, and can better be compared to a single point than to a road" (Hall & Hall, 1987, pp. 17–18). Many African, Asian, Latin American, Eastern European, Caribbean, and Mediterranean cultures are prime examples of P-time systems.

M-time people prefer to deal with conflict using a linear approach; P-time people prefer to handle conflict from a spiral viewpoint. For M-time individuals, conflict management time should be filled with problem-solving or decision-making activities. For P-time individuals, time is a "being" idea governed by the smooth implicit rhythms in the interactions between people. When two P-time individuals come into conflict, they are more concerned with restoring the disjunctive rhythms in the interaction than with dealing head-on with substantive issues.

M-time people tend to emphasize agenda setting, objective criteria, and clear time schedules to accomplish certain conflict goals. P-time people, in contrast, tend to work on the relational atmosphere and the contextual setting that frame the conflict episode. For M-time individuals, effective conflict negotiation means reaching and implementing tangible conflict outcomes within a clearly established timetable. For P-time individuals, the arbitrary division of clock time or calendar time holds little meaning if the relational rhythms between people are out of sync. For M-time people, a signed contract or written agreement signals joint explicit agreement to the solution of the conflict problem. For P-time people, however, once the appropriate level of relational rhythm or rapport is established, their words can mean more than a signed contract. Likewise, if they perceive that the relational rhythms are disjunctive, renewed face-related negotiation is needed to restore that delicate, face-honoring point. M-time people tend to define conflict using a short-term time line; P-time people tend to view time from a long-term, historical process. For P-time members, "deadline" is always subject to renegotiation, and human deadlines should be dealt with flexibly and patiently.

People move with different rhythms in conflict negotiation. Intercultural conflict between individualists and collectivists is magnified when the implicit rhythm of time plays a decisive role in the encounter. M-time individuals want to move faster to address substantive problems and resolve the conflict. P-time individuals prefer to deal with relational and contextual issues before concrete, substantive negotiation. M-time persons want to establish a clear timetable to achieve specific conflict goals and objectives. P-time people want to spend more time building trust and commitment between the conflict parties. Different rhythms of monochronic time and polychronic time thus can further polarize the individualists and the collectivists in the intercultural misattribution process.

Conflict Norms

Differences in norms of conflict interaction are the third factor compounding intercultural conflict. Norms are standards or guidelines for behavior. They are reflected in our expectations of what constitutes proper or improper behavior in a given setting.

Research has shown that individualists tend to prefer the equity norm (that is, the self-deservingness norm) in dealing with reward allocation in conflict interaction (Leung & Bond, 1984; Leung & Iwawaki, 1988). In comparison, collectivists prefer the communal norm (that is, the equal distribution norm) in in-group conflict, thereby preserving in-group harmony. The *equity norm* emphasizes the importance of individual reward and cost calculations, and of obtaining equitable rewards in resolving the problematic issue. The *communal norm* stresses the importance of taking in-group expectations into account in the calculation, and of satisfying the face needs of the in-group members that are involved in the conflict.

While the equity norm reflects the individualistic, outcome-oriented model in conflict, the communal norm reflects the collectivistic, process-oriented model. In addition, in collectivistic cultures different norms govern conflict interaction with in-group and out-group members. According to Triandis, *in-groups* are groups of individuals "about whose welfare a person is concerned, with whom that person is willing to cooperate without demanding equitable returns, and separation from whom leads to anxiety" (1995, p. 9). In-groups usually consist of people who perceive a "common fate" or shared attributes. *Out-groups* are groups of individuals "with which one has something to divide, perhaps unequally, or are harmful in some way, groups that disagree on valued attributes" (Triandis, 1995, p. 9). For very important conflicts, collectivists (similar to the individualists) prefer to use the equity norm when competing with out-group members (for example, people from another company) for needed resources (Leung & Iwawaki, 1988). However, for less important conflicts, collectivists prefer to use the communal, smoothing norm with either in-group or out-group members. Each culture also has different rules and meanings for proper or improper conflict behavior in dealing with in-group or out-group members in different situations.

By the norms of emotional expression, conflict is an emotionally distressing experience. In two extensive, detailed reviews of culture and emotions (Mesquita & Frijda, 1992; Russell, 1991), clear cross-cultural differences in emotional expression and interpretation are uncovered. On the basis of these reviews, we can conclude that there are cultural norms that regulate displays of aggressive or negative emotional reactions in conflict interaction such as anger, fear, shame, frustration, resentment, and hostility. For example, in many individualistic western cultures, open expressions of emotions in conflict are viewed as honest, engaging signals. In many collectivistic Asian cultures, however, restrained emotions are viewed as self-disciplined, mature signals in handling conflict. Thus, while basic emotions such as anxiety, shame, and fear can be viewed as pancultural conflict emotions, cultural display rules of when to express which nonverbal emotions (to whom and in what context) differ from one cultural community to the next. For example, for collectivists, the masking of negative emotions is critical to maintain a harmonious front during conflict. When collectivists feel embarrassed or perceive face threat in conflict, they may sometimes smile to cover up their embarrassment or shame.

Thus, different norms and rules govern the way individualists and collectivists deal with specific conflict issues. When an individualist prefers to use the equity norm to deal with a conflict issue and a collectivist prefers to use the communal norm, the hidden factor of normative expectations further splinters intercultural communication. In addition, the nonverbal/verbal dimension of emotional expression in conflict can vary along the individualism and collectivism schism, creating further tensions and gaps.

Conflict Styles

Findings from many studies indicate that people exhibit consistent cross-situational styles of conflict in different cultures. Culture assumes the primary role of conditioning certain preferred conflict styles or behaviors over others (Ting-Toomey, 1994b, 1994c). Differences in conflict styles are the fourth factor in intercultural conflict negotiation. Cultural differences in conflict style generate intergroup attribution errors and biases. For example, the following dialogue between Ms. Gumb (an African-American supervisor) and

Mr. Lee (a recent Chinese immigrant) in a U.S.-China joint-venture firm illustrates differences in conflict styles and attribution processes.

Example 6

Ms. Gumb (in the main office): Lee, where is your project report? You said you'd get it done soon. I need your part of the report so that I can finish my final report by the end of this week. When do you think you can get it done? [*Attribution: Lee is very irresponsible. I should never have trusted him. I thought I was giving him a break by putting him in charge of this report.*]

Mr. Lee (hesitantly): Well, Ms. Gumb . . . I didn't realize the deadline was so soon. . . . I will try my best to get it done as soon as possible. It's just that there are lots of details I need to cross-check. . . . I'm really not sure. [*Attribution: Ms. Gumb is sure a tough lady. Anyway, she is the supervisor, why didn't she tell me the exact deadline early on? Just last week, she told me to take my time on the report. I'm really confused. In China, the supervisor always tells the workers what to do.*]

Ms. Gumb (frustrated): Lee, how soon is soon? I really need to know your plan of action right now. You cannot be so vague in answering my questions all the time. I believe I've given you plenty of time to work on this report already. [*Attribution: Lee is trying to be sneaky. He does not answer my questions directly at all. I wonder if all Chinese are that sneaky? Or maybe he is not comfortable working for a black female? Anyway, I have to press him to be more efficient and responsible. He is in America; he has to learn the American way.*]

Mr. Lee: [*a long pause*] . . . Well, I'm really not sure, Ms. Gumb. I really don't want to do a bad job on the report and disappoint you. I'll try my best to finish it as soon as possible. Maybe I can finish the report next week. [*Attribution: Ms. Gumb is sure a pushy boss. She doesn't seem to like me and she is causing me to lose face in front of all my peers. Her voice sounds so harsh and blunt. I have heard American people are hard to work with, but she is especially rude and overbearing. I better start looking for a new job tomorrow.*]

In Example 6, while Ms. Gumb is assertive and direct in dealing with the problem, Mr. Lee is hesitant and indirect in answering her questions. Ms. Gumb has a "straight-talk," low-context approach to dealing with the work problem; Mr. Lee has a "face-talk," high-context approach. If both understand concepts such as low-context and high-context communication styles, they may arrive at a better understanding of each other's behavior.

Conflict style differences between cultural or ethnic group members profoundly influence the meanings we attach to each other's behavior. We typically use our own habitual scripts and interaction styles as a baseline to judge and evaluate others' behavior. While Mr. Lee is using his high-context scripts to evaluate Ms. Gumb's behavior as rude and overbearing, Ms. Gumb is using her low-context attribution (for example, "Lee is trying to be sneaky") and historical script (for example, "maybe he is not comfortable working for a black female") to make sense of Mr. Lee's high-context approach. If Ms. Gumb and Mr. Lee understand the cultural and historical conditioning of their own and the other's behavior, they may learn to be more culturally sensitive in their attribution process. They may learn to respect each other's stylistic scripts and work more adaptively in achieving a common ground in their interaction.

Ms. Gumb may learn to talk privately to Mr. Lee rather than to engage in such direct face-threatening behavior in public. Mr. Lee may learn to be more direct and open in answering his supervisor's questions and to pause and hedge less in their interaction. On the strategy level, individualists in conflict appear to prefer direct verbal assertions, direct verbal questioning, direct requests, and direct clarifications and answers in conflict. In contrast, collectivists prefer qualifiers (for example, "*perhaps* we should meet this deadline together"), tag questions (for example, "*don't you think* you'll feel better if you finish it and get it out of the way?"), disclaimers (for example, "*maybe I don't understand* what's going on here"), and indirect requests (for example, "*if it's not too much trouble,* let's try to finish this report together") to convey a softened approach to working out differences.

Research across cultures (for example, China, Hong Kong, Japan, Korea, Taiwan, Mexico, and the United States) clearly indicates that individualists tend to use styles in managing conflict that are more self-oriented, controlling, and competitive than those of collectivists, who tend to use mutual face-saving, integrative, and compromising styles in dealing with conflict. Furthermore, the styles of collectivists in task-oriented conflict situations tend to be more obliging and avoiding than those of individualists (Chua & Gudykunst, 1987; Ting-Toomey et al., 1991; Trubisky, Ting-Toomey & Lin, 1991). Silence is a critical strategy in dealing with both in-group and out-group conflicts in collectivistic cultures. Silence may signal approval or disapproval in collectivistic conflict interaction. In silence, the conflict parties incur no obligations. Silence may also be interpreted as an ambiguous "yes" or "no" response. On the other hand, silence may be viewed as an admission of guilt or incompetence in an individualistic culture.

Finally, several researchers indicate that collectivists tend to prefer an *informal* third-party conflict mediation procedure (such as seeking help from relatives or from wise teachers or gurus) more so than individualists (Cohen, 1991; Leung, 1987, 1988; Ting-Toomey, 1985, 1988). In mediated conflicts individualists prefer objective advice and facilitation from an impartial, formal third-party mediator (such as a certified mediator; see Chapter 10), and collectivists prefer to seek help from someone who already is informed about the conflict and whom they can trust and respect.

Different cross-cultural conflict styles create different attribution biases and tensions. In attributing meanings to collectivistic, indirect conflict styles, individualists tend to view collectivists in the conflict as trying to sidestep genuine issue discussions. Conversely, collectivists tend to perceive individualists as pushy, rude, and overbearing because of their confrontational conflict style.

Ethnocentric Lenses

Although we often rely on the knowledge of our own cultural approach, rhythms, norms, and styles to explain the behavior of other people from our culture, the same criteria may not be applicable to another culture. Being unfamiliar with the other party's cultural norms creates problems that can exacerbate an already tense intercultural conflict episode. An examination of such problems is a natural extension of the discussion on differences in conflict styles.

Ethnocentrism is defined as "the view of things in which one's own group is the center of everything, and all others are scaled and rated with reference to it" (Sumner, 1940, p. 13). When members of different cultures believe that their own approaches are the correct or natural ways to handle conflict, they tend to see the conflict behaviors of other cultures as deviant from the standard. Interestingly, the word *ethnocentrism* is derived from the two Greek words *ethnos,* "nation," and *kentron,* "center." In the context of the Greek culture in the Golden Age, those who spoke Greek were viewed as the "cultured" people, while anyone who did not speak this eloquent language was labeled a *barbarikos,* "barbarian" (that is, someone whose language was incomprehensible and sounded like a repeated chatter, or "barbar" sound).

According to Triandis (1990b), all cultural beings display the following ethnocentric tendencies: (1) to define what goes on in their culture as natural and correct and what goes on in other cultures as unnatural and incorrect; (2) to perceive in-group values, customs, norms, and roles as universally valid (that is, what's good for us is good for everybody else); (3) to feel proud of the in-group; and (4) to practice in-group favoritism and out-group distance or hostility. Accordingly, a rigidly held ethnocentric attitude promotes a climate of mistrust in intergroup conflict and is a hidden barrier to constructive conflict resolution.

Individualists with strong ethnocentric tendencies tend to view the outcome-oriented model as superior and more efficient in conflict resolution than the process-oriented model. Conversely, collectivists with strong ethnocentric lenses tend to view the process-oriented model as more desirable and personable than the mechanistic outcome-oriented model. Ethnocentrism reflects our comfort with familiar cultural habits and practices. Individuals are often unaware of their own ethnocentric behaviors and evaluations. They have internalized the standards and norms of their culture as the "proper" and "right" ways of behaving.

Individualists and collectivists also may engage in different attribution processes during interpersonal conflict. Overall, individualists tend to use more dispositional attributions than do collectivists to explain the conflict problem. Individualists might explain conflict by making negative personality statements such as "She's late because she's lazy" or "He's just too dumb to get it." Collectivists, on the other hand, tend to use more situational attributions than do individualists to explain problems. For example, they make statements such as "Maybe she's late because the traffic is really bad" or "Maybe he's confused because the manager did not explain the project clearly." Individualists tend to hold the person accountable for the conflict; collectivists tend to emphasize the context that contributes to the conflict.

Individualists and collectivists sometimes use similar attributions in making sense of conflict. Stewart and Bennett, in commenting on how ethnocentrism leads to more intensified intercultural miscommunication, observe: "When communicators engage in mutual negative evaluation, the recriminatory interaction may be enough to block communication. If the communicators then attempt to overcome the difficulty through ethnocentric procedures, the communication event may deteriorate even further. . . . With each turn of this regressive spiral, negative evaluations are intensified" (1991, p. 165). The lack of specific information about each other's conflict assumptions or styles often creates negative interaction spirals that deepen the cultural schism. The lack of communication skills to handle such problematic intercultural episodes appropriately and effectively also compounds the miscommunication chasm.

Our ethnocentric lenses push us to judge the behavior of another culture evaluatively and negatively. Ethnocentrism creates biased attributions and expectations in intercultural conflict. Thus, cultural differences in conflict assumptions, conflict rhythms, conflict norms, conflict styles, and ethnocentric lenses act as invisible barriers that widen the gap of intercultural conflict. Individualists and collectivists typically collide over their use of an outcome-oriented model or process-oriented model in dealing with conflict. They also collide over the rhythms, the norms, and the styles of how to approach conflict appropriately and effectively. Ethnocentric lenses creep into our attribution process and create further evaluative biases and binary mind-sets (that is, my way is the *right* way and your way is *wrong*).

COMPETENCE IN INTERCULTURAL CONFLICT

According to Spitzberg and Cupach (1984), communication competence has two criteria: effectiveness and appropriateness (see Chapter 2). *Effectiveness* is the degree to which communicators achieve personal goals in a given situation. *Appropriateness* is the degree to which behaviors are regarded as proper and match the expectations generated by the culture. Using these two criteria, we can define competence in intercultural conflict as the ability of individuals from two different cultures to uphold the impressions of effective and appropriate behaviors in a given conflict situation. Judgments of competence in intercultural conflict rely heavily on the perceptions of the disagreeing parties in evaluating each other's performance. What in one culture may appear effective can be viewed as ineffective and inappropriate in another cultural context. Different cultures may possess different notions of communication competence, and these different interpretations further complicate our understanding of constructive management of intercultural conflict.

Spitzberg and Cupach (1984) identify three dimensions of communication competence: knowledge, motivation, and skill (see Chapter 2). *Knowledge* is the cognitive or experiential understanding that helps one communicate effectively and appropriately in a given situation. *Motivation* is the cognitive or affective readiness, or mind-set, to communicate effectively and appropriately with others. *Skill* is the ability to perform behaviors that are considered effective and appropriate in a given situation. This section examines the effectiveness and appropriateness criteria of competence in intercultural conflict and concludes with some recommendations for enhancing our knowledge, motivation, and skill in managing intercultural conflicts competently.

Criteria for Conflict Competence

Major problems arise when individualists and collectivists hold different definitions and interpretations of effective and appropriate practices in conflict. For individualists, a conflict is resolved effectively when personal opinions are voiced and acknowledged, interests are defined and clarified, mutual goals are reached or compromised, and action plans are drawn. In addition, individualists perceive themselves to have acted appropriately when they display sensitivity to the immediate timing, relationship, and context of the conflict.

For collectivists, a conflict is managed effectively when conflict parties help each other attain mutual face-saving fronts in conjunction with consensus on substantive issues. A conflict is appropriately and competently tended to when parties acknowledge the expectations of the relevant in-groups and learn to give honor and attention to the in-groups. To the collectivists, a conflict situation has group-based and long-term implications. It entails fulfilling mutual face needs during disagreement and repaying any incurred obligations and face debts from a long-term perspective.

Overall, the individualistic, outcome-oriented model promotes effectiveness over appropriateness. Conversely, the collectivistic, process-oriented model emphasizes appropriateness over effectiveness. However, achieving one criterion may help achieve the other. For individualists, appropriate and cordial interaction between parties may follow naturally from effective resolution of the substantive issues in conflict. From a collectivist point of view, acting appropriately (in accordance with one's status and position) in the conflict situation and inducing facework cooperation can ultimately bring about effective outcomes. For collectivists, making strategic face moves and incurring face debts from the other conflict party are goals often much more important than "winning" or "losing" a conflict. From a collectivist perspective, "losing" a conflict in the moment can be interpreted as "winning" in terms of long-term facework indebtedness. Of course, the facework negotiation sequence differs according to individualistic and collectivistic value tendencies.

Knowledge, Motivation, and Skill in Intercultural Conflict

To act effectively and appropriately in interactive conflict, individuals have to enhance their cultural knowledge and motivation in applying adaptive interaction skills. Of all the dimensions of managing intercultural conflict, knowledge is the most important and underscores the other dimensions of competence.

Without culture-sensitive knowledge, parties cannot learn to uncover the implicit ethnocentric "lenses," or assumptions, they use to interpret and evaluate events in different intercultural conflict situations. "Knowledge" here refers to in-depth understanding of certain phenomena via a range of information gained through conscious learning and personal experiences and observations.

In addition to individualistic and collectivistic value tendencies, individual differences within cultures, such as independent-self versus interdependent-self concept, contribute to the interpretation of intercultural conflict. To manage intercultural conflict competently, we must take other people's cultural perspectives and personality factors into consideration. If others are interdependent-self collectivists, we may want to pay extra attention to their process-oriented assumptions about conflict. If others are independent-self individualists, we may want to be sensitive to their outcome-oriented assumptions about conflict. Although this chapter provides general knowledge for understanding individualistic and collectivistic cultures, knowledge concerning cultural and ethnic conflict assumptions and styles should also be pursued. This chapter emphasizes intercultural conflict differences rather than ethnic differences (for example, African-American versus Mexican-American interaction style in the United States) in conflict. However, the general concepts (that is, differences in conflict models, rhythms, norms, styles, and ethnocentric lenses) should serve as a good working basis in managing any kind of group-based difference in conflict. Both general and specific knowledge of other cultures and ethnic groups can increase our motivation and skill in dealing with people who are culturally and ethnically different.

In addition, while individualists and collectivists have different frames of reference in conflict negotiation, it is important to remember that most conflicts involve some common interests. Rather than harping on positional differences in conflict, parties to intercultural conflict should learn to uncover or cultivate common interests that bind them in the conflict (Fisher & Ury, 1981). Learning about cultural differences and moving toward mutual interest–based negotiation (for example, we both want the computer project to be on time, even though we have different ways of approaching this problem) can serve as the first step toward competent intercultural conflict management. If conflict parties do not develop in-depth knowledge of the implicit theories or scripts that drive intercultural conflict, the root causes of the intercultural conflict may remain unresolved.

"Motivation" in intercultural conflict competence refers to our cognitive and affective predispositions with regard to communicating with people who are different from us. Motivation is a conflict *mind-set* issue. To have an open mind-set in dealing with people who are different, we need (1) to suspend judgment of unfamiliar behavior, (2) to develop a mindful attitude in conflict, and (3) to engage in ODIE (observe, describe, interpret, evaluate) analysis.

Suspending evaluative judgment in intercultural conflict requires us to accept the fact that we engage in ethnocentric evaluations of culturally unfamiliar behavior. Ethnocentrism colors our attitudes and behavior in any intergroup conflict. To act competently in intercultural conflict, we must first acknowledge the ethnocentric lenses we put on in interpreting and judging unfamiliar behavior. As Stewart and Bennett comment:

> Participants in a cross-cultural situation need to consider first the possibility that a negative evaluation might be based on unrecognized cultural difference rather than the result of astute cross-cultural analysis. Each person needs to be aware that he or she is evaluating the other, often on similarly ethnocentric grounds, and seek to suspend these kinds of evaluations until the potential spiraling effects of the action have been considered. . . . swift evaluation is likely to be ethnocentric and detrimental to effective intercultural communication. (1991, p. 167)

Acknowledging our own ethnocentric biases and suspending our reactive evaluations are critical aspects of managing intercultural misattribution. By withholding our gut-level negative judgments about unfamiliar behavior, we are giving ourselves and others a chance to understand the cultural nuances that exist in a problematic situation.

Mindfulness is a motivational concept in managing intercultural conflict competently. Langer's (1989) concept of mindfulness encourages individuals to tune in consciously to their habituated mental scripts and expectations. According to Langer, if mindlessness is the "rigid reliance on old categories, mindfulness means the continual creation of new ones. Categorization and recategorization, labeling and relabeling as one masters the world are processes natural to children" (1989, p. 63). To engage in a mindfulness state, an individual needs to learn (1) to be open to new information, (2) to create new categories, and (3) to be aware that multiple perspectives typically exist in viewing a basic phenomenon (Langer, 1989, p. 62).

To acquire new information in conflict interaction, conflict parties must listen responsively to each other even when they are disagreeing. In intercultural conflict, disagreeing parties have to learn to listen attentively to the cultural perspectives and assumptions expressed in the interaction. They have to learn to listen responsively, or *ting* (" 聽," the Chinese character for "listening" means listening with our "ears, eyes, and a focused heart") to the sounds, tones, gestures, movements, nonverbal nuances, pauses, and silence in the conflict situation. They must mindfully notice the verbal, nonverbal, and meta-nonverbal contexts that are being conveyed in conflict negotiation. Creating new categories means learning to create or apply culturally sensitive concepts such as low/high-context communication styles in making sense of variations in conflict behavior. Finally, being aware that there are multiple perspectives means that individuals can apply different frameworks (for example, both individualistic and collectivistic perspectives) in analyzing and interpreting conflict and can come up with a creative, synergistic solution.

The third aspect of motivation is *ODIE analysis* (observe, describe, interpret, and then evaluate). Rather than making snapshot, evaluative attributions, we should first learn to *observe* attentively the verbal *and* nonverbal signals that are being exchanged in the conflict process. We should then try to *describe* mentally and in behaviorally specific terms what is going on in the conflict situation (for example, "she is not maintaining eye contact when speaking to me"). We should then generate *multiple interpretations* (for example, "maybe from her cultural angle, eye contact avoidance during conflict is a proper behavior; from my cultural angle, this is considered an improper signal") to make sense of the behavior we are observing and describing. Finally, we may decide to accept or respect the differences as genuine cultural differences and to adapt ourselves by integrating the differences or by *evaluating* them (for example, "I understand that eye contact avoidance can be either a cultural or a personal habit, but I still don't like it, because I feel invalidated by the person's lack of eye contact"). The idea of the sequence observe-describe-interpret is to allow ourselves a more open-ended evaluation or judgment of unfamiliar behavior. We may realize that the discomfort we experience in the conflict negotiation process is based, in part, on communication style differences. We may want to sample a wide range of people (in a wide variety of contexts) from this cultural group to determine whether eye contact avoidance is a cultural or individual habit. Or we may decide to approach the person (with the low/high-context styles in mind) directly or indirectly to talk about such differences.

Interaction skills, abilities that help us communicate effectively and appropriately in a given situation, are useful in promoting competence in intercultural conflict. The three skills that appear to be most pertinent are face management skills, trust-building skills, and communicative adaptability.

Parties to intercultural conflict should learn to cultivate *face management skills* in order to deal competently with intergroup conflicts. Face management skills address the fundamental issue of social self-esteem. Most human beings like to be respected and affirmed in their daily interaction with colleagues and loved ones. However, the behaviors that reveal the need for self-respect and that show respect and dignity to others differ from one culture to the next.

Individualists may want to learn to "give face" to the collectivists in the conflict negotiation process. Giving face means not humiliating or embarrassing the collectivists in public, and acknowledging collectivists' in-group concerns and obligations. Collectivists, on the other hand, may want to reorient face maintenance concerns and learn to pay more attention to the substantive (or task-relevant) issues. Collectivists may also want to recognize that individualists often separate substantive issues from socio-emotional issues in conflict. Conversely, individualists may want to pay more attention to the link between substantive issues and facework or relational issues when negotiating disagreements with collectivists. Thus, although the concern for face maintenance is universal, how we manage face issues is culture-specific.

Critical to competent management of intercultural conflict are *trust-building skills*. If parties in conflict do not trust each other, they tend to move away (cognitively, affectively, and physically) from each other rather than struggle side by side. According to Fisher and Brown (1988), trust is often viewed as the "single most important element of a good working relationship" (1988, p. 107). When we do not trust someone's words or actions, we tend automatically to turn off our listening devices in conflict. We may hear the words, but we are not listening. Trust building is both a mind-set and a communication skill. Especially in intercultural conflict situations, when we are experiencing high anxieties with unfamiliar behavior (for example, accents, nonverbal gestures), we may automatically withhold our trust. Well-founded trust is critical in any effective and appropriate management of intercultural conflicts. Trusting someone, however, entails risks.

In emphasizing the importance of developing a good working relationship as a base for conflict management, Fisher and Brown (1988) recommend that we learn to be "trustworthy" but not necessarily "wholly trusting." We should also learn to carefully analyze the risk of trust in an intercultural conflict situation. To be trustworthy means we should make our behavior more reliable so that others can depend on our words or actions over time. To avoid wholly trusting someone, we should be neither more nor less trusting than the risks dictate. Well-founded trust is based on a mindful analysis of risk. For individualists, such analysis probably is based on the conflict situation at hand. For collectivists, such analysis is often based on a long-term, contextual view of the layers that enwrap the conflict situation. Well-founded trust, in short, is a mind-set, an attitude. It is also a behavior that is developed via consistent, competent communication skills of managing differences.

Communicative adaptability is one of the key interaction skills in the negotiation of intercultural conflict. Communicative adaptability is the ability to change conflict goals and behaviors to meet the specific needs of the situation (Duran, 1985). It signals our mindful awareness of the other person's perspectives, interests, and/or goals, as well as our willingness to modify our own interests or goals to adapt to the conflict situation. Communicative adaptability can also imply behavioral flexibility. By mindfully observing what is going on in the intercultural conflict situation, both parties may modify their nonverbal and/or verbal behavior to achieve more synchronized interaction.

SUMMARY

Competence in intercultural conflict requires that we communicate effectively and appropriately in different intercultural conflict negotiation situations, and effective, appropriate communication requires adaptation. To manage conflict competently, we must understand and respect different world views and ways of dealing with conflict. We must be sensitive to the differences and similarities between individualistic and collectivistic cultures. We must also be aware of our ethnocentric biases and culture-based attributions in making snapshot evaluations of other conflict management approaches.

Competent conflict negotiation promotes flexible, adaptive behaviors in attuning to both the process and the outcome of an intercultural conflict episode. Although intercultural conflict is complex, understanding conflict along the individualism/collectivism continuum is the first step toward understanding cultural variations on conflict.

DISCUSSION QUESTIONS

1 Individualism and collectivism promote two rather different orientations to conflict. How are these differences reconciled in an intercultural conflict? One person could completely adapt (conform) to the other person's orientation. For example, a collectivist could take on an individualist orientation during conflict with an individualist. Would this approach be communicatively competent? Why or why not? What are some alternative ways for reconciling differences in values so that conflict can be managed successfully?

2 Think of a difficult conflict you've had with a relative stranger (possibly someone from another culture). Can you explain any of the difficulty in the conflict as being

due to the fact that you and the other person had (1) different conflict assumptions, (2) different conflict rhythms, (3) different conflict styles, or (4) different ethnocentric lenses? What happened that leads you to infer any of these differences?

3 Among the dimensions that facilitate communicative competence, knowledge is the most important for managing intercultural conflict. What is meant by knowledge? Do you agree or disagree? Why or why not? Can knowledge about another's culture ever lead you to be incompetent? If so, how? (Hint: If you meet a Chinese man and presume he possesses collectivistic values and treat him accordingly, do you run the risk of unduly stereotyping him?)

4 The desire to maintain face seems to be culturally universal, even though face issues are managed differently in different cultures. Does this universality suggest any general guidelines that would help communicators seek common ground when managing intercultural conflict?

5 The most important skills for competently managing intercultural conflict are (1) face management skills, (2) trust-building skills, and (3) communicative adaptability. Do you agree? Do you think that these three skills might be the most important for managing interpersonal conflicts in general? What other important skills for intercultural conflict competence would you add to these?

8

COMPETENCE IN ORGANIZATIONAL CONFLICTS

Dr. Michael Papa is associate professor of interpersonal communication at Ohio University. Dr. Papa earned his Ph.D. from Temple University. His areas of expertise include organizational communication, conflict management, and economic development programs.

Dr. Wendy Papa earned her doctorate from Ohio University, where she now works as assistant professor in the School of Interpersonal Communication. Dr. Papa is an expert in instructional methods, organizational and small-group communication, and conflict.

CHAPTER OUTLINE

Case Study: Grameen Bank versus Moneylenders

The Grameen Bank in Bangladesh has become an international 'icon' of organizations that focus on empowerment of the poor. Over the past fifteen years the Grameen Bank has successfully mobilized more than a million poor people in Bangladesh into an organizational framework in which they interact, generate income through self-employment, and improve their socioeconomic status (Auwal, Papa & Singhal, 1994; Auwal & Singhal, 1992; Fuglesang & Chandler, 1988). However, as the Grameen Bank has expanded its offices throughout rural Bangladesh, its workers have come into increasing conflict with an organized group of moneylenders. These moneylenders have become an accepted part of Bangladeshi society, even though they charge very high interest rates that trap the poor into an economic relationship from which they can rarely exit. When a landless, poor family is denied access to conventional bank loans, the moneylenders surface as the only available source of credit. Although the Grameen Bank has successfully undermined the power base of this corrupt group in certain areas of Bangladesh, numerous conflicts have surfaced between moneylenders and Grameen Bank workers.

One story illuminates how a group of Grameen Bank workers managed a conflict with a group of moneylenders (Shehabuddin, 1992). Three moneylenders threatened to break the legs of a Grameen Bank worker who walked each day along a path in front of their office on her way to work. When the thirty women workers of the local bank heard about this threat, they showed up at the office of the moneylenders. They told the moneylenders that they could threaten the bank worker only if they were prepared to lend the local poor the money they needed on the same terms as those of the Grameen Bank. The moneylenders were not willing to give up their exorbitant interest rates, but they promised to stop harassing the bank workers as well as the members of the local community who no longer came to them for money.

The Grameen Bank story gives us a few important insights into the management of conflict between members of two different organizations. The workers of the Grameen Bank recognized that in Bangladesh there are no government regulations to help them manage their problems with the moneylenders. Furthermore, the moneylenders have become an established part of Bangladeshi society, despite their unfair treatment of the poor. The bank workers realized that the moneylenders were confident in their ability to continue business, so the workers adopted a specific goal that addressed their immediate concerns. The bank workers wanted to prevent the moneylenders from threatening and harming bank workers and local community members who were the recipients of bank loans. The conflict management strategy of the bank workers was to confront the moneylenders directly in an organized group of thirty women. As Shehabuddin observed, "There is power in numbers: Thirty women can intimidate wealthy men if they join forces to show their collective strength" (1992, p. 83). Their affiliation with the Grameen

Bank empowered these women to feel confident in their ability to oppose an oppressive force. Although moneylenders continue to operate in the local community, the Grameen Bank workers established their right to offer alternative economic assistance to the poor. This story is one example of the many types of conflict that can surface in and between organizations.

Organizational researchers have long recognized that conflict is an inevitable and pervasive part of organizational life (Baron, 1984, 1985; Fisher, 1993; Jones & White, 1985; Katz & Kahn, 1978; Morrill & Thomas, 1992; Papa & Pood, 1988a, 1988b; Perrow, 1979; Pondy, 1967; Putnam & Poole, 1987; Tjosvold & Chia, 1989). In this chapter the term *conflict* refers to any incompatibility between people or other organizational units (Deutsch, 1973), especially incompatibility regarding valued goals (Hocker & Wilmot, 1991). As the Grameen Bank case study shows, incompatibilities often arise because of differences in orientations (for example, what sort of loan programs should the poor be offered, or what means of persuasion are acceptable to manage conflict) as well as in goals. Once orientations are clarified, conflict can be managed productively.

Putnam and Poole (1987) observe that organizational conflict occurs in primarily four arenas: (1) interpersonal (for example, coworkers involved in a dispute, or a superior and a subordinate in confrontation); (2) bargaining and negotiation (for example, labor versus management, sales representative versus buyer); (3) intergroup (for example, departments fighting over scarce resources); and (4) interorganizational (for example, organizations competing for market share). Each of these areas is important to explore for a comprehensive understanding of organizational conflict. In this chapter we rely on phase theory (described shortly) for insight into how individuals or other organizational units can communicate competently during conflict episodes. More precisely, this chapter outlines what we mean by competence in organizational conflicts. Following our clarification of competence, we discuss how individuals or other organizational units within organizations manage conflict, relying on phase theory.

ORGANIZATIONAL CONFLICT VIEWED FROM A COMPETENCE-BASED APPROACH

Recently, Spitzberg, Canary, and Cupach (1994) explained what is meant by a "competence-based" approach to the study of conflict. First, a competence-based approach examines the *impressions* of a person's communication behavior, not just the behavior itself. Second, a competence-based approach utilizes criteria that are often equated with communication quality. Two criteria that can be applied to conflict episodes are appropriateness and effectiveness (Canary & Spitzberg, 1987, 1989; Spitzberg & Canary, 1985). Communication is *appropriate* when it does not violate relationally or situationally sanctioned rules, and *effective* when it achieves the valued objectives of the interactant. Thus, the more appropriate and effective an interactant is, the more that person optimizes the possible outcomes of conflict (Spitzberg, Canary & Cupach, 1994).

The applicability of appropriateness and effectiveness (see Chapter 2) to organizational conflicts is linked to the fact that most of these conflicts are between parties (individuals, groups, departments, organizations) that have a relational history and expect to have a relational future. For example, when two employees come into conflict over a work task, their relationship will probably continue after the dispute is managed. Since most organizational relationships do not end at the conclusion of a conflict episode, the balancing of appropriate and effective behavior becomes important. Each party in the conflict needs to engage in behavior that is viewed as effective, because such behavior increases the probability that each party will obtain valued objectives. However, each party also needs to engage in behaviors that are viewed as appropriate, given the nature of the relationship between parties, so that future problem solving can be productive. Phase theory describes a general, competent manner in which conflict can be managed.

PHASES OF CONFLICT

Phase models describe the sequences of behaviors that interactants display as conflicts unfold over time. For example, Walton (1969) characterizes conflict in terms of two broad phases: differentiation and integration. During *differentiation,* positions and differences are clarified. *Integration* is the convergence on agreement between positions. To move from differentiation to integration, we believe, requires another phase: *mutual problem definition.* In this phase the conflicting parties describe the problem they are confronting in mutual terms (for example, a problem that requires the efforts of each party to reach an acceptable solution). Thus, in this section we consider the behaviors that appear to be optimizing—that is, behaviors that should lead to appropriateness and effectiveness evaluations—during the differentiation, mutual problem description, and integration phases of organizational conflict.

Differentiation

During differentiation interactants raise the conflict issue, clarify positions, pursue the reasons behind those positions, and acknowledge the severity of positional differences (Folger, Poole & Stutman, 1993). The importance of differentiation to conflict management is perhaps best summarized by Deutsch, who notes that without differentiation, the probability of finding a solution—"one in which the participants are all satisfied with their outcomes—is a hit or miss venture" (1973, p. 17).

Although differentiation is an essential part of conflict management, it is difficult in the context of an ongoing conflict. When two people recognize that a conflict exists between them, often each person initially perceives his or her partner as a barrier or stumbling block to obtaining goals or rewards (Hocker & Wilmot, 1991). How can the potential problems of differentiation be avoided? In the differentiation phase, optimizing communication behaviors are *information sharing* (explaining your perspective on the issue of dispute) and *information seeking* (soliciting the other person's perspective). Information sharing is crucial to each party's understanding of the perspective advanced by his or her partner. In this discussion the primary purpose of information sharing is to enable the other person to understand our position for joint advantage (Putnam & Jones, 1982). Research suggests that sharing information during a conflict increases the likelihood of reaching a creative solution that meets the needs and goals of each party (Papa & Pood, 1988a, 1988b).

Information seeking is important because it allows interactants to confirm the accuracy of their perceptions of a partner's views on the conflict issue. Without seeking information, each conflict interactant may have difficulty attaining a clear understanding of his or her partner's views on the conflict. Furthermore, as Fisher and Ury (1981) argue, when people seek information during a conflict, the likelihood of understanding increases because "questions generate answers" and, therefore, lead to insight. Information sharing and seeking require that each party to the conflict explain his or her perception of the conflict issue. This exchange entails defining the problem that is creating the dispute, and in the process, each side may discover that different perceptions of the problem exist. Any perception that is different should be discussed, since it represents a starting point toward eventual management of the conflict.

Once the conflict participants agree on a definition of the problem (and each person accepts responsibility for his or her role in creating and maintaining the problem), they can identify their individual positions on the dispute and, importantly, their reasons for those positions. In explaining the reasons supporting a position, an interactant supplies his or her partner with insight into what is important about this particular conflict. Moreover, the strength of commitment to the position becomes clear.

How is information shared and sought during differentiation? Each party to a conflict clearly explains his or her position on the issue of dispute, and the reasons underlying that position. After party A describes his or her position and the underlying reasons for that position, party B must seek clarifying information to make sure that B understands A's position and reasoning. The two parties to the conflict should then switch roles so that A can gain a clear understanding of B's positions on the conflict and the reasons supporting these positions.

Mutual Problem Description

The mutual problem description phase is a bridge between the differentiation and integration phases. Mutual problem description can be considered competent for two reasons. First, in describing a conflict in mutual terms, each party accepts responsibility for the conditions of conflict and socially constructs the conflict in understandable terms. Second, the problem is described as one demanding the efforts of each party to identify a solution that achieves the goals of each party. Thus, through mutual problem description, each party becomes invested in obtaining an optimal outcome.

The preceding section emphasized the importance of presenting personal positions during conflict. While presenting positions and defining the conflict issue, each side should acknowledge his or her mutual role in creating and sustaining the conflict, thus contributing to a mutual problem description. Unfortunately, such mutuality is not always acknowledged. The feelings of anger that sometimes simmer before an individual expresses his or her opinions about a problem with a coworker, for example, may prevent the objective reasoning necessary to cast a problem in mutual terms (Freud, [1900] 1953, 1949). Such a person can feel justified in pointing a finger of blame at the coworker and simultaneously see no contradiction in absolving him- or herself from any involvement in the creation or maintenance of the problem.

The first step toward mutual problem description when conflicting parties are stuck defining the problem from their individual perspectives is *recognizing relational interdependence*. As Papa and Canary recently observed:

> When two parties are involved in an open struggle and each perceives the other as a stumbling block to personal goal attainment the two parties are *interdependent*. So, the issue becomes how to get each party to recognize what is already present in their relationship. Competence in communication then is reflected in the actions of the person (or persons) who makes the move to define relational interdependence. (1995, p. 163)

Even when conflict interactants accept the fact that it is in their best interests to negotiate an outcome that is mutually satisfactory, deadlocks can obstruct problem description. One way to remove such deadlocks is to *restructure the problem*. As Sycara observes, "problem restructuring is the process of dynamically changing the structure of the conflict problem to achieve momentum towards agreement" (1991, p. 1248). The first step in restructuring the problem is for each side to put all of their desired outcome goals (both short-term and long-term) on the table. Once these goals are known, the parties can search for relations among the goals that indicate a dovetailing of interests. According to Sycara, "by having access to information concerning goals and relations among them, [conflicting parties] can produce promising problem reformulations" (1991, p. 1249).

Mutual problem description can be considered an optimizing response to conflict because it ensures that the needs of each party are addressed. Thus, each party has the potential to be effective in obtaining his or her objectives when the final outcome is negotiated. Mutual problem definition also forces each party to be attentive to the needs of his or her partner. When party A focuses on the needs of party B during problem description, party A is being attentive to their relationship and thus is behaving appropriately.

Integration

After defining their problem in mutually constructed terms, conflict participants are prepared to move toward integration. During the integration phase, competent communication behaviors include (1) displaying cooperative tactics, (2) generating alternative solutions, (3) evaluating the positive and negative aspects of each solution, (4) selecting and clarifying the solution to be implemented, and (5) establishing a monitoring system to determine if the solution is being implemented correctly. Such communication behaviors help the conflicting parties remain focused on the problem and commit to identifying a solution that meets the goals of each party.

Displaying Cooperative Tactics Various conflict strategies and tactics have been identified in the literature (see Chapter 3). A strategy is the general approach a person takes to manage conflicts; tactics are the specific behaviors that institute the strategy (Newton & Burgoon, 1990a). Three general strategies identified by communication researchers are *integration, distribution,* and *avoidance* (Putnam & Wilson, 1982; Sillars et al., 1982). In the integrative strategy (not to be confused with the integrative *phase* we are now discussing), parties unite resources to manage the conflict. Integrative tactics include behaviors such as considering a full range of alternatives, seeking a mutually beneficial solution, and compromising after a period of competition. The distributive strategy is competitive and includes behavioral tactics such as criticizing the partner, shouting, and using threats and sarcasm. Finally, the avoidant strategy seeks to distract attention from the conflict by denying the presence or severity of the conflict or by shifting the partner's focus to another issue. As a rule, the more cooperative behaviors are those that seek to integrate resources. In addition, such behaviors have been positively associated with perceptions of appropriateness and effectiveness (Canary & Spitzberg, 1990). Using integrative, cooperative tactics helps align, instead of malign, orientations to the problem (Papa & Canary, 1995).

Generating Alternative Solutions Solutions should not be advanced until both parties agree on the nature of the problem (Graham & Papa, 1993; Papa & Graham, 1990). One reason for withholding solutions is that standards for evaluating the effectiveness of the solution are based on meeting all exigencies presented by the problem. Two strategic approaches to generating solutions are collaboration and compromise. *Collaboration* involves seeking a solution that satisfies both parties' goals, whereas *compromise* refers to splitting the difference between parties' goals. Collaboration is often held as the preferred approach for problem solving; by definition, it is an optimizing response to conflict. As Hocker and Wilmot (1985) observed, however, collaboration is also costly in terms of time and energy. Not all conflicts merit the investment of energy required to collaborate. On the other hand, although compromise may be seen as cooperative and appropriate, the solutions reached through compromise may be temporary. Compromise also precludes the emergence of creative alternatives.

Solutions to problems should satisfy standards agreed to by all parties. Papa and Canary (1995) offered six such standards, describing the optimal solution as:

1 *Feasible:* The solution should be both doable and desirable.

2 *Ethical:* The solution should not violate standards for personal conduct.

3 *Fair:* Neither party should take advantage of the other.

4 *Efficient:* The solution should reduce the amount of work currently done to manage the problem.

5 *Permanent:* The solution should be effective over the long term as well as in the immediate present.

6 *Inexpensive:* The solution should not cost the company more money than it will receive in long-term benefits.

Standards that guide choices of solutions can also be used to monitor the effectiveness of solutions.

Evaluating, Selecting, and Monitoring   Hirokawa (1985, 1988) has argued that solutions should be evaluated for both positive *and* negative consequences. While employees may be eager to offer supporting arguments for solutions, they should also consider the possible negative ramifications of alternative solutions, including relational outcomes. To accomplish this task practically, parties to the conflict can write the positive and negative consequences separately and then jointly discuss their lists, or the parties can exchange their assessments orally. In either case, this activity can optimize the conflict situation. Although one cannot identify all the merits and problems associated with a solution before it is implemented, one may minimize hardships by anticipating negative as well as positive consequences of solutions (Papa & Graham, 1990).

After discussing both positive and negative aspects of alternative solutions, the parties need to select one solution. If the parties have engaged in the phases of differentiation, mutual problem description, and integration, the selection of a solution should be relatively straightforward.

Finally, the conflict parties should establish a monitoring mechanism to ensure that the solution selected continues to operate over time. Two obvious criteria that can be used to assess the efficacy of the solution are appropriateness and effectiveness. Accordingly, we can assess how optimizing the solution is by determining whether it has resulted in promoting the fulfillment of organizational expectations and relational features, such as trust, which reflect appropriateness issues. In addition, the solution can be assessed in terms of its effectiveness; that is, one can ascertain whether the solution accomplishes both parties' goals.

The implementation of a monitoring system can prevent conflicting parties from reverting to prior destructive behaviors. Old ways of thinking and behaving are difficult to abandon. Some individuals even seek out information that convinces them that the new idea should never have been adopted (Rogers, 1983). Thus, one purpose of monitoring is to ensure that each side follows the agreements that were part of the solution.

APPLYING THE PHASE MODEL TO ORGANIZATIONAL CONFLICT

Having identified conflict behaviors that are optimizing within the general framework of phase theory, in the following sections we examine how conflicting parties can display competence in the four main arenas of organizational conflict: (1) interpersonal, (2) bargaining and negotiation, (3) intergroup, and (4) interorganizational. In each of these contexts we demonstrate the utility of phase theory with examples. However, these examples do not exhaust how phase theory can guide other types of conflict.

Interpersonal Conflicts in Organizational Settings

Within organizational settings interpersonal conflict arises primarily in two types of dyadic relationships: (1) superior-subordinate, and (2) coworkers. The literature on the behaviors that surface in these conflicts suggests that when superiors are in conflict with their subordinates, they tend to use forcing or competitive strategies that rely on their power within the organization (Howat & London, 1980; Kipnis & Schmidt, 1982; Morley & Shockley-Zalabak, 1986; Phillips & Cheston, 1979; Putnam & Wilson, 1982). Conversely, subordinates tend to avoid, compromise, or smooth over issues when in conflict with their superiors (London & Howat, 1978; Putnam & Wilson, 1982; Renwick, 1975).

The literature regarding conflict between coworkers does not reveal as clear a set of behavioral tendencies. When positional power is removed from an organizational relationship, a wider range of behaviors seems to emerge. Researchers examining coworker conflict have focused more on how perceptual issues or informational and organizational environments influence behavioral choices. For example, Papa and Pood (1988a, 1988b) observed that when organizational actors enter a conflict with accurate knowledge of one another's views on the issue of dispute, they are more likely to enact friendly influence strategies (for example, "Larry can you help me understand why we should target this consumer group next month?"). Less knowledge is more likely to engender assertive behavior (for example, "Look, Larry, these figures make no sense whatsoever."). An organization's history or "conflict management culture" can also influence employee behavior. For instance, Tjosvold (1982, 1983) observed that when an organization has developed a problem-solving history, members are more likely to ask questions and integrate issues when involved in disputes.

Let us now turn to our model of displaying competence in conflict by closely examining an organizational conflict at the interpersonal level. As part of their research program examining organizational conflict, Papa and Pood (1988a, 1988b) videotaped fifty-four dyads who were involved in a dispute over their company's proposed plan to adopt a participative decision-making system. In these dyads, one person supported the company's proposal to adopt the system, and the other person opposed the system. Presented below are specific statements from a conflict in which the participants reported satisfaction with the outcome of their discussion.

Manager: I like the proposed system because it includes input from more employees about how we get things done around here. Managers aren't the only ones who know how to get things done. People like you know as much about how things are done around here as anyone else.

Subordinate: I haven't liked the system since I first heard about it. We're overworked now, and this new system will increase our workload. Plus, I don't think that many of the managers around here are going to back down and listen to one of our suggestions. What makes you think things will get better if we implement this system?

Manager: I've heard some of the other people in our unit ask the same question. I know you all feel overworked, but if we could all start talking more about how work is accomplished around here maybe we could improve our efficiency and make things a little less hectic. We just keep plugging away on a day-to-day basis and never take the chance to think about whether there is a better way. Do you at least think that the people in our unit can put our heads together to improve things?

Subordinate: I know you've been sympathetic to our workload in the past, and I appreciate that. I also know you're optimistic that if we put our heads together we can figure out a way to sort through all the craziness of juggling twenty different cases every day. I guess I'm just tired of listening to management talking about how things are going to get better, when they only seem to get worse. But we do help each other out, at least in our department. Maybe there's some hope. I'm just not sure.

In the preceding dialogue, the manager and the subordinate successfully work through the differentiation phase of their conflict by engaging in the optimizing behaviors of information sharing and information seeking. Both the manager and the subordinate state their positions on the issue of dispute (the proposed participative decision-making system) and the reasons for their positions. Both interactants ask questions of one another. These questions help each person to understand a little bit more about their partner's perspective on the conflict issue. We return to this discussion as the interactants begin to frame a mutual problem:

Manager: You know I'm getting pressure from the regional manager to move this system along. But I know you're hesitant to spend time you don't have on a system you're skeptical of. Isn't there some way we can work together on this?

Subordinate: Well, I just want to feel that we're really going to be given a voice on this. I don't want to waste time talking about how we're going to participate, when nothing really changes. Can we get together and talk about how we're going to *share* responsibility to get things done? I think some of us in this department have some good ideas about how to streamline some procedures, but we have to be given the chance to try these ideas out without having to go through five levels of management to get the OK.

Manager: I think you're right. I want to be an equal partner with the rest of you in deciding how to improve things. I don't just want to be a gatekeeper who gets the OK for our group from upper management. I also don't want to stand in the way of what you and the others think is a good idea. We just have to try some new ideas first and see what happens. Of course, I think my opinions deserve to be considered like everyone else's. How does that sound?

Subordinate: I think we're going in the right direction here. If you're willing to listen to us and give us the chance to try some different things, maybe this participative decision-making plan will work. If we're really a team here and you aren't going to stop what the rest of us think will work, I'll feel more positive. I guess we can at least talk about what some first steps will be.

In the preceding dialogue, both interactants talk about how they have to work together if the new system is to be effective. From the subordinate's viewpoint, the manager's statement about wanting to be an *equal* member of the department on discussions of work changes is important. This statement helps meet the subordinate's concern that potentially good ideas can be vetoed by the manager. However, the manager also emphasizes that his opinions on new ideas deserve to be considered. Thus, in this short dialogue, the manager and the subordinate merge on the description of the problem that confronts them. These two people perceive themselves to be part of a work team. They are considering a shift in how decisions are made, and they need one another's help for the system to work. Let's return to the conflict as it approaches the integration phase:

Subordinate: How about we start by talking about increasing our financial authority to negotiate settlements with claimants? It's really a problem when we have to have so many of our decisions okayed by management.

Manager: I think that may be a good idea, but let's not rush things. How about we get everyone together to talk about the things that are causing the greatest problems and address them one at a time?

Subordinate: I don't know; that may just be a gripe session. What if we all write down the things that we'd like to change first, and then we can figure out what we can tackle first?

Manager: That sounds more organized. Everyone can give their list to me.

Subordinate: Wait a minute, how about everyone submit their ideas to me? That will show me and the others that you are trying to be a team player. Maybe I can get together with the other seven people in our unit and we can prioritize the list.

Manager: That sounds good, but shouldn't I be part of that meeting too? I won't be there to say yes or no to each idea, but I should have input too.

Subordinate: Oh yeah, of course.

In this portion of their conflict discussion, the interactants generate alternative ideas for establishing a participative decision-making system. As the alternatives are discussed and evaluated, the coworkers eventually arrive at one that is mutually acceptable. These statements meet the problem-solving criteria of evaluating and selecting solutions (Hirokawa, 1985, 1988). Now let's move to the final part of the integration phase—monitoring:

Subordinate: I'm still worried that we're going to wind up spinning our wheels. What can we do to make sure that we keep on track? You know, so we know we're making progress.

Manager: How about we get together once a month to talk about how our new ideas are working? That way we can keep track of what's going right and what problems need to be worked out.

Subordinate: Maybe we can work this out. Have you talked to the others in the department yet?

Manager: You're the last one. I think this program is finally going to get off the ground.

In this final part of the discussion, the manager and the subordinate agree on a monitoring system. Establishing such a system helps ensure that enacted changes continue to be implemented correctly. By taking this step, the manager and the subordinate help prevent old problems from resurfacing.

Bargaining and Negotiation

In bargaining and negotiation, parties exchange proposals as a means of reaching mutual agreement. *Bargaining* means negotiating for someone else; *negotiation* means arguing for your own outcomes. One type of bargaining that is receiving a great deal of attention in the literature is the collective bargaining process between labor and management. The agreements reached through collective bargaining can have a strong impact on the economic profitability of an organization, as well as influence the nature of the relationship between labor and management. In this section we discuss collective bargaining as it relates to labor and management.

Walton and McKersie (1965) first identified a distinction between distributive and integrative bargaining. *Distributive bargaining* is commonly described as involving the division of resources. The parties exchanging proposals believe there is a fixed supply of some resource, so one party's gain is the other's loss. *Integrative bargaining* refers to situations in which the negotiators cooperatively face a common problem. In integrative bargaining the parties search for solutions that meet the needs of all the participants (Andes, 1992; Mumpower, 1991; Nunamaker et al., 1991).

During the differentiation stage of negotiation, the parties need to clarify their positions on the issue in dispute. Integrative bargaining involves the most sharing of information and an accurate disclosure of each party's needs and objectives (Walton & McKersie, 1965). Through information sharing and information seeking, each side comes to a clear understanding of the issues that need to be negotiated.

Another key component of successful negotiation is arriving at a mutual definition of the problem. The first step in this process is to discuss differences in each party's initial perceptions of the problem (Walton & McKersie, 1965). Next, the parties need to separate and prioritize the subissues of the conflict so that they can redefine and clarify the problem (Putnam & Bullis, 1984). This process may result in a restructuring of the problem as the parties recognize relationships among their goals. Ultimately, the parties must determine how they are interdependent so that they can identify superordinate goals that unify them in the search for mutually acceptable solutions.

During the integration stage of negotiation, alternative solutions are identified that meet the goals of each party. To be effective, negotiators must drop their defensive barriers and listen carefully to their opponents' affective and substantive meanings (Lewicki & Litterer, 1985). Once solutions that meet the needs of each party are identified, a means of implementing the solutions should be discussed. Finally, a monitoring mechanism should be identified so that the groups can ensure that the solution remains intact as they continue to work with one another.

To assess the relevance of our phase model to collective bargaining situations, let's examine an example that was discussed extensively in the media: the collective bargaining agreement reached by the National Basketball Association (NBA) in 1983. The NBA owners and players were locked into the age-old labor-management dispute over wages. The owners believed that player salaries had escalated to a level that threatened the existence of some teams. Indeed, during the early 1980s, discussions among the owners focused on issues such as *how many* franchises would fold and on whether or not the NBA itself was a viable business venture (Chapin, 1993). The players believed that since their careers are limited (by injury or age), they needed to maximize their earnings while playing. The players also argued that owners were receiving too high a percentage of total revenue, given that the players are the product that the public pays to see.

During the early stages of this conflict, each side defined the problem from its own perspective. The players felt they deserved higher levels of compensation because of their specialized talents and their limited careers. The owners felt that as business owners, they deserved a reasonable return on their financial investment in the teams. The two sides reached a deadlock less than a week before the strike deadline (Goldaper, 1983).

The players' strike was averted three days before the deadline by creative problem restructuring and the introduction of new goals. The players' association and the owners' group, after carefully analyzing projected revenues for the league, realized that a new superordinate goal existed—league survival. Most important was the mutual realization that the league could not survive unless both the owners and the players could agree on how to meet escalating costs and on how to share profits equitably. Salary escalation was threatening the survival of several teams, so the nature of the player-owner relationship needed to change. Instead of maintaining an adversarial labor-management relationship, the players and the owners entered into a partnership that addressed their mutual concern for league survival. The players agreed to the imposition of a salary cap to meet owner concerns for maintaining a certain level of profitability. The owners agreed to guarantee the players 53 percent of total annual league revenue to meet player concerns that the players had not been receiving a fair share of league profits (Serrin, 1983). This agreement would not have been possible without a mutual problem description.

Between 1983 and 1993, the NBA owners group and the players formed a partnership based on common interests. The players accepted an important role in marketing the game: They appear in public service announcements (for example, the stay-in-school campaign, antidrug messages) and in commercials that advertise NBA games. When players endorse products on television, they not only increase their income, they also give the game of basketball greater public visibility. The players' agreement to compete in the Olympics in 1992 helped promote the game internationally. Finally, their agreement to accept a tough drug policy helped maintain the integrity of the game (Chapin, 1993).

During the five seasons from 1989 to 1993, more than 15 million people attended NBA games and the NBA earned approximately $900 million. The NBA owners have negotiated a television contract that guarantees them $750 million and could bring in considerably more. The owners have continued to view the players as partners, and the two groups often work together in establishing policies for the teams (Chapin, 1993).

Although the NBA has established a player-owner partnership, recent problems have emerged between the two groups. The collective bargaining agreement ended after the 1993–1994 season. In February 1994, the NBA Players Association indicated that they would push for the elimination of the college draft to recruit players, and for the elimination of the salary cap. Furthermore, the players wanted more liberal rules regarding free agency (making it easier for players to switch teams). Finally, the players want increased revenue sharing with the owners (Brown, 1994).

If the collective bargaining agreement between the NBA owners and the players was so good, why are the players dissatisfied? One problem could be that there was no monitoring mechanism to ensure that the agreement would remain satisfactory over time. When the initial agreement was reached in 1983, the NBA was struggling financially. By 1994, the NBA had established itself as the most economically successful professional sports league. In addition, NBA Merchandising has increased league revenue by marketing and selling NBA products. Whereas in 1982 retail sales of NBA products totaled $10 million, in 1992 sales reached $1.4 billion (Chapin, 1993). Players do not presently share this revenue with the owners, and they believe they should. Thus, players and owners need to address the issue that the financial health of the league has changed over time. The improvement in the economic performance of the NBA warrants a reconsideration of some of the agreements that were part of the previous collective bargaining contract.

Negotiations between NBA players and owners took a negative turn in 1995. On June 21, 1995, a select group of players (led by Michael Jordan and Patrick Ewing) sought to decertify the players union for not bargaining effectively with the owners. The primary concern of this group was the imposition of a luxury tax on teams that exceeded the agreed-upon salary cap. Two days later, the league owners approved the new labor deal negotiated by the players union, despite the objections of Michael Jordan and other players. However, when the players tabled the vote and demanded that union leaders reopen negotiations with the league, the owners responded with a player lockout and a suspension of all league operations (Pedullah, 1995).

On September 12, 1995, union decertification was rejected by the players by a margin of 226 to 134. The labor deal was then finalized when the owners and the elected union representatives approved the collective bargaining agreement (Nance, 1995b). Central to the new labor agreement was the decision to allocate 57 percent of league revenue to player salaries (a decision which should result in average annual player salaries of $3 million at the conclusion of the contract in the 2000–2001 season), and an elimination of the luxury tax on teams exceeding the salary cap limit. Players will also now share $25 million annually in the sale of NBA products (up from $500,000 in 1994–1995) and become unrestricted free agents (free to sign with any team) after three years. Finally, a rookie salary cap was negotiated, as well as a decision to limit the college draft to two rounds through 1997 (one round after 1998) (Swan, 1995).

Reflecting on the NBA labor-management agreement of 1983, Pierce noted that "it worked during the lean years, but it was not designed to withstand prosperity" (1995, p. 78). Now an agreement has been reached that more equitably divides total league revenue among players and owners, and players have been given greater freedom to move from team to team, thereby increasing their bargaining power. Owners are now guaranteed 47 percent of league profits, which totaled $924.6 million in 1993–1994 (Nance, 1995a). Although the negotiation was difficult, by sorting through all the complex issues and equitably distributing league revenue, the owners and players have struck an agreement that will carry into the twenty-first century. The recent agreement represents the first step toward reestablishing the player-owner partnership that contributed to the NBA's success from 1983 to 1995.

Intergroup Conflict

The study of intergroup conflict requires a focus on aggregates rather than on individuals. In this approach the group is viewed as a homogeneous entity. Since groups are made up of independent members, however, many views toward a given conflict issue can exist within the group. Thus, one key issue in intergroup conflict is "how groups become and remain homogeneous in order to present a coherent voice and to engage in unified action" (Putnam & Poole, 1987, p. 574).

The development of a coherent voice within a group is linked to the processes of social categorization and group differentiation as well as to the emergence of group ideologies (Folger, Poole & Stutman, 1993). *Social categorization* is the process by which people determine membership in different groups. For example, a worker may view herself as part of the "labor" group, which views itself as distinct from the "management" group. Many different social categories are possible in a large organization. Social categories not only create a sense of identification for group members; they also determine which groups oppose others (for example, line workers versus staff, male versus female, blue-collar versus white-collar, Caucasian vs. African American). Social categorization creates communication barriers as in-group members develop perceptions about other-group members that are never tested. For instance, men develop perceptions about women by talking with other men. However, men are not likely to test these perceptions by talking to women about them. As Folger, Poole, and Stutman (1993) conclude, when people accept social categories, they are likely to act toward others on the basis of attributions developed within in-groups, reducing the likelihood of competent organizational conflict management.

Group differentiation refers to polarization between groups. This polarization results from group stereotyping. Furthermore, when groups compete with one another, member expressions of loyalty to their group tend to increase. Eventually, a self-reinforcing cycle of polarization and hostility develops between the competing groups. As Coser (1956) explained, in-group members begin to believe that the other group is responsible for their problems. These in-group members will attend only to information that portrays the other group as negative, and they do not test their perceptions through interaction.

For example, during a period of economic decline, an organization may have limited resources to increase worker pay. Conflict can develop between Caucasians and African Americans who view themselves in competition for scarce economic rewards. Caucasians may argue that affirmative action programs unfairly compensate African Americans for *who* they are rather than how productive they are. Conversely, African Americans may point to the Caucasian male power structure that dominates top-level decision making and the distribution of economic rewards in most organizations in the United States. Such finger-pointing only weakens the relationship between the opposing groups and minimizes their ability to work together productively.

Once two groups have been in conflict for a prolonged time period, intergroup ideologies surface. *Intergroup ideologies* are organized belief systems that "describe the differences between groups in terms that present the in-group in a favorable light and explain the conflict from the in-group's perspective" (Folger, Poole & Stutman, 1993, p. 37). Once intergroup ideologies develop, the opposing groups feel justified in displaying aggression toward each other. For example, a Caucasian supervisor may purposely give an African-American worker unfavorable work assignments, offer only negative feedback on performance, and encourage others in the work group to sabotage this worker's work efforts. The supervisor justifies these behaviors because of ideologies formed with other Caucasians about African Americans and because of the corporate affirmative action program that he believes places him at a disadvantage.

Given such deep-rooted animosities and the emergence of intergroup ideologies, is it possible for competing groups to manage conflict with each other? To address this question, let's turn to our phase model of conflict management. The first step in managing an intergroup conflict is to initiate differentiation by sharing and seeking information. Groups that have formed ideologies of one another on the basis of stereotypes developed within in-groups need to separate fact from fiction by talking with one another. For example, women can speak and behave in ways that distinguish them from men. People of African, European, Central or South American, or Asian descent can speak and behave in ways that are unique to their cultural background. However, differences in the use of language or in behavioral patterns does not justify unequal treatment. Let's consider language use from the perspective of the power elite in the United States (mostly Caucasian males). Radical humanists argue that organizations oppress women and people of color through language and meaning inherent in the system (Burrell & Morgan, 1979). In other words, sexual harassment and racial or ethnic prejudice can be viewed as the result of a language that dehumanizes people. Dreyfuss observes that to "survive population shifts and to prosper among them, companies are training workers to be more tolerant of language and cultural differences, to identify and reject any racial and sexual prejudices, and to be more accommodating to the handicapped" (1990, pp. 165, 168).

As different groups come to terms with the thoughts and behaviors that distinguish them from one another, they can begin to focus on mutual problem description. Given the changing demographics of the American workplace, workers will need to adapt to people with many different ethnic and racial backgrounds. In addition, workers will need to adjust to men and women who work in nontraditional positions for their gender. Part of this mutual adaptation can be facilitated if people of different groups work together on common tasks. For example, management can integrate work groups by gender and by ethnic or racial background. The members of these groups can be trained to perform activities that mesh in a division of labor to support a larger work effort. By placing members of different groups in contact with one another, and by requiring them to work together to accomplish task objectives, management can help tear down the barriers that separate people.

One way to create a mutual problem definition is to *identify a superordinate goal*. However, unless groups "develop a culture of understanding each other and a different set of communication patterns, superordinate goals are not likely to work" (Putnam & Poole, 1987, pp. 578–579). Thus, it is critical for human resource departments to develop training and education programs for employees to facilitate the transition to a culturally diverse workplace that does not tolerate discrimination based on gender, ethnic or racial heritage, religion, or physical disability.

Once members of different social groups develop a culture of understanding each other, they can work on tasks that require interdependent efforts. The successful completion of tasks in a group of men and women from different cultural backgrounds can help promote a level of relational harmony not possible before the integrated group was formed. However, this process of joining people together from different social categories should not be viewed as simple. Animosities and prejudices that have developed over time are not diminished through a couple of training sessions and a few work projects. All members of the management team must display their commitment to diversity and their intolerance of discrimination. In such an organizational environment, superordinate goals can help unify members from different social categories.

How can the members of different social groups reach a point of integration in managing their conflicts? One way to address this question comes from feminist theory. Fine is particularly interested in how employees from diverse backgrounds "can create organizations in which each of their voices is heard and respected and all of their voices work together productively" (1991, p. 260). Fine (1991) proposes a framework for creating multicultural communication within the workplace that is based in feminist theory and includes two processes: (1) resisting privileged discourse and (2) creating harmonic discourse. *Privileged discourse* involves language that oppresses people and separates the power holders from those who are subject to their control. To create *harmonic discourse* means first to recognize language differences and then to integrate these differences for the good of the group. Again, this is not a simple process. The creation of harmonic discourse requires widespread organizational support. Finally, as noted by Thalhofer (1993), management must clearly indicate through behavior that different languages and behaviors are equally valued throughout the organization.

The final step of conflict management is the establishment of monitoring mechanisms to prevent old prejudices from surfacing and once again dominating intergroup relations. The members of different social groups should meet periodically to share success stories as well as talk about the problems associated with working together. These discussions should center on how to repeat successes and avoid the problems of the past. Group members need to receive reinforcement for disallowing discrimination and for striving for superordinate goals. Such a monitoring mechanism will minimize the reemergence of conflict between members of different social groups within an organization.

Interorganizational Conflict

Interorganizational conflicts typically arise in the marketplace as "organizations attempt to carve out and maintain niches or domains" (Putnam & Poole, 1987, p. 581). One way to examine such conflicts is to focus on economic variables (percentage of market share, net profits/losses, and so on). Another way to learn about conflict between organizations is to examine how these disputes are managed by public or private regulatory agencies. For example, a company may be required to address charges that it has violated the provisions of the Antitrust Act. However, when examining interorganizational conflicts over market share, the adoption of a communication perspective is somewhat restrictive. The competing organizations view one another as adversaries, and any action allowed by private and/or public regulatory agencies will be pursued.

One area of interorganizational conflict that includes a mixture of motives to compete and cooperate is strategic alliances. *Strategic alliances* are "relatively enduring interfirm cooperative arrangements, involving flows and linkages that utilize resources and/or governance structures from autonomous organizations for the joint accomplishment of individual goals linked to the corporate mission of each sponsoring firm" (Parkhe, 1991, p. 581). The reason we focus on these alliances to depict interorganizational conflict is that alliances have become an integral part of contemporary corporate strategic thinking (Ernst & Bleeke, 1993). IBM, for example, has entered more than 400 strategic alliances with companies in the United States and abroad (Sherman, 1992). Furthermore, Ernst and Bleeke (1992) report that the rate of strategic alliance formation between U.S. companies and international partners has been growing by 27 percent annually since 1985.

The phase model advanced in this chapter clearly applies to the conflicts that surface during strategic alliances. These partnerships offer a mixture of motives to cooperate and compete. Cooperation is relevant within the context of the agreement reached between the two organizations. For example, a computer manufacturer may enter into an alliance with a firm that specializes in marketing computer systems. However, the two firms remain in competition with one another regarding the marketing of other high-technology products.

The mixture of motives to cooperate and to compete in strategic alliances is analogous to the tension that exists between the appropriateness and effectiveness dimensions of competence during conflict. Appropriateness involves attending to the needs of the partnership—for instance, addressing the issue of how the two firms can combine their resources to produce and market a product more effectively. Effectiveness involves attending to self (organizational) needs such as survival and profitability. Thus, members of both management teams recognize that an important part of their job is to withhold certain proprietary information from their partners because such information could reduce their organization's competitive advantage. Of course, the two sides must disclose relevant information concerning the specific products or services that are marketed under the terms of the alliance, but information about organizational functioning that is beyond the terms of the alliance must be protected. Let's apply our phase model to the management of interorganizational conflicts that are the product of strategic alliances.

In the beginning stages of establishing a strategic alliance, management team members from each organization need to work through the differentiation process by seeking and sharing information. Why is information exchange so important? Consider Lei and Slocum's (1992) observation that the most productive alliances are between firms that have different core competencies. For example, one firm is more adept at manufacturing, while the other excels at product marketing. Building a strategic alliance requires that each side gain information about their potential partner's core competencies and motives for seeking the alliance. Furthermore, Lei and Slocum (1992) contend that if each party understands the other's strengths and weaknesses, an initial balance can be achieved that facilitates the eventual structuring and development of the alliance.

In working through the differentiation process, each party to a strategic alliance must acknowledge that mutual cooperation is not automatic. Although the members of an alliance must cooperate with one another for the alliance to succeed, the members of each organization are also motivated by self-interest. For example, by providing one another with access to organizational resources and personnel, each organization sets up the possibility that their partner will uncover proprietary information or technology that is not linked to the alliance.

One type of information sharing that must be part of differentiation in forming strategic alliances is a discussion of the risks of the alliance. As Lei and Slocum observe, without clearly "identifying the risks inherent in alliances, collaboration may unintentionally open up a firm's entire spectrum of core competencies, technologies, and skills to encroachment and learning by its partners" (1992, p. 82). In the consumer electronics industry, no U.S. manufacturer produces its own color television sets, VCRs, stereo equipment, or compact disc players. All electronic products sold under U.S. brands (Kodak, General Electric, RCA, Zenith, and so on) are made by foreign alliance partners and imported into the United States. In most instances the U.S. firms lost their competitive edge in manufacturing by unwittingly letting critical technology flow out of their corporations through poorly implemented alliance mechanisms (Lei & Slocum, 1992).

To lessen the risks associated with alliances, the alliance agreement must be carefully crafted from the outset. During differentiation, the potential partners should discuss their mutual incentives for opportunism. In addition, prospective punishments that are applied after the fact can be instituted. "These ex post deterrents consist of contractual safeguards, or stipulations in a formal partnership agreement, that inflict penalties for the omission of cooperative behaviors or commission of violative behaviors" (Parkhe, 1993, p. 804).

During differentiation the partners to a strategic alliance must come to terms with the mixture of motives to cooperate and compete. This process is facilitated when each party clearly communicates its goals for the alliance in the short and long term. A mutual discussion of goals helps the partners understand what each is supposed to contribute and learn from the alliance. As Lei and Slocum conclude: "The process of thinking through this duality of simultaneous collaboration and competition provokes questions that need to be raised before the alliance can be structured and the reward system fashioned" (1992, p. 96).

A discussion of the goals of the alliance brings the parties to the mutual problem description phase of their conflict. In framing a mutual problem description, the parties to the potential alliance need to focus on the competitive advantages of forming a partnership. Ultimately, competing firms form strategic alliances when they perceive that such a partnership will enhance each firm's competitive position against *mutual* rivals (Shan, 1990). One part of the mutual problem description process, then, is to identify how the proposed alliance will benefit the competitive position of each partner.

During mutual problem description, potential partners need to compare the immediate gains that each side can receive from cheating with the possible sacrifice of future gains that might result from violating an agreement. By talking about the relative advantages of maintaining the partnership, each side begins to recognize the value of cooperating rather than competing. Part of this discussion should include a specific list of expected economic benefits from the partnership and a description of punishments linked to agreement violation (Parkhe, 1993).

When the proposed partners of a strategic alliance agree that there are specific advantages to the partnership and that there is a stronger mixture of motives to cooperate than to violate the agreement, they are prepared to move on to the integration phase of conflict. In establishing the alliance, the members of each firm must set up a communication system that allows for frequent communication between the organizations (Axelrod & Keohane, 1986). A system in which there is frequent interaction allows the partners periodic assessments of the outcomes of the alliance. In addition, Parkhe (1993) recommends promoting high behavioral transparency between the partners. *Behavioral transparency* refers to the speed and reliability with which alliance partners learn about each other's actions. Behavioral transparency is thus a means for each organization to monitor the other's actions.

Frequent interaction and behavioral transparency can be facilitated if the partners are willing to exchange workers. For example, in a recently formed alliance, IBM and BASF permanently transferred some staff and senior managers in charge of an alliance in order to improve their ability to conduct business with their partner. As Jones concluded: "In the future, strong interpersonal linkages will be required to sustain learning and to provide the glue for keeping an alliance together" (1992, p. 54).

To deal with the possibility of agreement violations, each party to a strategic alliance may wish to absorb bonding costs when they enter the exchange. Each partner must then set up monitoring mechanisms to detect any opportunistic actions that would require forfeiture of the bond. Although monitoring mechanisms are in the best interests of each partner, the cost of maintaining such mechanisms reduces the economic value of the alliance (Parkhe, 1993). Thus, each side should work toward the establishment of a trusting relationship that reduces the need for expensive monitoring mechanisms.

As two potential partners attempt to build a trusting relationship during the integration phase, they may wish to incorporate flexibility into the proposed alliance. For example, consider the recent merger of the U.S. pharmaceutical company Merck with the Swedish firm Astra (a discount retailer of pharmaceutical products). Their alliance started in 1992, when Merck obtained the U.S. rights to market Astra's new drugs. This phase of the alliance required very little capital investment from either firm, and it gave the senior managers on each side a chance to assess the potential value of the partnership. During the next phase of the alliance, in 1993, Merck set up a new corporation to handle the partnership's $500-million-a-year business. Merck and Astra evenly shared the cost of this new business. This mutual financial commitment was undertaken only after the initial rewards of the alliance were carefully analyzed by each firm (Parkhe, 1993).

In the integration phase the potential partners can agree to commit nonrecoverable investments to the alliance. Nonrecoverable investments include special physical assets, such as buildings and equipment, and human resources. The more nonrecoverable assets each side is willing to commit to the alliance, the more likely a trusting relationship will develop between the parties. Mutual investment of such assets exhibits commitment to the success of the partnership and reduces the likelihood that either side will engage in opportunistic behavior (Smith & Aldrich, 1991).

The preceding examination of strategic organizational alliances exemplifies how our phase model can be applied to interorganizational conflicts. For a strategic alliance to work, two organizations must manage the tension that exists between incentives to cooperate and incentives to compete. This tension is best managed through the display of competent conflict behavior as representatives of the two organizations work through the differentiation, mutual problem definition, and integration phases. During differentiation, the two sides describe the abilities, assets, and objectives that each brings into the partnership. During the mutual problem description phase, each side needs to focus on the rewards that are linked to continued partnership, rewards that exceed the benefits linked to opportunism or to exiting the alliance. During integration, the two parties need to engage in interaction that builds trust between the parties. This trust can be exhibited through an exchange of nonrecoverable assets that are committed to the partnership. Finally, the two organizations should establish monitoring mechanisms to ensure that the terms of the alliance are upheld by each side.

Although the behaviors identified in this chapter can contribute to effective problem solving and conflict management, there are limitations. First, the history that social actors have established with respect to conflict management can impede their ability to display optimizing behaviors. For example, coworkers who have maintained an aggressive-defensive pattern of problem solving for years will find it extremely difficult to change their behavior. Even if coworkers commit to change, entrenched patterns of behavior are very difficult to alter. Thus, in relationships in which dysfunctional problem-solving patterns may become entrenched, a third party may be needed to help facilitate the shift toward more competent behaviors.

At a more general level than relational context is the organization's culture. Organizations establish cultures that influence the choices people make when involved in conflict. For example, one organization may have developed a collaborative, problem-solving culture, while another may have established a competitive, win-lose culture. Individuals within organizational systems that do not support a competence-based approach to problem solving may find it impossible to obtain personal goals by displaying competent behavior in conflict. Thus, individuals need to make choices during conflict that reflect the reality of their organization's culture.

Perhaps most important is the need to recognize that organizational conflicts may emerge that demand an approach very different from the competence perspective advanced here. For example, if an African-American employee is subjected to racial slurs by coworkers, given the least favorable work assignments by supervisors, and ignored for promotions despite superior work performance, the approaches we have discussed appear naive. Such a person has the right to focus on self-oriented concerns. He or she should demand equal treatment from coworkers and superiors and insist that the racial slurs cease. This employee should also seek legal counsel to ensure that personal rights are respected and to obtain compensation for the injustices experienced on the job.

In the future, researchers need to scrutinize carefully the relevance of a competence-based approach to managing organizational conflicts. As explained in this chapter, this approach offers many opportunities for creative problem solving, but it also has limitations. In the final analysis, the more we learn about how to manage conflicts competently in organizational settings, the more we will know about how to sustain supportive and productive work environments.

SUMMARY

The purpose of this chapter was to explain how conflicts in organizations can be optimized through the display of competent communication behaviors across three phases: differentiation, mutual problem description, and integration. At a general level, we examined how organizational actors can balance the dual criteria of appropriateness and effectiveness in the management of different types of disputes. More specifically, within the context of phase theory we presented a model of competent communication during conflict that focused on the following behaviors: (1) information exchange to establish positions on the conflict issue, (2) construction of a mutual definition of the conflict problem, and (3) cooperative problem solving. This model was then applied to the four arenas of organizational conflict: interpersonal, bargaining and negotiation, intergroup, and interorganizational.

Although the differentiation, mutual problem description, and integration processes we discussed may not apply to all organizational conflicts, they are appropriate in most situations. Coworkers who approach conflict as a win-lose game may end up damaging a potentially productive working relationship. If coworkers can construct their conflict in mutual terms for the purpose of identifying a solution that meets the needs of each party, they should attempt to do so. When labor and management meet during collective bargaining sessions, it is usually in the best interests of the organization for them to view one another as partners that must work together to guarantee the continued survival and success of the organization. When people from different social categories discover how to manage their differences, the entire organization benefits, for example, from the relational harmony that results. Finally, as strategic alliances become more prevalent, the leaders of organizations need to learn more about how to solve problems across organizational boundaries. Successful alliances require an attention to individual corporate goals as well as to the goals of the partnership. Thus, our perspective of conflict management holds relevance for dispute resolution across the four main arenas of organizational conflict.

DISCUSSION QUESTIONS

1 Information sharing is very important during the differentiation phase. People can become more accurate in understanding each other's positions through information sharing. Have you experienced a conflict at work or elsewhere that was never resolved in part because people simply did not understand each other? Are there special instances where understanding someone might hurt the relationship or company? Elaborate on your answers.

2 How might you bring about—through communication—differentiation, mutual problem description, and integration? Should one do this informally, without relating what one is doing, or should one begin these phases more formally, with an explicit agenda? Give examples to illustrate your opinion.

3 Compare the example of NBA negotiation discussed in this chapter with others that have not worked as well—for example, the negotiations between President Clinton and the Republican Congress over the budget, the Major League Baseball dispute, the air traffic controllers strike of 1980, or any other negotiation that you understand. In your opinion, what phase is missing from the "failed" negotiations?

4 An effective way to achieve mutual problem definition within intergroup conflict (for example, between departments) is to identify a bigger, superordinate goal that the two groups share. Discuss this idea in terms of groups that appear to be opposed to each other, but who actually share a common, superordinate goal. What might you recommend to these groups in terms of mutual problem description and integration?

5 Strategic alliances are ways that organizations differentiate themselves, for example, by noting how their resources can complement one another. However, organizations using strategic alliances must balance their need to compete with each other and their need to cooperate with each other. Does this tension between cooperation and competition also apply to interpersonal conflicts? Give examples to support your opinion.

9

VIOLENCE IN INTIMATE RELATIONSHIPS

Dr. Brian Spitzberg is professor of speech communication in the School of Communication at San Diego State University. He earned his Ph.D. from the University of Southern California. Dr. Spitzberg enjoys an encyclopedic mind of scholarly information and is published widely. His topics of expertise include communication competence, interpersonal conflict, and emotion. In addition to being a leading authority on interpersonal communication competence, Dr. Spitzberg conducts original research in the area of violence and abuse in close relationships.

A peculiarity accompanies the discussion of competence and violence in the same context. A natural reaction is that violent behavior is entirely incompetent. But this view is too simplistic.

This chapter examines the complex interplay of competence and violence, with an emphasis on violence in intimate relationships. After a discussion of some conceptual issues that surround competence and violence, several myths about violence in intimate relations are examined. Following the development of grounding maxims or principles about violence, some models of the process with implications for competent management of relational violence are presented.

It is important to note that courtship violence is a serious problem—in general, a much more serious problem for women than for men—because this chapter reaches many conclusions that could be interpreted as deemphasizing the severity of many individuals' experiences and the deep personal turmoil that people face as a consequence of violence. Further, a conception of communication that accepts the principles of process and interdependence will properly avoid issues of blame and responsibility. This chapter examines the complex ways in which risk factors (for example, background characteristics, emotions, cognitions, and actions) of *both* parties result in violence. In the long run, such a discussion should be more empowering than the rhetoric of blame and victimization, especially if a means of recognizing, deescalating, and transforming the pattern that leads to severe violence can be identified.

This chapter concentrates primarily on courtship violence among young adults (rather than parent-child, marital, or sexual violence). More and more research suggests that these instances of violence are distinct types, presumably because the relationships themselves are unique. Children, relative to their parent(s), have much less power, less interactional skill, and stronger physical and economic constraints on their behavior. Married partners typically share long relational histories, are legally and economically interdependent, and tend to face great social stigma and psychological disruption if they separate. Sexual violence, particularly date rape, appears to have a motivational profile very different from that of relational violence in general. This chapter also is generally not about pathologically abusive, battering relationships. The intent is to concentrate on "normal" intimate violence, although research from marital and sexual violence will occasionally be mentioned.

Performing competently means behaving both effectively *and* appropriately. Perhaps nowhere is this dual accomplishment more problematic than in contexts of conflict and violence (Spitzberg, Canary & Cupach, 1994). Violence seems to be a direct attempt to force compliance or otherwise effectively control a situation (deTurck, 1987), yet to most people violence is intrinsically inappropriate.

To understand the nature of the relationship between competence and violence, violence should be separated from other common but related terms. Abuse, aggression, and violence are often considered synonymous, although there may be useful distinctions among them. *Abuse* is an ongoing, repetitive pattern—psychological, emotional, or behavioral—of pain infliction. The term *abuse* carries negative connotations; for example, it is difficult to visualize justified abuse. *Aggression* implies intent (Gergen, 1984). To engage in aggression is to intend harm against another; the perpetrator and target are clear. To think of aggression in the context of self-defense is difficult (Marshall, 1994). *Violence*, however, may result from accident and from expressive motives in addition to instrumental motives (Stets, 1992). That is, people may occasionally inflict physical pain purely out of heightened arousal and an impulsive need to express that arousal, rather than to obtain an intentional or preconceived goal.

Violence—behavior that potentially or actually causes harm to person or property—is more often assumed in the nature of behavior than defined conceptually. We ask people to say how often they have been on the receiving or giving end of behaviors such as a hit, slap, or kick. Such behaviors are presumed to be violent, even though the person exhibiting the behavior is not usually asked whether he or she intended the action to be harmful. *Violence* is sometimes defined as behavior that is intended to cause harm to another person (Sugarman & Hotaling, 1989), even though hitting an object is often given as an example of violence.

The subtle distinctions that characterize abuse, aggression, and violence are blurred because the three overlap. For example, violent behavior often is aggressive and abusive. If nothing else, violence is undeniably a form of social interaction (Felson, 1984; Gergen, 1984; Harris et al., 1984).

THE INCIDENCE AND TYPES OF VIOLENCE

The most commonly used measure of violence is Straus's (1979) Conflict Tactics Scale (CTS). Table 9-1 summarizes several studies that have investigated the incidence of many of the behaviors assessed by the CTS.

TABLE 9-1

INCIDENCE OF VIOLENCE[a]

Tactic[b] (references)	Percentage of respondents who reported having experienced tactic		
	Males	Females	Total[c]
Abuse verbally (4, 6)	65%	58%	
Push or shove (1, 2, 3, 4, 5, 6, 7, 8, 9, 10, 11, 12, 13)	29	32	36
Slap (1, 2, 3, 7, 8, 9, 10, 11, 12, 13)	37	23	28
Threaten with violence (4, 5, 6, 7, 9, 10)	24	24	24
Slap, hit, grab, or scratch (4, 5, 6)	21	25	
Punch or kick (5, 6, 7, 8)	24	14	
Threw object at victim (2, 3, 4, 5, 6, 8, 9, 10, 11, 12, 13)	22	14	15
Kick, bite, or hit with fist (1, 2, 3, 9, 10, 11)	16	12	21
Try to hit with something (2, 3, 4, 9, 10, 12, 13)	14	12	12
Hit with hard object (6, 7, 8, 11, 12, 13)	6	16	5
Hit with fist (1, 12, 13)	1	2	18
Kick (5, 8, 12, 13)	15	5	1
Throw victim (12, 13)	0	3	1
Bite (8, 12, 13)	1	3	0
Choke (5, 6, 7, 12, 13)	1	3	0
Beat up (1, 2, 3, 5, 8, 9, 10, 11, 12, 13)	4	5	3
Threaten with weapon (1, 2, 3, 5, 8, 9, 10, 11, 12, 13)	3	3	2
Assault with weapon (2, 3, 4, 6, 7, 8, 10, 11, 12, 13)	3	3	1

Notes:
[a]This sample of studies is by no means exhaustive. Studies were selected primarily based on their similarity of assessment and reporting.

[b]Studies cited use similar but not always identical wording of items. Some interpretation was employed in categorizing the information.

[c]Percentages varied considerably across many of the tactics and studies. Percentages represent the average across the studies reporting an estimate. For example, for "Threaten with violence," four studies reported the data by male and female victimization (studies 4, 5, 6, and 9), and two other studies (7 and 10) reported only totals across sex. Consequently, the percentages are not directly comparable between the sex columns and the total column. A blank space appears when none of the studies reported a total percentage.

References:
[1] Cate, R., Henton, J. M., Koval, J., Christopher, F. S., and Lloyd, S. (1982). Premarital abuse: A social psychological perspective. *Journal of Family Issues, 3,* 74–90.

[2] Deal, J. E., and Wampler, K. S. (1986). Dating violence: The primacy of previous experiences. *Journal of Social and Personal Relationships, 3,* 457–471.

[3] Henton, J., Cate, R., Koval, J., Lloyd, S., and Christopher, S. (1983). Romance and violence in dating relationships. *Journal of Family Issues, 4,* 467–482.

[4] Lane, K. E., and Gwartney-Gibbs, P. A. (1985). Violence in the context of dating and sex. *Journal of Family Issues, 6,* 45–59.

[5] Laner, M. R. (1985). Unpleasant, aggressive, and abusive activities in courtship: A comparison of Mormon and non-Mormon college students. *Deviant Behavior, 6,* 145–168.

[6] Laner, M. R., and Thompson, J. (1982). Abuse and aggression in courting couples. *Deviant Behavior, 3,* 229–244.

[7] Makepeace, J. M. (1981). Courtship violence among college students. *Family Relations, 30,* 97–102.

[8] Makepeace, J. M. (1986). Gender differences in courtship violence victimization. *Family Relations, 35,* 383–388.

[9] Marshall, L. L., and Rose, P. (1987). Gender, stress, and violence in the adult relationships of a sample of college students. *Journal of Social and Personal Relationships, 4,* 299–316. (split samples)

[10] Marshall, L. L., and Rose, P. (1988). Family of origin violence and courtship abuse. *Journal of Counseling and Development, 66,* 414–418.

[11] Plass, M. S., and Gessner, J. C. (1983). Violence in courtship relations: A southern sample. *Free Inquiry in Creative Sociology, 11,* 198–202.

[12] Roscoe, B., and Callahan, J. E. (1985). Adolescents' self-report of violence in families and dating relations. *Adolescence, 20,* 545–553.

[13] Roscoe, B., and Kelsey, T. (1986). Dating violence among high school students. *Psychology, 23,* 53–59.

Table 9-2 identifies types of violence and their causes. *Psychological violence,* as defined by Marshall (1994), is the undermining of another person's sense of self or self-competence. Although physical violence may have this effect, psychological violence more often appears to take the form of distorted communication patterns that blame, confuse, criticize, bind, or otherwise constrain another person. Marshall's research reveals a variety of psychologically abusive tactics (Table 9-3). Part of the terrible nature of psychological violence is that it is often employed in the context of positive messages. For example, in a study by Shupe, Stacey, and Hazlewood (1987), many victims of batterers reported that during the previous month their

TABLE 9-2
BASIC TYPES OF VIOLENCE AND THEIR CAUSES

I. Psychological violence

1. Anger/hostility (e.g., getting angry with someone for little or unpredictable things)
2. Emotional control (e.g., blaming someone else for being upset)
3. Jealousy/possessiveness (e.g., constantly checking up on someone and someone's whereabouts)
4. Isolation/restraint (e.g., keeping someone from seeing friends)
5. Bind/dilemma (e.g., putting someone in no-win situations)
6. Disconfirmation (e.g., treating someone as stupid or inferior)
7. Withdrawal (e.g., becoming cold or indifferent toward someone)
8. Insult (e.g., calling someone names)

II. Symbolic/verbal violence

1. Hot heated arguments (e.g., constantly getting into shouting matches)
2. Same old issue (e.g., constantly raising the same issue)
3. Coercion (e.g., wearing someone down with constant demands or arguments)
4. Threat
    a. Mild (e.g., shaking a finger or fist at someone)
    b. Moderate (e.g., destroying something of value to someone else)
    c. Serious (e.g., threatening to hurt someone)

III. Physical violence

1. Mild (e.g., holding someone down, pushing/shoving)
2. Moderate (e.g., slapping someone with the palm or back of hand)
3. Serious (e.g., stomping on, choking, or hitting with object)

IV. Sexual violence (e.g., demanded sex, physically forced sexual intercourse)

1. Sexual coercion (e.g., persistently arguing with or threatening)
2. Sexual aggression (e.g., forcing petting against expressed consent)
3. Rape (e.g., forcing intercourse against expressed consent)

Adapted from Buss and Perry (1992), Caulfield and Riggs (1992), Kasian and Painter (1992), Marshall (1994), Rodenburg and Fantuzzo (1993), and Shepard and Campbell (1992).

TABLE 9-3
PSYCHOLOGICALLY ABUSIVE TACTICS

Control activities	Intrude on activities
Control emotions	Intrude on privacy
Control information	Isolate emotionally
Control thinking	Isolate physically
Corrupt	Exhibit jealousy
Degrade	Demand loyalty
Denigrate	Monopolize perception
Dominate emotionally	Act omnipotent
Dominate physically	Be possessive
Double-bind	Punish
Embarrass	Reject
Make dependent on	Enact unreasonable rules
Exploit	Sabotage
Inflict mental fear and anxiety	Enforce secrecy
Inflict physical fear and anxiety	Denigrate self
Fight or create conflict	Shift responsibility
Humiliate	Use surveillance
Induce emotional debility	Threaten emotionally
Induce physical debility	Threaten physically
Induce guilt	Show verbal aggression
Induce powerlessness	Withdraw

Source: Marshall (1994).

attacker had "made me feel wanted and needed" (77 percent), "shown affection toward me" (82 percent), and "shown interest in what I say" (65 percent). The reinforcement provided by such messages and the debilitating nature of the confusion they cause may be what makes psychological abuse so potent.

Symbolic/verbal violence is the use of words in a directly threatening manner. Whereas psychological violence does not typically imply direct danger or ultimatum, verbal violence involves threats of harm, relentless or intense verbal fights, and coercion (for example, threatening to break up if the partner will not comply). Neither psychological nor verbal violence may seem to be appropriate forms of the concept of violence, because we tend to stereotype violence as involving intense physical harm. As Marshall (1994) notes, psychological abuse is relatively uncorrelated with physical violence and is more highly correlated to symptoms of mental and emotional distress than to physical violence.

There are many levels of *physical violence*. Pushing and shoving that develops out of an innocent pillow fight might qualify as mild or minor violence. Moderate violence would likely involve acts more akin to slapping or throwing a nonlethal object at the other person. Serious violence is potentially

BOX 9-1

THE SPECIAL CASE OF DATE RAPE

According to numerous studies, between 5 and 24 percent of adult women are raped in their lifetime (Koss, 1989, 1993; Muehlenhard & Linton, 1987; Russell, 1982). Males also report victimization, but at much lower rates than women (Struckman-Johnson, 1988). Males report lower perpetration rates than would be expected from the percentage of women who report victimization. This discrepancy may be the result of self-serving underreporting on the part of males, or it may mean that some males rape more than one victim.

A gray area of sexual aggression is sexual coercion. Results of coercion include actions such as giving in to sex because of constant arguments, threats to break up, threats to violate relational secrets, and so on. Rates of sexual coercion tend to be more than 50 percent of college-age women (Mahoney, Shively & Traw, 1986; Muehlenhard, 1991).

Most of the evidence, and there is not a lot, indicates that date rape is not strongly motivated by power (as some people assume), but is instead motivated by sex. Date rapists tend to report that they expect sex to occur, but not rape (Kanin, 1984). Beating and other types of physical aggression appear to be relatively rare in date rape. The extent of nonsexual physical force employed in most date rapes involves holding or pinning the woman down, using the male's weight and strength to advantage.

Although the male who rapes on a date may not intend to, studies of adolescent and college attitudes reveal a disturbing picture. Goodchilds and Zellman (1984) found nine "conditions" that make date rape more acceptable to both men and women who generally strongly oppose date rape. There were, from least to most justifying:

(1) He spends a lot of money on her, (2) he's so turned on he can't stop, (3) she is stoned or drunk, (4) she has had sexual intercourse with other guys, (5) she lets him touch her above the waist, (6) she says she's going to have sex with him and then changes her mind, (7) they have dated a long time, (8) she's led him on, (9) she gets him sexually excited. (Goodchilds and Zellman, pp. 241–242)

Several contextual features predict date rape. Sexual aggression is more likely to occur when alcohol consumption by either or both persons has been excessive, when the male perceives the female as seductively dressed, when there has been foreplay, when the situation is private (Kanin, 1984; Muehlenhard & Linton, 1987), and when there is stress in the relationship (Marshall & Rose, 1988; Mason & Blankenship, 1987).

Large percentages of women who have been forced to engage in intercourse against their expressed will (that is, raped) systematically choose not to apply the label "rape" to their experience (Koss, 1989). This may explain in part why about 40 percent of victims continue dating and having sex with their assailant (Koss, 1989; Stets & Pirog-Good, 1989). Regardless of its label, rape has a significant negative impact on the victim's psychological well-being (Resick, 1993), although few studies have specifically examined "date" rape.

One intriguing hypothesis is that there are two different types of date rapist: the *socially incompetent* and the *socially hypercompetent*. The incompetent date rapist would likely be frustrated, lonely, and unable to perceive the subtle courtship cues of others. Instead, he would fall back on the social stereotypes that men should pursue and women should feign resistance. The hypercompetent date rapist would, in contrast, use manipulation, guile, and sleight of symbol to coerce sex with the woman. Muehlenhard and Falcon (1990) found some evidence in support of this hypothesis. Interestingly, unwanted sex is least likely to be thwarted when verbal persuasion is employed rather than physical force (Murnen, Perot & Byrne, 1989).

or actually injurious, or otherwise appears to qualify as felonious assault. *Sexual violence,* although generally not a component of most types of physical violence, nevertheless involves physical restraint and/or force, and qualifies as a form of violence (Kanin, 1984).

THE RELATION BETWEEN VIOLENCE AND COMPETENCE

How are violence and competence connected? First, if competence is the ability to interact well, it follows that competent communicators avoid undesired violence. Research has found a lack of communicative skills among violence-prone couples (Lloyd, 1990; Margolin, John & Gleberman, 1988) and sexually aggressive individuals (Lipton, McDonel & McFall, 1987; McDonel & McFall, 1991), as well as in nonviolent but distressed couples. The important implication is that incompetence may produce relational maladjustment, which then contributes to the use of violence.

Second, acting violently seriously impairs our ability to appear competent. Perceiving someone as behaving inappropriately appears to be a necessary, and biased, condition of aggressive behavior (Gergen, 1984; Mummendey, Linneweber & Loschper, 1984). The violent actor views his or her own violence as much more justified and appropriate than does the partner (Mummendey, Linneweber & Loschper, 1984). In addition, violence by females appears to be viewed as more appropriate (or excusable) than violence by males (Harris, Gergen & Lannamann, 1986; Struckman-Johnson & Struckman-Johnson, 1992). By definition, violence jeopardizes the partner's ability to pursue personal goals (and is thereby seen by the partner as inappropriate), or it incites violence as a response (which thereby jeopardizes the actor's effectiveness).

Third, despite the intuitive belief that violence is incompetent, research indicates that "competent violence" is not as paradoxical as it seems. For example, more than 90 percent of American adults approve of physical punishment in disciplining children (Pagelow, 1984). Ruane's study of tolerance for using force with children concluded, "Use of force is judged reasonable if such force counteracts disturbing or outrageous behaviors by the child" (1993, p. 299).

Social acceptance of violence is directed not only at children. Arias and Johnson (1989) found that many respondents perceived slapping a partner as legitimate in the case of self-defense (62 to 81 percent), defense of a child (82 to 86 percent), the discovery of sexual infidelity by a partner (32 to 33 percent), and reciprocation of being slapped (34 to 44 percent). Roscoe (1985) found that almost 50 percent of college students surveyed considered slapping to be an acceptable form of violence between dating partners, and 14 to 23 percent considered shoving/pushing, punching, kicking, and restraining to be acceptable forms of physical force. Studies also reveal a number of conditions under which many adolescents (males especially) believe that forced sex is justifiable (Cook, 1995; Goodchilds & Zellman, 1984; Malamuth, 1984). People see their own use of aggression as particularly justified, especially as a response to another person's affront or initiation of violence (Mummendey, Linneweber & Loschper, 1984).

Violence is not inherently wrong or incompetent. The question is, Under what conditions is violence incompetent? As Harris, Gergen, and Lannamann state, "In effect, given the rules of Western culture, physical aggression has an appropriate place" (1986, p. 254). To address this "place," we need to examine some myths and maxims of violence. It is perhaps no surprise that an area as socially volatile as courtship violence is widely assumed to have mythical qualities (Burt, 1991; Marshall & Vitanza, 1994). The section that follows considers some of these myths.

MYTHS OF INTIMATE VIOLENCE

Case Study 1: "If only . . . "

David and Kathy both came from violent families. David's dad used to beat both David and his mother. Kathy's parents didn't beat her, but often made her feel worthless with their constant fighting and criticism. David seemed sort of helpless, and Kathy wanted to take care of him; to give him a life they had missed when growing up. They were in love—perhaps too much in love. David constantly checked up on Kathy's whereabouts. He criticized her, and when she would look hurt, David would say that it's only because he cares so much that he wants her to be perfect. Still, David would often go into rages when they would argue, seemingly over minor things. Afterward, they would make up and these were the times that Kathy felt closest to him. But these times started becoming too brief between the fights, and the fights started getting worse and worse. David would throw and kick things, and threaten Kathy with violence. Finally, during one fight, David became so out of control that Kathy slapped him, at which point David hit her with his fist. He excused himself by saying he just "went crazy" and that it would not happen again. But, a few fights later, he started beating Kathy, screaming that she "just doesn't learn." Kathy often blamed herself and felt awful for having driven David to such rage. She felt that if she simply tried hard enough, he would change (adapted from Jenson, 1991, pp. 46–49).

This case illustrates a prototype of violence. David is a victim of a violent upbringing, and his female partner has been entrapped by his psychological and physical abuse. The violence grew gradually, and in the context of positive behaviors that sustained hope of eventual reform. This image of intimate violence is so clear in our public conscience that it is hard to imagine that the reality is far more complex. This is not to deny that such abuse happens. It happens all too frequently. To assume that this case typifies the nature of intimate violence, however, reinforces many of the myths of intimate violence.

Myth 1: Intimate Violence Is Obvious

This myth follows the logic espoused about pornography: "I don't know how to define it, but I know it when I see it." Many have tried to provide a precise and comprehensive measure of violence. There seems to be a normative continuum of violence, from psychological and verbal forms, to mild forms of physical violence, to more physically injurious forms. However, physically injurious violence is not necessarily the most incompetent or harmful. Marshall's (1994) research suggests that psychological well-being is impaired more by psychologically abusive behavior than by physically violent behavior. Indeed, people who have been victims of date rape (Koss, 1989), violence (Stets & Pirog-Good, 1989), and battering (Margolin, John & Gleberman, 1988) often do not consciously perceive themselves as victims.

Myth 2: Intimate Violence Is about Power

At one level, this statement is almost definitional. But once we accept that violence may be expressive, this myth applies equally to self-defensive behavior as it does to aggressive behavior. Violence may be largely expressive in many instances (Berkowitz, 1983; Burke, Stets & Pirog-Good, 1989). Anger, jealousy, frustration, confusion, and even love are common meanings attributed to violence (Henton et al., 1983; Roscoe & Kelsey, 1986). Sexual coercion may be motivated by sexual pleasure instead of retributive justice or domination (Felson, 1993).

Some research indicates that in explaining violence, men are more likely to claim motives of intimidation, retaliation, or uncontrollable anger, and women are more likely to claim motives of hurting the other person, possibly in self-defense (Makepeace, 1986). One study found that women acknowledge control and power motives for perpetrating violence more than twice as often as men, and both motives represented a minority of uses of violence (29.2 percent and 13.6 percent, respectively; Follingstad et al., 1991). Men also differ among themselves in the degree to which they find power desirable (Prince & Arias, 1994). Thus, although intentions can be attributed, violence often seems to arise from relatively uncontrollable emotional outbursts. As such, violence may always be a *form* of power, but not necessarily a function of power *motivations.*

Myth 3: Intimate Violence Is Masculine

A related myth holds that violence provides a way for men to control women, and as a corollary, that men are intrinsically more violent than women (White & Kowalski, 1994). In fact, the research is far more interesting. Most recent research indicates that women report engaging in more violence, and men report receiving more violence (McNeely & Robinson-Simpson, 1987; Sugarman & Hotaling, 1989). Research on aggression and anger finds gender differences to be relatively minor (Bjorkqvist, 1994; Cupach & Canary, 1995).

Several explanations have been offered for this surprising finding. First, males may be more reluctant to admit to violating the social ethic of never hitting a female. On the other hand, males are also likely to report less victimization, because of the presumed social stigma of being weaker than females. Second, the finding that women are more violent could reflect that women feel compelled to resort to violence to balance any perceived status inequity. However, men similarly face a power deficit during conflict management, since they are consistently found to be less verbally (Maccoby & Jacklin, 1974) and nonverbally (Hall, 1984) skilled than women.

Third, the sex difference may indicate that women engage in more self-defensive violence than men (Saunders, 1986). Women are more likely to receive injury and use violence for self-defense, whereas men use violence to intimidate others or to force compliance (deTurck, 1987). However, given the generally greater physical size and strength of men, it would take less effort for a man to inflict injury. It cannot be presumed that women's behavior is self-defensive; women may initiate a flurry of violent but noninjurious acts, and men may respond with a single violent and injurious act. Follingstad and colleagues found that "males who used force reported that they were more likely to be retaliating for being hit first and female victims also reported this to be the case" (1991, p. 56). Similarly, Billingham and Sack found that 59 percent of relationships experiencing violence reported that the violence was "mutual," and of those reporting that only one member had used violence, "an almost equal percentage of males (6.0%) and females (5.8%) report themselves as having been the victim of the violence" (1986, p. 318).

Finally, the difference may be due not to biological gender, but to psychological gender (Thompson, 1991). That is, people who adopt more masculine identities, regardless of biological sex, may be more prone to violence. However, research indicates that expressiveness (which is more closely associated with femininity) is more likely to lead to violence than is masculinity (Burke, Stets & Pirog-Good, 1989). Research also suggests that lesbian relationships are as violent as heterosexual relationships (Lie et al., 1991; Renzetti, 1992). A masculinity model, whether biological or psychological, might have some difficulty accounting for such a finding. Unfortunately, there is minimal evidence to resolve these issues.

Myth 4: Intimate Violence Is Repetitive

A common assumption is that there are violent people and violent relationships. Violence is thought to recur continually in relationships as a function of the violent person. Although violent battering, or abusive, relationships exist, by no means do they account for all violent episodes. The research is mixed in its findings; some studies report that the average relationship experiences nine to ten violent acts (Sugarman & Hotaling, 1989), and others find this number to be one to two violent acts over the life of the relationship (Sigelman, Berry & Wiles, 1984). The National Crime Victims Survey reported that of women who were victims of violence, one in five had been a victim of three or more similar episodes of violence. However, "for assaults in general in 1992, fewer than 1 in 10 victimizations involved this type of victimization" (Bachman, 1994, p. 2). Data on sexual aggression reflects similar variation (Sorenson et al., 1991).

Studies have begun unraveling the difference between couples who experience only one or an occasional episode of violence, from those who experience ongoing violence (Follingstad et al., 1988; Kasian & Painter, 1992; Stets, 1992). The clearest conclusion is that couples experiencing just one violent episode are more like couples who have never experienced violence than they are like couples who experience repeated violence.

In one of the few longitudinal studies of couples from engagement to early marriage, nearly half of the couples had never been physically aggressive over thirty months, and 17 percent of the women and 8 percent of the men were considered stably aggressive (O'Leary et al., 1989). Thus, the isolated occurrence of violence in a relationship does not mean that the relationship or the individuals in it are inherently violent.

Myth 5: Intimate Violence Is Intergenerational

Another myth is that people who witness or experience violence as children are likely to be violent or be victims as adults. The reasoning is that children model the behaviors they observe and experience. Despite widespread acceptance of this assumption, the research is not particularly supportive. Studies that have found a significant influence of family or origin often have focused on severe forms of battery rather than on violence in general. Most studies have failed to find either strong or consistent support for the link between violence in a child's home and later violence (Stets & Pirog-Good, 1987; Sugarman & Hotaling, 1989; Widom, 1989).

Myth 6: Intimate Violence Is Individual

Violence is often seen as the product of a disturbed personality, a pathological nature, or a culturally conditioned individual character. The basic notion is that violence-prone people behave violently. Yet, most research finds only a small correlation between personality and violence (O'Leary, 1993 for review) and between personality and sexual aggression (Murphy, Coleman & Haynes, 1986). Rather than no effect, the effects of personality either are very inconsistent across studies or tend to be relatively minor (Sugarman & Hotaling, 1989).

People who have a high acceptance of violence and who believe that heterosexual relationships are fundamentally adversarial in nature tend to be more violent (Christopher, Owens & Stecker, 1993; Follingstad et al., 1988; Sugarman & Hotaling, 1989). However, factors other than personality and personal attributes appear to be more important in predicting violence. As Busby concludes, "whether a spouse is violent is more important in determining personal violence than attitudes against violence" (1991, p. 376).

Other studies suggest that contextual features, such as conflict history and problems in the specific relationship, strongly predict violence (Riggs, 1993; Riggs, O'Leary & Breslin, 1990). Research on date rape also reveals the importance of situational factors more than personality factors (Muehlenhard & Linton, 1987). Thus, while violent people undoubtedly exist (Gondolf, 1988; Shields, McCall & Hanneke, 1988), situational and relational influences are probably more important in the explanation of most violence.

Myth 7: Intimate Violence Is Abnormal

A related myth holds that violence is abnormal. Violence happens to someone else, but not to "normal" people. In fact, however, surveys suggest that violence *is* the norm. Competition appears to be an integral aspect of courtship itself (Laner, 1989). Most Americans support the use of physical punishment with children. More than 80 percent of children experience sibling violence (Straus, Gelles & Steinmetz, 1980). Sugarman and Hotaling's (1989) summary of research on overall lifetime dating violence prevalence rates revealed an average of almost 37 percent. Marshall (1994) concludes that 75 percent of college students report having inflicted and 75 percent report having received threats of violence in an intimate relationship, and more than 50 percent actually inflicted or received violence, although most of this violence was minor.

Research shows similarly extensive rates of sexual aggression. Across numerous studies, between 5 and 39 percent of women have been victims of sexual aggression, and much higher percentages report some form of sexual victimization or coercion (Koss, 1989; Muehlenhard & Linton, 1987). Studies of date rapists and sexually coercive males suggest that they are surprisingly "normal" in comparison to nonrapists (Kanin, 1984; Koralewski & Conger, 1992). In summary, we live in a culture in which violence is normative in its use, in its tolerance, and in the character of its perpetrators.

Myth 8: Intimate Violence Is Traumatic and Dissatisfying

On the one hand, relational violence is clearly disturbing. The mythic aspect of trauma, however, is the idea that violence is the same as battering, spousal murder, and ruined lives. These things do occur all too frequently (Marshall & Vitanza, 1994). About 15 percent of all homicide victims in the nation are spouses or lovers of their attackers (U.S. Department of Justice, 1994). On the other hand, much violence is relatively incidental, minor, and not massively harmful.

There are several ways of examining the extent of trauma resulting from violence. Self-report research shows that the experience of violence and date rape are correlated to distress, although in the case of violence, "the trauma is considered mild in the majority of cases" (Sugarman & Hotaling, 1989, p. 13). Further, it is commonly assumed that associations of violence with distress mean that violence is the cause of distress. Instead, they may *both* be symptoms of psychological abuse or general relational dissatisfaction (Marshall, 1994). Finally, as Laner (1990) reports, the causes of violence (for example, jealousy, arguments, sexual problems) are recalled as sources of relational discontent much more often than the violence itself.

Another approach examines whether relationships change significantly after the experience of violence. Here the picture is much more complex. "On average, the relationship has worsened because of the violence in about 40 percent of the cases, but in roughly six of every ten relationships that did not terminate, the violence is reported to have had no effect on, or to have actually improved, the relationship" (Sugarman & Hotaling, 1989, p. 14).

For example, some studies have found that relational dissatisfaction and/or termination are not strongly related to frequency of violence (Kasian & Painter, 1992; Murphy & O'Leary, 1989). Holtzworth-Munroe and colleagues (1992) found that almost 24 percent of their sample of "satisfied" married couples had experienced violence, 12 percent within the previous year. O'Leary and colleagues (1989) found that only about a fourth to a third of partners of stably aggressive individuals were dissatisfied with their relationship, whereas about 10 percent of partners of *non*aggressive individuals were dissatisfied. Although the differences were considered significant, they also indicate that the presence of physical aggression is not necessarily a sign of relational dissatisfaction or distress.

In fact, when asked to attribute a meaning to the violence, a sizable number of victims select "love" as a label (Sugarman & Hotaling, 1989). It may therefore be unsurprising that Roscoe and Benaske (1985) found that 30 percent of battered women eventually marry someone who abused them during courtship. Research on date rape similarly reveals that about 40 percent of date rape victims continue to be friends with, date, and/or have sex with their assailant (Koss, 1989; Mills & Granoff, 1992; Murnen, Perot & Byrne, 1989). In part, these results may reflect the fact that victims of physical and sexual aggression often do not label themselves as victims (Koss, 1989; Stets & Pirog-Good, 1989).

Many groups use the topic of violence in public debate to advance their social and political aims. In the process, groups often invoke a single explanation of violence (for example, intimate violence is about male domination or intimate violence is a pathology or a sickness). Most of these attempts to reduce the complex phenomenon of violence to simple causes limit our understanding of how violence grows and functions in relationships. In the next section, a more differentiated view of violence is offered. This view will establish the basis for speculating on how violence typically erupts in relationships, and how it is managed.

MAXIMS OF INTIMATE VIOLENCE

The myths of violence that we have examined are not entirely false. The nature of myths is that they may have some accuracy, although they are not entirely accurate. A responsible view of violence requires that it be considered for what it is: a form of interactional behavior. As such, violence is likely to be as complex as most forms of interactional behavior. The maxims developed in this section attempt to clarify some of these complexities.

Maxim 1: Intimate Violence Is Culturally and Ideologically Bound

Violence, like most forms of behavior, is valued differently in different cultural frames of reference (Levinson, 1989; Spitzberg & Duran, 1994). In some cultures, the notion of "an eye for an eye, and a tooth for a tooth" takes on literal and sacred overtones. In our own society, we give the state permission to enact violence in various forms, including capital punishment, police action, and war. In some countries, poachers who are hunting endangered species can be shot on sight. In other cultures, wives are considered property of the husband, and violence against one's own property is not generally viewed as punishable or unjustified. Conversely, some cultures have developed elaborate rituals of symbolic or actual property exchange to avoid violence and preserve order. Regional differences exist even within our own society. Sugarman and Hotaling (1989) and White and Koss (1991) found that the southern United States showed rates of violence almost twice as high on average as rates in any other region. In short, different cultures and subcultures adopt different attitudes toward violence.

Maxim 2: Intimate Violence Is Contextual

If our culture affects our view of violence, it follows that violence is a contextual phenomenon. Only occasionally, however, does violence appear to be attributable to personal factors, such as personality. Research has identified many situational factors that predict violence. For example, jealousy, the most common cause of violence in relationships (Sugarman & Hotaling, 1989), is defined as a blend of negative emotions resulting from a perceived threat of a third party to a valued relationship. Thus, although some people clearly are more jealous than others, something in the nature of the relationship or the situation likely activates the jealousy.

Other situational factors related to violence include economic dependency (Mason & Blankenship, 1987), relative isolation from a broader network of interpersonal relationships (Ponzetti, Cate & Koval, 1982), alcohol and drug consumption (Flanzer, 1993), unemployment and job stress (Ponzetti, Cate & Koval, 1982), and psychological stress (Marshall & Rose, 1987). Sexual violence also appears strongly influenced by situational factors, such as location, foreplay, and dating activities that involve no expense or male payment for the costs of the date (Muehlenhard & Linton, 1987).

Other obvious situational factors concern where and when violence occurs. The vast majority of violence occurs in private settings—a residence or a car, for example. Violence also generally occurs on weekends, and either late at night or early in the morning (Sugarman & Hotaling, 1989). These are more than just interesting findings. They indicate that people are not compelled to violence just anywhere or anytime, but that violence may be opportunistic in the sense that situations affect actions in systematic ways.

Maxim 3: Intimate Violence Is Relational

The type of relationship affects the incidence of violence. For example, both marital violence and date rape appear to happen earlier in relationships rather than later (Muehlenhard & Linton, 1987), whereas tendencies for verbal aggression increase as commitment to the relationship develops (Billingham & Sack, 1987; Kasian & Painter, 1992; Stets, 1992). Love appears unrelated to the level of violence in a relationship (Gryl, Stith & Bird, 1991). Cohabiting couples reportedly experience higher rates of violence than married couples, and remarriages experience more violence than first marriages (Busby, 1991; Ellis, 1989). Husbands are more likely to report "loss of control" (for example, anger, alcohol consumption) motivations for their violence than are dating males, who report more instrumental motives (for example, intimidation, gaining compliance; Sugarman & Hotaling, 1989).

Herein is one of the enduring ironies of intimate violence. Violence, a generally antagonistic action, occurs most with those for whom we feel the strongest positive feelings. There are several explanations for this paradox.

First, if violence is related to arousal, then those whom you care about are most likely to provide a source of arousal. Second, the closer a person is to you, the more likely she or he is to know which "buttons" to push. Third, as your relationship develops you become more interdependent, and therefore conflict is more probable.

Maxim 4: Intimate Violence Is Multifunctional

People use violence to influence interaction, which may or may not be a conscious motive. The question is, What functions does violence serve? When people resort to violence, they frequently view it as justified (Greenblat, 1983). Billingham (1987) speculates that violence in courtship relations often "tests" the resiliency of the relationship. Lloyd and Emery (1993) interpret intimate violence as a process used to negotiate psychological distance or intimacy in a relationship.

Violence can serve a number of other potential functions in relationships, including punishment for rule violation, as a form of reciprocity or "fair fight" ritual, and in self-defense (Felson, 1984; Follingstad et al., 1991). Finally, as indicated previously, violence is often expressive. None of these functions necessarily justifies violence, but they suggest that violence concerns more than simply winning an argument or putting someone else in his or her place. Violence is multifunctional, and a balanced examination of its functions yields insight into its meaning.

Maxim 5: Intimate Violence Is Verbally Facilitated

Violence most often occurs during conflict. Several studies have found that in violent relationships, the level and frequency of conflict are closely linked to the onset of violence (Coleman & Straus, 1986; Gryl, Stith & Bird, 1991; Riggs, O'Leary & Breslin, 1990). In a study with more than 6000 interviews, Stets concluded that "only rarely does physical aggression occur without verbal aggression (from .2% to .4%)" (1990, p. 508). In an interview of 250 single, never-married adults, Stets (1992) found that couples with high levels of conflict are 75 to 100 percent more likely to experience violence than couples with less conflict. Conflict appears to generate a set of features, discussed in the next section, that make physical violence more likely.

Maxim 6: Intimate Violence Is Reciprocal

Violence generally does not occur without perceived provocation of some sort. Most people avoid the label of "initiator" of violence (Sugarman & Hotaling, 1989); across many studies, evidence indicates that violence in intimate relationships is typically "mutual" (Gryl, Stith & Bird, 1991;

Sigelman, Berry & Wiles, 1984) or that the amount of expressed violence is highly correlated to the amount of received violence (Bookwala et al., 1992; White & Koss, 1991). The concept of provocation does not excuse violence. Nor does it deny the injury frequently experienced by one or both parties. But it does provide a context in which to understand the use of violence. Intimate violence is often a mutually constructed activity in which the lines between perpetrator and victim become blurred.

Violence does not occur in a vacuum. It is a complex, multilayered phenomenon. Violence appears to be a product of relational conflict and, generally, a product of factors other than individual pathologies. It serves many functions in the relationship and may represent a conflict tactic of last resort for the participants. To gain a thorough understanding of violence requires considering its place within a larger model of relational and conflict processes.

A GENERAL MODEL OF VIOLENCE

The Meanings of Violence

There are two obvious windows into the meanings of violence. First, what conversational or conflict topics appear to bring about violence? Such information would suggest the areas of our lives that are so arousing and intense as to provoke violence. Second, what meanings do people give to violence? Regardless of how the violence actually functions in relationships, people apply psychological meanings to label their experiences. These labels may play an important role in allowing the person to accept or reject the violence.

Jealousy is by far the most common subject that instigates violence in couples (Stets & Pirog-Good, 1987). Dating couples also often cite sexual refusal and drinking behavior, as well as arguments over friends and parents. Important identity issues related to one's own sense of virility (sexual refusal) and others' attractiveness (jealousy) and issues of high interdependence (children, money, and so on) most commonly evoke intense emotions that lead to violence. Such studies probably miss the emotional component and the structure of the interaction that stimulated the emotion. In other words, talking about money is likely to elicit violence only if one's partner has done something or is proposing to do something financially that violates one's sense of identity represented by issues of finance. That is, the extent of violation, rather than the topics themselves, best explain the outbreak of violence.

Meanings attributed to violence are particularly informative. The most common attribution is anger (Sugarman & Hotaling, 1989). The second most common attribution is confusion. Interestingly, confusion suggests a minimal responsibility on the part of the violent person. That is, people who are confused are less responsible for their actions than are people who clearly know their intentions.

The most striking and unanticipated finding is that approximately one-third of victims of courtship violence associate love with the act of violence. The logic appears to be that "s/he wouldn't hit me if s/he didn't love me." This logic helps absolve the other person, since the motives are pure even if the actions are not. Clearly, just as the behavior of violence is multifaceted, so is its meaning. However, the evidence indicates that violence is perceived to be wrapped up in the realm of emotion. An understanding of emotions, and the activities that arouse them, will help us understand violence.

The Dynamics of Transgression and Affront Management

Case Study 2: "He dived for me"

We were having an argument about something. I think it was money. I'm not exactly sure but probably because we didn't have the money for him to go out—that was what usually caused all the arguments. It was the first time he really hit me. It wasn't just a slap, you know, he didn't give me a black eye at first, but it was a really sore one, you know, a punch. Before then he used to shout and bawl messages, you know; I wouldn't answer back, didn't open my mouth. I used to just sit there or go and wash the dishes or something. But this time I started shouting back at him and that was it. He got angry and made a dive for me and starting thumping me about.

At what point in the argument did he actually hit you?

When I answered him back, you know. He dived for me. No, I mean you couldn't really reason with him; he's too big headed, he's right. Even when he knows himself he's wrong, he won't admit it, you know. (Dobash & Dobash, 1979, p. 103)

In this case study, the wife's decision to shout back at her husband was an affront to his sense of legitimate conflict behavior and relationship definition. *Affronts* are actions that call the other person's face, or impression, into question, and are often likely to violate a rule in the process (for example, you should not criticize me in front of others; Honeycutt, Woods & Fontenot, 1993).

A *relational transgression* is a particular type of affront—a violation of a relationally relevant rule, tied to particular standards or limits of behavior—and requires explanation or repair to neutralize the resulting negative emotions (Metts, 1994). In other words, a coactor violated some expectation the actor had for the coactor's behavior. Most transgressions appear to fall into one of six basic categories (Jones & Burdette, 1994; Metts, 1994): (1) sexual infidelity, (2) privacy or secrets, (3) unfulfilled commitments, (4) underprivileging the primary relationship (for example, spending too much discretionary time with others rather than with the partner), (5) interaction management (for example, fighting unfairly), and (6) inappropriate emotions (for example, unreciprocated love or affection).

Upon discovering or recognizing a transgression, an actor is likely to demand an account of a coactor's behavior. An actor may employ accusation, reproach, or innuendo, depending on the severity of the transgression (Schönbach, 1990) and the certainty with which the coactor's guilt is presumed. Typically, the coactor will have several response options: confession, apology, justification, excuse, and so on.

Affronts and transgressions may unfold in a basic sequence (Newell & Stutman, 1988). In general, an affront or discovered transgression leads to an expression of disapproval or evaluation, which leads to some form of accounting process, which then leads to acceptance or argument over the legitimacy of the account. If the argument escalates, it is likely to become a conflict concerning the legitimacy of the rule(s) violated, the seriousness or nature of the transgression, and/or the legitimacy of the account offered. There is considerable flexibility in this basic pattern. At any point the interactants may diverge onto other topics, avoid the issue, counterattack, or continue and escalate the conflict.

Evidence indicates that violence tends to occur in situations of affront (Tuppen & Gaitan, 1989) or rule violation (Felson, 1984). Specifically, threats to personal integrity and jealousy are common sources of anger, and both are obvious forms of affront and transgression (Fitness & Fletcher, 1993; Mathes & Verstraete, 1993). Studies indicate that anger itself rarely leads to violence. However, when anger is experienced along with a perception of having no control (Betancourt & Blair, 1992), or having been shamed (that is, rejected) by the partner, violence is much more likely (Retzinger, 1991; Scheff & Retzinger, 1991). Such shame could easily be a result of predicament and criticism, in which the actor loses face.

People who respond to interpersonal conflict with anger tend to be more violent-prone (Bird, Stith & Schladale, 1991). A particularly interesting bind suggested by the case study in this section is the common relational rule that one shouldn't get angry (Honeycutt, Woods & Fontenot, 1993). Conflict in general and transgressions in particular are likely to evoke anger, yet the expression of anger may well violate another rule. As such, the expression of anger itself is often viewed as a relational transgression by the target of the anger.

Different studies provide widely varying estimates of the frequency with which apologies are offered after an episode of violence (Baumeister, Stillwell & Wotman, 1990; Dobash & Dobash, 1984). Some research indicates that apologies increasingly give way to excuses as the relationship, and use of violence, progress (Wolf-Smith & LaRossa, 1992). Such a shift reflects an increasing denial of responsibility for the violence (Schutte, Malouff &

Doyle, 1988). Interestingly, almost all women accept the apologies for the first incident and do not expect the violence to recur, but by the final incident, 92 percent no longer honor the accounts offered. Apologies significantly tend to reduce aggressiveness but are not indefinitely believable (Ohbuchi, Kameda & Agarie, 1989; Sitkin & Bies, 1993).

Divergent Attributions

A complicating factor in episodes of anger and violent transgression is that the two parties tend to have divergent and self-serving perceptions of the process (Andrews, 1992; Baumeister, Stillwell & Wotman, 1990). "Across studies, the majority of respondents (ranging from 75 to 100 percent) do *not* label themselves as initiators of the violence," although large percentages blame *both* themselves and their partners collectively (Sugarman & Hotaling, 1989, p. 12). Mummenday, Linneweber, and Loschper also indicate that re- gardless of whether one is initiating or responding, "one's own behavior is judged as more appropriate than the similar or identical behavior of the other person involved" (1984, p. 84). This bias, combined with the perception of transgression or affront, likely has a very powerful influence.

A picture of typical violence begins to emerge. An actor's affront or transgression stimulates arousal, and probably some anger, in a partner. The partner demands an account, and if the account is not considered en- tirely legitimate, the conflict escalates. Conflict tends to be self-perpetuating (Vuchinich, 1986, 1987); that is, our tendencies to perceive our own behav- ior as appropriate and the partner's behavior as inappropriate allow us to escalate the conflict. Both people therefore feel justified in responding as they do.

Actor perceives coactor at fault, and vice versa. Both see the episode's causes and effects differently (Bernal & Golann, 1980) and thereby feel jus- tified not only in entrenching themselves in their own position, but in attack- ing the partner for attacking oneself unjustifiably. Rather than ending the con- flict, violence reveals a very strong reciprocal effect; that is, violence is likely to be met with violence (Vivian & Langhinrichsen-Rohling, 1994). All the while, anger is likely to continue to escalate (Margolin, John & Gleberman, 1988) as each interactant's routine is further disrupted by the "unreasonable" partner (Sillars & Parry, 1982).

Conflicts characterized by violence tend to escalate both because violent couples generally seem to lack communication skills that might defuse the dispute (Holtzworth-Munroe & Anglin, 1991; Infante et al., 1990) and be- cause violent couples engage in fewer minor squabbles that might ease the tensions of relating to one another (Lloyd, 1990). Violence seems to brew in the volatile conditions of transgression, intense emotions (shame, anger, rage), perceptual differences, and self-reinforcing cycles of conflict. In the midst of such storms, the lightning and thunder of violence are played out.

THE AFTERMATH OF VIOLENCE

When the storm of violence has passed, you may often wonder why people choose to stay where they are, knowing the risk exists that the storm will return. Makepeace (1989) found that people had many reasons for not terminating their relationship after an episode of violence, including emotional attachment, making up, and a perceived lack of seriousness of the violence.

Several theories explain why people stay in abusive relationships. The simplest explanation is that they get something out of it. *Social exchange theory* posits that people stay in punishing relationships because the alternatives are viewed as more punishing. Loneliness, security, love, children, commitment, marriage, and other concerns may seem too fragile outside the primary relationship with the partner.

Another theory is *learned helplessness,* a condition in which your actions do not appear related to what happens to you. For example, if you are hit for talking back on one occasion and not on another, the resulting confusion becomes debilitating. You no longer know how to behave, and your confidence diminishes.

Both social exchange theory and learned helplessness assume a fair degree of rationality: You add up rewards and costs relative to alternatives, or you link your actions to outcomes. Two theories that depend less on assumptions of rationality are paradoxical punishment and rationalization theory.

Paradoxical punishment explains how punishment can be rewarding. This theory suggests that battered women ignore the current pain for a more powerful future reinforcer (Long & McNamara, 1989). Several processes are at work. If a honeymoon, or making up, phase follows violent episodes, the actors learn to associate that reward with the activity of fighting, and abuse actually becomes a stimulus for positive reinforcement. Second, abuse may end a period of anxious anticipation and fear. That is, a person in an abusive relationship may experience so much fear and distress wondering when the next abusive episode will occur, that when it finally does, it is a source of relief and satisfaction.

Rationalization theory bases its analysis on interviews with batterers. Ferraro and Johnson (1983) found that victimized wives stayed in abusive relationships by rationalizing their situation in ways that tended to absolve the batterer, to blame self, or to provide a desirable role for self to play. These investigators identified six rationalizations:

1 The *appeal to the salvation ethic* allows the victims to see themselves as providing the nurturance that their "sick" husbands need.

2 The *denial of the victimizer* involves connecting the abuse to some external force (for example, loss of job) beyond the control of the abuser.

3 The *denial of injury* refuses to recognize any injuries. When hospitalization is not required, the routines of daily life seem to go on as normal shortly after the episode of violence, so perhaps the violence simply is not that bad.

4 In *denial of victimization,* the victim accepts blame for the violence, thereby absolving the abuser.

5 The *denial of options* supposes that there are neither tangible resources (alternative housing, income, protection, and so on) nor emotional resources (friends, helpers) available, and therefore the violence must be endured.

6 The *appeal to higher loyalties* locates an overarching commitment, such as God or the sanctity of marriage, that requires acceptance of the situation for the sake of the higher good.

Ferraro and Johnson note that people are unlikely to view themselves as true victims unless and until significant changes occur, such as changes in the severity of the violence, economic resources, relationship status, public visibility of the violence, and so forth.

Most of these explanations for why people stay in relationships are psychological and ignore the role that the partner plays in creating and reinforcing rationalizations. These explanations also seem more relevant to disturbed relationships than to "normal" relationships. Nevertheless, a partner can promote such punishments and rationalizations and may even be a victim of the same distorted interactional patterns. Subtle and highly complex forces, both behavioral and psychological, keep people in abusive relationships.

COMPETENT VIOLENCE?

Several threads run between conflict and competence. Let's examine ways in which violence in interaction can be competently reduced. The essential bind of violence in relationships can be presented as a series of propositions. No single process envisioned by the proposition is problematic, but when the propositions are combined, the system begins to become complex and the propositions viciously interwoven.

1 Conflict brings about perceptual differences, such that an actor views his or her own behavior as more appropriate (that is, competent) than the partner's behavior. This perceptual discrepancy has been demonstrated with aggressive behavior as well (Mummendey et al., 1984).

2 Conflict often involves the violation of relational rules (Metts, 1994).

3 Relational rules often require integrative conflict behavior, which includes the management of anger (Jones & Gallois, 1989).

4 Jealousy helps incite violence (Sugarman & Hotaling, 1989). The combination of anger and jealousy reduces the possibility for integrative communication, especially if shame is experienced (Scheff & Retzinger, 1991).

5 The greater the transgression, the greater the tendency toward distributive tactics and divergent perceptions.

6 The more one person employs distributive tactics, the more likely the partner will reciprocate in kind.

7 The greater the tendency to reciprocate distributive tactics, the greater the tendency for emotions to become more relationally interdependent and for rational tactics to be chosen less frequently.

8 The collective impact of the previous propositions is that violence becomes increasingly likely, and one person's violence tends to reinforce the partner's violence (Sugarman & Hotaling, 1989). Furthermore, the use of violence maximizes personal effectiveness at the cost of relational appropriateness, while passivity and avoidance maximize appropriateness at the cost of personal effectiveness.

In short, violence inherently jeopardizes competent performance by all interactants involved, whether violent or not. Yet, given the structure suggested by these propositions, violence seems inevitable as the pattern reaches a crescendo.

Violence does not have to be inevitable. Several levels of mitigation can decrease the likelihood of violence. At the simplest level, reciprocity is a mutual process. Episodes of violence sometimes occur "out of the blue," but most occur in the context of conflict. Defusing the conflict by shifting the dialogue to less emotional topics, or to a discussion of the rules for engaging in conflict, may break the escalation cycle.

Competent rule management may prevent violence. Both the rules of conduct and the rules of negotiating the rules of conduct can establish norms for nonviolent action and costs for violent action. The most appropriate competent behavior for this form of mitigation is metacommunication (that is, communication about communication). Being able to draw the topic away from the specific transgression and onto the pattern of interaction may allow a less emotionally charged breather, as well as parameters for the ongoing conflict.

Mitigation at the level of transgression is of several types. Reproach requires sensitivity to the nature of hurtful messages and complaints. In a counterintuitive finding, research indicates that informative messages (for example, "You aren't a priority in my life") in a complaint tend to be more hurtful than direct accusations or insults (for example, "You are a liar"), presumably because it is easier to dismiss an accusation as biased or simply untrue (Vangelisti, 1994). To the extent that reproaches are presented in the form of complaints, research indicates that people prefer that complaints be expressed in a calm, conversational, specific, and clear manner (Alberts, 1989).

Next, assuming these levels of mitigation have not succeeded, conflict can be mitigated at the level of anger management. Research has indicated that relatively nonassertive (Sereno, Welch & Braaten, 1987), integratively oriented (Guerrero, 1994) forms of expressing anger are most competent (as perceived by American college students). Listening to your partner's side of the story, showing fairness, and sharing feelings with your partner are viewed as more appropriate and effective forms of managing anger than are screaming, criticizing, threatening, trying to prove your correctness, or simply denying or hiding your feelings.

Mitigation at the level of account is the final form of managing violence. Certain types of accounts are more aggravating (for example, denials or justifications), whereas others, such as apologies and concessions, are more effective (Hickson, 1986; Ohbuchi, Kameda & Agarie, 1989; Riordan, Marlin & Kellogg, 1983). Generally speaking, accepting some of the blame and indicating some level of remorse are acceptable patterns for deescalating conflict encounters.

Perhaps the most difficult topic in the realm of violence is a consideration of the conditions, if any, under which interpersonal violence is called for, or competent. Some have argued that both anger and aggression can play a role, if appropriately managed, in fulfilling the potential of a relationship (Bach & Goldberg, 1974). We have already seen that the enacting party tends to see his or her own violence as more appropriate and competent than the other person's aggressive actions. Further, recipients become the initiator, as reciprocity and the blurring of who is at fault enter the interaction.

We have also seen that many people believe that violence is justifiable in the event of (1) defense or protection of self and (2) protection of others, especially helpless others (for example, infants). Another, more ambiguous situation could be (3) impression management (Felson, 1981) and deterrence of future attack. Establishing an impression of power, emphasizing the importance of an issue to one's face, and establishing one's position in a relationship may sometimes be served more effectively by a display of aggression than by other less salient means.

However, it is in this regulatory function that our society has received extensive criticism. To the extent that males possess advantages over women (for example, social status, economic independence, physical strength) violence becomes a tool for domination and female censorship. On the other hand, to dismiss violence out of hand for this reason commits the fallacy of sweeping generalization. Violence is not all of one type. It is multifaceted and complex. The presumption that no violence can function in competent interpersonal relations is thus difficult to justify.

On a personal note, I believe unequivocally that societies, families, and relationships, are better off without violence, *all things being equal.* Violence clearly is, in most of its applications, a destructive force, and one that is philosophically problematic in an ideal world. But all things are not equal, and this is not an ideal world. As a result, science has a responsibility to examine phenomena, *as much as is possible,* stripped of ideological biases and cultural presumptions.

SUMMARY

The phrase "red in tooth and claw," coined by Alfred Lord Tennyson, was employed by Charles Darwin to provoke deep insight into the essence of nature. The violence of nature is not a moral issue viewed in the grand scheme, for violence both causes great individual suffering, and also functions to constrain the course of evolution and change. Had the dinosaurs not been extinguished through some form of violence, humans probably would never have evolved. However, viewed from the frames of human perception, society, and culture, violence *must* be a moral issue.

This chapter has attempted to view violence as an "objective" phenomenon. In this frame, violence is found to be commonly misconceived as more harmful, more individually-based, more masculine, and more pathological than it actually is. From the strictly scientific frame, violence is often relatively harmless (even though it is also often very damaging, and often deadly), isolated, and co-constructed in the context of verbal conflict. But morally, it is important to ask questions such as "How much violence is acceptable in society?" and "Even if both sexes are violent, how should our society cope with the fact that far more women are seriously injured in intimate conflict than men?" These are moral questions that science can illuminate, but not answer.

DISCUSSION QUESTIONS

1 Which is worse, in your opinion, verbal violence or physical violence? Support your answer.
2 This chapter offers many interesting and controversial findings regarding violence. For example, about half of college students see slapping as acceptable in dating relationships, and 75 percent of college students report having inflicted and received violence with their dating partners. Given these findings, discuss when you think slapping (or other forms of violence against) a dating partner is appropriate.
3 Several studies have shown that men do not necessarily use violence more than women. Women might even use violence more than men. Discuss why sex differences may not be as large as people assume and provide personal examples (if you wish).

4 Which myth of violence is the most surprising to you? That is, which myth do you think is most reasonable to accept and why do people largely accept it? Can you disbelieve this myth, or do you need more evidence? Please elaborate.

5 Which maxim of violence is the most insightful to you? That is, which maxim increases your understanding of relational violence? Why?

6 Have you ever witnessed violence that emerges from an affront or a transgression? Describe the specifics of your experience to determine if the general progression discussed in the section "The Dynamics of Transgression and Affront Management" applies to your experience. What insights does that general progression to violence give you?

7 Which explanation of violence do you find most useful (learned helplessness, paradoxical punishment, rationalization theory, etc.)? Elaborate and give examples.

10

MEDIATING CONFLICT

Dr. Claudia Hale is professor of interpersonal communication at Ohio University. Dr. Hale's ideas about mediation come from her extensive research and professional practice. Her research interests include alternative dispute resolution, children's communication, and conflict.

Dr. Amy Thieme is assistant professor of communication at Eastern Kentucky University. Having recently completed her doctoral work at Ohio University, Dr. Thieme remains active in the research and practice of mediation. She also helps direct Eastern Kentucky University's alternative dispute program.

CHAPTER OUTLINE

In an ideal world, if two or more parties found themselves in disagreement, they would confront each other in a constructive manner, talking through their individual perspectives and needs. These discussions would continue until the parties managed, via joint negotiation and problem solving, to find a way of working together to resolve their disagreements.

Obviously, we do not live in an ideal world. We live in a world where individuals vary widely in their skills as communicators and in their willingness to collaborate when faced with disagreements. Even individuals who are, under normal circumstances, excellent communicators and problem solvers can find themselves confronted with situations that tax the limits of their abilities. Emotions might run too high and/or trust too low for the involved parties to coordinate their efforts appropriately. Cultural and social differences might impose additional barriers to effective communication and conflict management.

Left on their own, unresolved conflicts can grow until they eventually result in outbreaks of violence and/or cases that unnecessarily clog our court system. This does not have to be the end result, however, because a variety of *alternative dispute resolution* (ADR) mechanisms exist for people who wish to find a constructive venue for addressing their conflicts. One such alternative is dispute mediation.[1]

In the United States in the past ten years the use of mediation as an ADR approach has increased dramatically. However, mediation (even if unfamiliar to many readers of this chapter) is not new. Mediation has an extremely long and rich history that crosses cultural, national, and religious boundaries. Mediation was the principal means of dispute resolution in ancient China (Brown, 1982) and continues to be practiced today (Folberg & Taylor, 1984). Various forms of mediation and conciliation have rich histories within Japanese law and customs (Henderson, 1965), Native American tribes (LeResche, 1993), and African communities (Gulliver, 1979). In the United States, the American Jewish community established the Jewish Conciliation Board, and the early Quakers practiced mediation to resolve commercial disputes and marital disagreements (Folberg & Taylor, 1984).

Today, mediation is used as an approach for conflict management in a wide variety of contexts. Not only do we have the familiar use of mediation to address labor-management disputes, but some states (for example, Alaska, California, Maine) mandate the use of mediation as an approach for resolving some of the controversies that emerge during divorce. (By "mandate" we

---

[1] As is true of most of our communication colleagues who work in the area of conflict management, we adhere to the position that no conflict is ever truly resolved. Rather, conflicts are managed. Nonetheless, we might occasionally use the terms *resolve* or *resolution* at least in part because of the formal designation of mediation as an ADR mechanism. Even if "resolution" is a façade, the language of resolution is well established within the literature and the vocabularies of many individuals who work in the area of ADR.

mean only that the parties have to appear at a mediation session. It is not possible to require enthusiastic participation or to dictate that agreements be reached.) Many communities look to mediation as an approach for handling family disputes, neighborhood disagreements, gang-related conflicts, landlord-tenant difficulties, and customer-merchant problems. In some communities, mediation programs attempt to bring together victims of crime and their victimizers to bring about a form of restitution or reconciliation. (These programs are typically referred to as Victim-Offender Reconciliation Programs, or VORP. For more information about such programs, see Umbreit, 1993, 1989; Woolpert, 1991.) An increasing number of school systems employ peer mediation programs as a way not only of empowering youngsters to manage their own conflicts but of teaching problem-solving skills.

Our objective in this chapter is to introduce readers to dispute mediation. We hope that the information we offer will help you gain an understanding of both the process of dispute mediation and the constructive role that mediation plays in addressing interpersonal conflicts. Our discussion is organized around the following topic questions: (1) What is mediation? (2) How are mediations conducted? (3) What skills and knowledge contribute to competence on the part of mediators? (4) What skills and knowledge contribute to competence on the part of disputants? Our own backgrounds in mediation come not only from our activities as researchers but from training and experiences as participants in community mediation programs. That training and those experiences provide lenses through which we view both the promise and the problems associated with conflict management via dispute mediation.

WHAT IS MEDIATION?

Simply put, *mediation* is a process involving two or more parties who are in conflict with each other and an "uninvolved" third party (the mediator).[2] Ideally, the mediator serves as a neutral and impartial guide, structuring an interaction that enables the conflicting parties to find a mutually acceptable solution to their problems. The mediator remains neutral to the extent that she or he does not have a relationship (personal or professional) with any of the disputants and thus, at least in theory, will not act in a way that privileges one of the disputants over the other(s). The concept of neutrality often applies specifically to the proposed solutions and to whether those solutions seem fair to all involved parties. A mediator is considered to be impartial to the extent that he or she does not act as an advocate for one party or assume an adversarial role (arguing against the position of one of the parties).

---

[2] What is presented here is a picture of mediation as it is generally practiced within the United States. Cross-cultural comparisons of mediation would reveal interesting variations. In some cultures, for example, the mediator is typically a well-known and respected community elder as opposed to the unknown, neutral third party that is common in the United States.

Although neutrality and impartiality represent fundamental ideals, they are not trouble-free concepts. Almost without exception, documents that prescribe ethical behavior for mediators caution the mediator to assume responsibility for ensuring that the final agreement entered into by the disputants is fair. In at least some instances, this responsibility for ensuring fairness seems to call on the mediator to be quite positional, perhaps noting problems with or concerns about a proposal that is acceptable to one disputant while significantly disadvantaging the other disputant. Questions have also been raised about *how* a mediator acts neutrally and/or impartially (Cooks & Hale, 1994; Rifkin, Millen & Cobb, 1991). It is one thing to tell someone that they are to be neutral and impartial; it is another thing to explain what these concepts mean within the reality of a specific mediation.

Mediation can be easily distinguished from arbitration and adjudication (that is, decision making through the courts): During mediation, the people in conflict are the decision makers. The mediator serves not as a judge but as a *facilitator*. He or she tries to set the stage for conversation, encouraging the disputing individuals to work cooperatively to resolve their problems. One of the by-products of a successful mediation can be the discovery of new ways of communicating that are constructive and productive. Such skills can be especially important in an ongoing relationship (for example, between a landlord and tenants, between neighbors, within a family, between roommates, or between divorced parents who continue to share parenting responsibilities for their children).

Although a mediator does not control decision making with respect to issues of substance, the mediator does control (or, at least, attempts to control) the communication process during the mediation. This is one of the primary differences between decision making through negotiation and decision making through mediation. In direct negotiations, the disputing parties control both the process and the solution. When they enter into mediation, however, the disputing parties agree to relinquish to the mediator at least some control over the process.

A wide variety of people in different professional organizations have been involved in efforts to define mediation. Some such organizations are the Academy of Family Mediators, the American Bar Association, the American Arbitration Association, the Association of Family and Conciliation Courts, the National Association of Social Workers, and the Society of Professionals in Dispute Resolution. Despite that diversity, researchers and practitioners agree on the basic principles that define mediation. Primary among those principles is that mediation is a dispute management process that attempts to promote self-determination. That is, dispute mediation emphasizes that the conflicting parties reach *voluntary, uncoerced* agreements that reflect *autonomous* decision making on their part.

Another defining principle of mediation centers on the ideal that disputants make informed decisions, both about their participation in the mediation and about their commitments to (or rejections of) proposed solutions. In some cases, mediators recommend that each of the disputants seek the advice of an attorney prior to making final commitments to the proposals that emerge during the mediation. The intent of this recommendation is to ensure that the disputants consider all options and make informed decisions concerning the proposals that have been put forward.

The final defining principle we will mention here is confidentiality. Mediation is a confidential process, and the mediator typically reassures the parties that, at least as far as he or she is concerned, nothing said during the mediation will be communicated outside of the mediation setting (at least not to inappropriate parties and/or not in a way that would identify the mediation participants). There are limits, however. Should information be revealed that points, for example, to possible child abuse, the mediator is ethically bound to communicate that situation to appropriate authorities.

While there is agreement concerning the basic principles that define mediation, the goal of the process is a matter of some dispute. Some practitioners believe that the primary goal of mediation is to resolve interpersonal conflicts by reaching agreements (see McIsaac, 1983). In this approach to mediation, any emotional or relational issues within the conflicts are secondary concerns. Other practitioners believe that the primary goal of mediation is to assist disputants through the emotional issues, with resolution of substantive issues defined as a secondary concern (see Milne, 1978). Campbell and Johnston (1986) emphasize that the manner in which mediators allow emotional issues to enter the mediation process varies depending on the model of mediation used by the practitioner. Thus, the mediator's own ideology regarding the goal of mediation can influence the methods (strategies and tactics) that the mediator uses. Figure 10-1 provides a spectrum of the goals of the mediation process.

To the extreme left of the continuum are the practitioners who believe that mediation reflects a goal-directed, issue-oriented process aimed at achieving an agreement. This model assumes an orientation of humans as rational beings who can contain their emotions and proceed logically to resolve their disputes (McIsaac, 1983). Coogler (1978), the pioneer of this philosophy, advocates a very systematic, structured approach to mediation that provides legally enforceable agreements between disputants. A mediation session will stop, at least temporarily, if the disputants need to work out emotional issues elsewhere (for example, in family counseling) before proceeding with substantive discussions.

The middle of the spectrum is occupied by a group of practitioners who recognize that feelings are not so easily separated from the conflict, and that,

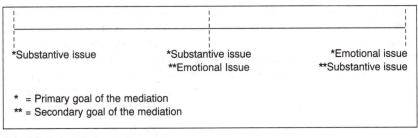

FIGURE 10-1
THE RANGE OF MEDIATION GOALS

for an agreement to be reached, the mediator must address the emotional issues (Folberg & Taylor, 1984). The mediator addresses emotional issues by using communication skills such as active listening, paraphrasing, and reflecting. The idea is to address the emotional issues and encapsulate them, and then resolve the substantive issues (Campbell & Johnston, 1986).

Finally, at the far right of the spectrum is a group of practitioners who view mediation as a therapeutic event. This type of mediation is advocated for high-conflict cases such as divorce or child custody disputes. The primary goal of this type of mediation is to assist the disputants through the emotional issues that have divided them (Haynes, 1982).

A key question for anyone involved in a conflict is, Which dispute management procedure will best help me meet my objectives? Sander and Goldberg (1994) reviewed a variety of binding and nonbinding procedures in an attempt to answer that question. Dispute mediation is considered a nonbinding procedure because, with its emphasis on disputant self-determination, any proposed and accepted agreements are maintained *voluntarily* by the disputants. By contrast, the courts and, typically, arbitration provide binding decisions concerning how a conflict should be handled. Sander and Goldberg argue that if the disputants' objectives are (1) to obtain vindication, (2) to obtain a neutral opinion concerning the merits of their individual positions within the conflict, (3) to establish a formal precedent, or (4) to maximize recovery and/or minimize loss, then mediation is probably not the best approach for resolving their conflict. However, if the disputants are interested in (1) minimizing their financial costs, (2) having relatively speedy access to a conflict management process, (3) engaging in a process that will be private and confidential in nature, and perhaps most importantly, (4) maintaining or even improving their relationship with each other, then mediation is ideal. Sander and Goldberg also argue that, in comparison to some other dispute management processes, mediation more likely helps disputants overcome barriers to settlement that might exist because of poor communication skills, the need to express emotions, and constituent pressures (that is, pressures exerted by individuals or groups who are being represented at the table by the disputant/ negotiator; we could extend the idea of constituents to include friends of the disputants or other family members—anyone whom the disputant views as an advisor or "opinion leader" with respect to the dispute in question).

HOW ARE MEDIATIONS CONDUCTED?

Mediations do not just happen. A trained mediator follows an established set of sequential and developmental stages. The progression of these stages is important because each builds on the work accomplished in the previous stage. For example, in the initial stage of the mediation, a mediator typically explains his or her role to the disputants and establishes any ground rules to guide the sessions. Mediation proceeds only after the mediator has obtained agreement from all disputants to those ground rules. Often, one of the ground rules concerns engaging in behaviors that exhibit mutual respect. One example of respectful behavior is not to tolerate interruptions. During the mediation, if the disputants begin interrupting each other or displaying other signs of disrespect, the mediator can regain control by, in part, reminding the disputants of their earlier acceptance of and agreement to the ground rules.

To help illustrate the process of mediation and to accompany the remainder of our discussion, we have created a transcript for a prototypical mediation (contained in Boxes 10-1 through 10-6). No two mediations are alike, and we have controlled the development of this one for our own purposes. However, this hypothetical case should provide at least a general idea of the various stages of mediation.

A mediator works at reducing tensions between the parties in conflict and at gaining trust and commitments to work together. Most mediation models are structured to move disputants from a "you-me" to an "us-we" orientation. This new perspective helps the disputants look for mutually satisfactory ways of resolving their conflict. If this change in perspective is not accomplished in the initial stages, the mediator runs the risk of having disputants polarize even further into their own positions. In the later stages, polarized disputants will have difficulty perceiving any areas of common ground and that difficulty, in turn, will affect their ability to reach an agreement. Therefore, an experienced mediator does not rush the process but rather takes the time needed to work through each stage. The amount of time spent in each stage depends on the intensity of the conflict, the type of conflict, and the negotiating skills of the disputants (Moore, 1986). As might be expected (because of space constraints), the example we have given represents a mediation that moves relatively smoothly and quickly from one stage to the next. In the real world, the picture is often quite different.

One other disclaimer is appropriate. We provide a very general description of the way in which mediation works at many community mediation centers;

however, variations exist. Not all centers handle the intake procedures in the same way, nor do all mediators establish the same sets of ground rules. The mediation centers where we have worked have tended to prefer a comediator model, with two mediators present to conduct any mediation session. For the sake of convenience, we describe our mediation as though only one person occupies the mediator role. Also for the sake of convenience, our discussion focuses on only two disputants, but it is certainly possible to have disputes that involve three or more parties (with almost any number of people making up a party). Despite these simplifications, we hope the description we provide will give you an adequate understanding of the way mediation works.

How Are Mediations Initiated?

Frequently, mediations are initiated by the disputing parties themselves, who, either unilaterally or bilaterally, solicit the assistance of a mediator or mediation agency. Although unilateral initiations are common, a dispute can be mediated only when at least two disputants agree to participate. It would be impossible, for example, to mediate a dispute between a husband and wife if the wife refused to participate in the mediation process. In the case of a unilateral initiation, the noninitiating party may refuse to participate or may react negatively to the mediator and to the mediation process. By contrast, bilateral initiation can signal a willingness on the part of both disputants to negotiate in good faith and actively to explore possible solutions to their problems.

Disputants might be referred to mediation by secondary sources, such as close friends, family members, social service agencies, police officers, or lawyers. Although secondary sources are not principal actors in the dispute, they are concerned about the consequences of the conflict, should it continue. In the Zappia-Spriggs dispute, the police officer might have referred the neighbors to mediation as a means of containing the conflict before it escalated into more property damage. Referral could also have come from spouses or mutual friends. We have structured a scenario in which the dispute was referred to mediation by the courts (see Box 10-1). If the dispute were not settled in mediation, it would be sent back to the courts for a ruling.

After parties to a conflict have been referred to a mediation center, an intake professional tries to educate the parties about the process of mediation and help them determine whether mediation is the most appropriate arena for resolving their dispute. Most mediation centers take a "multidoor" approach to case screening (Ostermeyer, 1991); that is, the intake professional not only determines if mediation is appropriate but also tries to determine whether other dispute management or support processes (such as family counseling) are necessary as well. To make this assessment, intake professionals ask parties about the history and nature of the dispute, whether or not violence or

---

BOX 10-1

ZAPPIA-SPRIGGS: A HYPOTHETICAL MEDIATION

Case History

Mike Zappia and Scott Spriggs are in conflict. They have lived next door to one another in a residential neighborhood for seven years. The conflict started (or escalated) between the two neighbors one afternoon when Mr. Zappia cut down some branches from Mr. Spriggs's maple trees. The branches were hanging over Mr. Zappia's property. When Mr. Spriggs learned about the destruction to his property, he stormed over to Zappia's house and declared that if Zappia ever did anything like that again he'd be sorry. Zappia responded angrily that if Spriggs had taken care of his own trees then Zappia would not have had to cut them in the first place. Spriggs, frustrated and angered by his confrontation with Zappia, called the police. The police warned Zappia not to cut down any more branches.

The conflict escalated the following week when Mr. Zappia was working in his yard. Still angry about the branches over his property, he raked up all the leaves in his yard and dumped them on Spriggs's front lawn. Spriggs decided he'd had enough and that the only way to settle this mess was to take Zappia to court. The judge assigned to the case noted that she could easily make a ruling that would solve the immediate problem but recognized that no court order could address the underlying conflict or necessarily help improve the long-term relationship between these two neighbors. Thus, the judge referred the case to mediation.

---

substance abuse is involved, what the parties hope to gain from mediation, and whether the parties are willing to resolve their dispute. If mediation is thought to be appropriate (and the disputing parties agree to participate in the process), the intake professional tries to match the case with a mediator (or mediation team) and to schedule a mediation.

Stage 1: Introductions

Although the individual who handles the intake process typically provides the disputants with information concerning the process of mediation, during the first meeting involving the mediator and the disputants, the mediator begins the session by taking a few minutes to give an overview of the process and to explain her or his role as mediator. Box 10-2 illustrates the introductory stage of the Zappia-Spriggs mediation. Mediators typically try to make clear that they are not judges and that, as mediators, they will not be trying to determine who is right and who is wrong, or dictating appropriate courses of action. Instead, the determination of appropriate actions is the responsibility of the disputants.

At the beginning of the initial mediation session, it is reasonable to expect that the disputants are feeling angry and frustrated with each other, and perhaps even distrustful of the mediator. As explained in Chapters 1 and 2, disputants can bring a great deal of "baggage" to any conflict in terms of cultural norms, personal dispositions, relational history, and prior conflict outcomes

---

BOX 10-2

MEDIATION—STAGE 1: INTRODUCTIONS

Mediator: Good afternoon. My name is Chris Jones and I have been asked to assist you in discussing the issues that brought you to mediation. First, I'd like to congratulate you both on agreeing to try to negotiate a solution to an issue that might have been difficult for you to discuss in the past. What we will be doing in this mediation is talking through the problems that have brought you here today. Once we have a clear understanding of the issues of concern, then we will turn our attention to a search for solutions that will satisfy your needs and interests. It is important for you to understand that, as a mediator, I am not here to judge who is right or wrong, or to tell you how to resolve your differences. What I will try to do is to assist you in identifying any problems or issues you want to talk about, guide you through a problem-solving process, and, generally, help keep you on track and focused. It will be up to you to create and agree upon a solution that is right for both of you.

So that everyone can feel comfortable talking openly, I want you to know that I consider these mediation sessions to be confidential. This means that I will not discuss what occurs or what is said with anyone not directly involved in this session. You will notice that I will be taking notes during the mediation, but these are just to help me keep track of the concerns that you raise. I promise you that these notes will be destroyed following the mediation.

Before we begin, there are some ground rules that I would like each of you to follow. These ground rules focus on demonstrating civility and respect for each other while we are involved in this process. Civility and respect can be demonstrated in a variety of ways. At the most simple level, I would like one party to speak at a time. While that party is speaking, I ask that the other party listen carefully and not interrupt. If you have a question about what is said, I ask that you hold it until it is your turn to speak. Is this agreeable to each of you?

Zappia: Yes.

Spriggs: Yes.

Mediator: Are there any questions before we begin? If not, then let's get started.

(recall Figure 2-2). In addition, mediators must keep in mind that individuals who have never experienced mediation can bring with them misconceptions (and even disappointments) not only about the conflict they are in but about the process of mediation. The first mediation that one of the authors conducted involved three current roommates and a former roommate. This mediation was particularly difficult at least in part because the former roommate wanted to be in a court of law (rather than in mediation) and wanted a person in authority (that is, a judge) to tell the other disputants that they had acted inappropriately. When we began the mediation session, she made her feelings clearly known, stating in an angry tone of voice: "All we're going to do is talk. We've already tried that. I can't see what possible good this is going to do." Fortunately, we were capable of getting beyond that point and achieving satisfactory agreements on a number of the problems the women had been experiencing with each other. However, this particular disputant remained disappointed at not having her position (weak as it proved to be in at least some respects) totally vindicated in a court of law.

During the early stages of the mediation, it is imperative that the mediator begin the session on a positive note, gaining the trust of the disputing parties. To build this positive tone, the mediator might begin by congratulating the parties on their willingness to come to mediation and on their openness to working on the problems they have been facing. This approach can reinforce the disputants' commitment to work together. The mediator needs to establish his or her position as a neutral and impartial third party whose role is to facilitate discussions. Typically the mediator emphasizes that the disputants will share in the decision-making process, and that the solutions they arrive at will be their own (as opposed to the mediator's). The mediator also explains that the sessions are confidential and that anything discussed during the mediation will not be disclosed (at least by the mediator) to parties outside the mediation.[3] This reassurance is designed to encourage the disputing parties to speak freely. Opening the channels of communication is central to the success of mediation.

Finally, during the initial stage of the mediation, the mediator establishes the ground rules, or guidelines and expectations, for the mediation sessions. Typically, these include the fact that parties are expected to listen carefully to what each other says and not to interrupt while another person is speaking. Parties are asked to agree to these guidelines before the mediation continues.

Throughout the introduction, the mediator attempts to build rapport and trust. Ideally, the physical setting will encourage communication and mutual

---

[3] If the mediation is conducted through a community program or agency, agreements reached or difficulties experienced with the mediation process are often reviewed with the director of the agency but would not be discussed with outside parties. In court-connected programs, the court might need to review any agreements reached, or at least be apprised of the fact that the parties have been able to mediate their differences.

problem solving. The mediator should be courteous and professional toward everyone involved in the mediation sessions. Through careful attention to the nonverbal cues of the disputants, mediators attempt to determine the emotional states of the parties and to assess their willingness to negotiate.

Stage 2: Telling the Story

Once the mediator has finished the introductory comments, answered any questions, and obtained agreement to the ground rules, the mediation proceeds to the story-telling phase. During this stage, the mediator asks each party, one at a time, to share his or her perspective concerning the problems that have brought them to mediation. As illustrated in the Zappia-Spriggs case (see Box 10-3), usually the mediator begins with the person who requested mediation. In essence, the mediator begins with the "complaining party," but that phrasing would not be used, since it might be perceived as insulting and thus undercut any rapport that has been developed. In a similar sense, the mediator would never refer to the other party as the "defendant," since such a label would define that person's position as one of defending himself or herself rather than one of sharing his or her perspective on the dispute. If the mediator believes that a power imbalance exists between the parties, he or she might decide to begin with the weaker of the parties. This action would be taken as part of an effort to build the power of the weaker party and thus enable that party to be at the table as an equal.

Situations of power imbalance pose great challenges for mediators and provide the basis for many of the concerns voiced by individuals who are critical of the mediation process (see, for example, Grillo, 1991; Lerman, 1984). The assumption is that, in a court of law, the rules that guide the process and the knowledge and skills of the professionals (that is, the attorneys and judges) protect those who need protection. Mediations, however, rely on the communication skills, intellects, and decision-making abilities of the participants. What if one of the parties is significantly less skilled as a communicator or has less power (however that term might be defined) than is possessed by the other disputant? In that case, we must rely on the ability of the mediator (1) to find an approach that balances the power of the disputants or (2) to recognize that, because of the problems and risks created by the power imbalance, the conflict is not amenable to mediation.

The story-telling phase of the mediation allows the mediator to hear the disputants' explanations and to begin defining the issues that need to be addressed. In addition, the story-telling stage provides a structured arena that forces the parties to listen, without interruption, to each other's perspective regarding the conflict. To check for accurate understanding, the mediator might even ask parties to paraphrase what they hear each other saying. Understanding does not indicate agreement, but it does indicate that each party at least

BOX 10-3

MEDIATION—STAGE 2: TELLING THE STORY

Mediator: Mr. Zappia, since Mr. Spriggs brought the matter to the attention of the courts, I'm going to begin by having him tell me his perspective on the issue. When he is finished, I will give you the same opportunity. Is this OK with you?

Zappia: Yes.

Mediator: Mr. Spriggs why don't you begin. Take a few minutes and tell me the concerns that brought you to mediation.

Spriggs: My family and I have lived in our house for twelve years. One of the reasons we moved into the neighborhood was that it was an older neighborhood in a wooded area and there were a lot of kids around to play with our children. We have always gotten along with all our neighbors, and I just can't understand why Zappia keeps harassing us.

Mediator: Mr. Spriggs, could you just take a moment and explain to me in more detail exactly what you mean by "Mr. Zappia keeps harassing us"?

Spriggs: Well, it all started with trees. There are five maple trees that border the property between Zappia's house and my house. One day, I came home from work and found Zappia chopping the branches off my maple trees. I was shocked that he had done this and told him that he had no right to destroy my property. Zappia swore and threatened to continue cutting. So, I called the cops. I mean, what would you do if you were in this situation? He was destroying my trees.

Mediator: I'm not sure what I would have done, but if I'm understanding you clearly, you felt it was appropriate to call the police when you saw Mr. Zappia cutting down the branches on your maple trees. Is that accurate?

Spriggs: Yeah. That's right.

Mediator: Mr. Spriggs, what do you mean when you say that the trees were "destroyed"?

Spriggs: Well, Zappia cut off all the branches on the side of the trees that borders his property. Not only do my trees look bald on one side, they will probably die from the shock of the slicing. Parts of the trees are open and exposed. I'm afraid all sorts of insects and other bugs will get in there and eat away at my trees. The trees will probably rot.

Mediator: Is there anything else that you think I should know about this situation?

Spriggs: It just seems like this guy is out to get me. If it's not one thing, it's another. Just the other day, I found the guy dumping leaves from his yard onto my yard. He told me he did that because they were

BOX 10-3 *(continued)*

the leaves from my trees. How can I be responsible for the leaves that blow into his yard? It's always something with him. The guy is nuts.

Mediator: Is there anything else you want to talk about?

Spriggs: No. I just want him to pay for the damages to my trees and leave me and my property alone.

Mediator: Let me see if I can summarize what your specific concerns are. First, you are worried about the health of your trees because some of the limbs were removed, and you believe Mr. Zappia should be responsible for the cost of their damage. Second, you are uncertain about who is responsible for the maintenance of the leaves from your tree. Is that basically the situation from your perspective?

Spriggs: Yes, and the fact that I don't know why he's doing all this.

Mediator: Thank you very much, Mr. Spriggs. Mr. Zappia, I appreciate your listening to Mr. Spriggs's statement. Now, I would like to have you take a few minutes to explain your perspective on the situation.

Zappia: Basically, I think this guy is full of it. He is acting like everything is my fault, and besides, he doesn't get along with any of his other neighbors.

Mediator: Is Mr. Spriggs's relationship with his other neighbors causing problems for you that you want to discuss?

Zappia: No. That's his problem. Not mine.

Mediator: Mr. Zappia, why don't you give me your perspective on the situation.

Zappia: I'll tell you about the situation. It's like this: Spriggs doesn't care about anybody but himself. As long as his lawn and trees look all right, he's happy. He doesn't care what effect his stuff has on anyone else.

Mediator: Could you be a bit more specific. What "stuff" are you referring to?

Zappia: Yes. His trees.

Mediator: What effect are Mr. Spriggs's trees having on you?

Zappia: Well, for one thing, they're too big. The branches are overtaking my driveway. Seedlings and leaves are always falling off all over my yard and my cars. They get stuck on the windows and make a big mess. Not to mention the mess the birds make on my cars.

Mediator: What do you mean when you say the leaves and the birds are making a big mess?

Zappia: Sometimes the leaves are sticky and they get the cars all sticky. Sometimes they get stuck on the car and leave leaf prints all over the place. And the birds perch in the branches all day and night and

BOX 10-3 *(continued)*

leave droppings all over the cars and driveway. I told Spriggs that, and he didn't do anything about it. So I just trimmed the branches back a little. It was no big deal.

Mediator: When you talked to Mr. Spriggs, what did you tell him?

Zappia: I told him that he had to do something about the trees. I told him that every morning when I come outside, my cars are filthy from the leaves and birds.

Mediator: Did you discuss what you wanted Mr. Spriggs to do about the trees?

Zappia: No. I guess I just thought it was obvious. What else would you do?

Mediator: You assumed that Mr. Spriggs knew you meant the branches should be trimmed back, and when he did not do it, you cut them down.

Zappia: That's right. I just trimmed them a little, though.

Mediator: What do you mean by "trimmed them a little"?

Zappia: Well, the branches from his trees hung over my lawn and driveway, so I trimmed them back to his property line.

Mediator: Approximately how far would you say that was?

Zappia: Seven or eight feet. I didn't hurt the trees any. I love trees as much as the next guy, but I would do something about them if they were interfering with someone's property. Then he goes and calls the cops. I told the cops that the branches were on my property, so I had every right to cut them down. The cops told me not to cut anymore and to have it settled in court. So, now I'm not allowed to cut the branches. He won't cut them. So my family and I are forced to park our cars in the street so we won't have to keep cleaning them. On top of that, the darn leaves from his trees keep blowing into my yard. So, I just started blowing them back into his yard.

Mediator: Is there anything else that you would like to discuss?

Zappia: No. I just want him to do something about those trees.

Mediator: What would you like to see happen?

Zappia: I would like him to cut them down.

Mediator: Let me see if I understand your perspective, Mr Zappia. The leaves that fall from Mr. Spriggs's maple trees are causing you some distress because they leave marks on your cars and you have to rake them up from your lawn. You believed that cutting down the limbs was a way of solving this problem. Is that basically correct?

Zappia: Yes.

Mediator: Thank you very much, Mr. Zappia.

comprehends the other's perspective. After both parties have had the opportunity to tell their story, any differences in stories are at least mentally noted by the mediator. The differences might indicate key areas of misunderstanding between the parties. The mediator might ask a series of closed-ended or open-ended questions to clarify and correct misperceptions and inaccurate assumptions.

The story-telling stage also allows for the venting of emotions. Moore (1986) states that the need to vent emotions in the beginning of the mediation is normal and should be expected. In fact, he believes that venting is almost a prerequisite for dealing with the substantive issues. However, intense emotions should be minimized, since they can be counterproductive to the mediation process. Such emotions might block a party's willingness to negotiate or interfere with a party's ability to reason. Moore suggests that mediators manage emotions by recognizing their existence, identifying them, and selecting appropriate interventions. If a mediator thinks that the expression of the emotion will not be counterproductive to the mediation, she or he should let the party vent. In fact, the venting might help enlighten the other party about the intensity of the conflict. If the mediator believes that the venting will be counterproductive, he or she might decide to caucus (that is, meet separately with the parties) to allow each party to vent in a neutral environment, or the mediator might initiate a break in the proceedings, giving each party a few minutes to compose themselves and the mediator a chance to refocus the mediation process.

The main goal during the story-telling stage is for the mediator to create a sense of shared perceptions concerning the dispute. Often conflicts are struggles over misperceptions of differing sets of assumptions. As explained in Chapter 1, in addition to parallel conflicts (that is, conflicts that have an objective basis), the disputants within a mediation can experience displaced conflicts, misattributed conflicts, and/or latent conflicts. The role of the mediator is to help the parties reshape and relabel the language of the conflict to ensure that they are talking about the same issues (Evarts et al., 1983; Kiely & Crary, 1986).

The mediator's role becomes one of translator of the disputants' messages; it is the mediator's responsibility to reshape the language in a form that makes sense and is acceptable to both parties. Terms that are unclear must be defined, and emotionally charged language must be reworded and neutralized. Throughout the process, the mediator should summarize important points in neutral, positive terms and continually emphasize areas of shared understanding and/or agreement. Looking back at the transcript in Box 10-3, note the points at which the mediator engages in each of the activities indicated here, seeking clarification about what is being said and reframing the disputants' contributions in clear, less negatively charged language.

Stage 3: Identifying the Issues

The information gathered during the story-telling stage is used to define the problems or key issues that must be resolved. One potential difficulty for the mediator at this point is that the issues might seem completely different for each party. For example, in the Zappia-Spriggs case (see Box 10-4), the issues for Mr. Zappia regard the mess the trees are making and his frustration at being ignored by Mr. Spriggs. Mr. Zappia would prefer the trees cut down and wants his needs and perspective as a neighbor to be respected by Mr. Spriggs. The issues for Mr. Spriggs revolve around his desire for his trees to be left alone; he wants to collect for damages to the trees, and he, too, is frustrated and wants respect from his neighbor. In essence, the parties argue from their own positions and world views. When parties argue from their own positions, how can a mediator help them find a satisfactory solution? The answer emerges from the dictates of principled negotiation (Fisher & Ury, 1983). The mediator must find a way to encourage the participants to focus on their underlying interests rather than on their positions.

BOX 10-4

MEDIATION—STAGE 3: IDENTIFYING THE ISSUES

Mediator: As I understand it, the situation between the two of you centers around a need for mutual respect for each other's property. Is that an accurate assessment?

Zappia: Yes. Definitely.

Spriggs: Sounds right to me.

Mediator: So, the issues that need to be resolved center on the care of the maple trees and finding a way that the leaves will not bother Mr. Zappia. Mr. Spriggs, would you agree that this is what the situation is about?

Spriggs: Yeah. That and the issue of who is responsible for paying the damage to my trees.

Mediator: So, from your perspective, you want to protect your trees. That includes attending to the damaged sections and finding a way to handle the problem of the leaves.

Spriggs: That's right.

Mediator: Mr. Zappia, do you agree with that statement of the issues?

Zappia: Yeah. That sounds right.

Fisher and Ury (1983) argue that *interests* are the motivating force behind positions. In other words, our interests shape the positions that we claim. The mediator's task is to discover *why* a person has chosen a particular position. Answering the "why" question can help the mediator uncover the disputants' common interests. In the Zappia-Spriggs case, although their positions are different, Zappia and Spriggs do share common interests: They each want their property and needs to be respected by the other party. If the parties agree about the shared interests, the mediator has changed the focus of the session from arguing over *positions* to trying to find solutions that satisfy *shared interests*—showing respect for each other's property and personal rights.

Once the issues have been identified and agreed upon, the parties are ready to move to the solution stage. We emphasize, however, that the mediator's summary must first be greeted with agreement from the disputants. If one or more of the disputants indicates that the mediator's summary is in error, before moving on the mediator must spend the time and energy required to discover how that summary (and identification of issues) needs to be revised.

Stage 4: Generating Options

With the issues identified and the parties in agreement concerning the importance of those issues, the disputants can begin to generate solutions (see Box 10-5). The mediator encourages the disputants to come up with several solutions and then evaluate them one by one as they try to find the best course

---

BOX 10-5

MEDIATION—STAGE 4: GENERATING OPTIONS

Mediator: I'd like to compliment you on the progress you have made so far. Now that we understand what the issues are, I'd like to talk with both of you in detail about the ways to handle this situation. Mr. Spriggs, since we started with you, I'd like to go back to you again and ask what, in your opinion, would resolve this situation.

Spriggs: Well, I will agree with Zappia and say the branches on the trees did extend over his driveway. However, until now, I wasn't aware that the problem was that bad for him. He says he talked with me, but I don't remember his ever saying anything. Had I known, I would have had them trimmed. However, as sorry as I am about that, I still don't

BOX 10-5 *(continued)*

think he had the right to cut down the branches without my approval. And I don't think I should get stuck paying for a tree professional to come treat the trees so that they don't rot.

Mediator: So, you are saying that you are now aware that the branches on the trees were troublesome for Mr. Zappia, but you would prefer not to be responsible for the cost of the tree professional.

Spriggs: Right.

Mediator: How would you resolve this?

Spriggs: I think Zappia should pay for the treatment.

Mediator: Thank you. Let me take this proposal to Mr. Zappia. Mr. Zappia, Mr. Spriggs has indicated that he now understands that the branches created a problem for you. Nonetheless, he believes that there is a need for a tree professional to treat the trees and that you should pay the cost of that professional. What do you think should happen in this situation? How would you resolve the problem?

Zappia: Well, as I said before, since the branches extended into my property, I thought I had every right to trim them back. If I have to pay for the tree professional, then he should pay for all my car washing bills and labor for raking his leaves over the years.

Mediator: Do I understand that you think the expenses to wash your car and maintain your lawn will equal the cost of having a tree professional come and treat the trees?

Zappia: Right. I have my receipts from the car wash right here and they total about $25 a month.

Mediator: So, you propose that you pay for your car washing bills and lawn maintenance, and Mr. Spriggs should pay for the tree professional.

Zappia: Right.

Mediator: Mr. Spriggs, Mr. Zappia has indicated that the expenses from washing his car and maintaining his lawn equal the cost of the tree professional. So, he feels that each of you should be responsible for your own bills. I'd like you to address that issue.

Spriggs: Well, I have an estimate from a tree professional. He determined that it would cost $150 to treat the trees. I don't think it's fair to attribute all the dirt on Zappia's cars to my trees, and for several months a year, there are no leaves on the trees. For the sake of settling this, I'd be willing to pay for $50 of the tree professional to even out some of his car washing bills.

Mediator: So, you would be willing to pay for $50 of the tree care?

Spriggs: Right.

BOX 10-5 *(continued)*

Mediator: Mr. Zappia, you heard what Mr. Spriggs said. What do you think?

Zappia: Well, I think $100 is too much for me to pay. I would like to have a breakdown of what the tree professional is going to do.

Spriggs: I have the form right here. $45 would be for three spraying treatments to prevent the openings on the trees from rotting or becoming infested with insects, $30 would be to even out the trimming, and $75 would be for labor.

Zappia: Well, since you said if you had known the effect the trees were having on us you would have had a tree expert come and trim the trees, you would have had to pay for that anyway. So, I would be willing to split the cost of the labor and the three spraying treatments if you pay for the trimming.

Mediator: So, you would pay for $37.50 for labor and $22.50 for the sprayings and Mr. Zappia would be responsible for the trimming fee?

Zappia: Correct.

Mediator: Mr. Spriggs, what do you think of that proposal?

Spriggs: I guess that sounds fair.

Mediator: Mr. Zappia?

Zappia: Sounds OK to me.

Mediator: Now, you need to determine when the tree professional will come, who needs to be there when he does the work, and how the two of you will set up payment. Mr. Spriggs, do you have any suggestions?

Spriggs: I have already scheduled him to come this Saturday. I will definitely be there, and I don't suppose Zappia needs to be, unless he wants to. Zappia can pay me his share and I will give the man the check.

Mediator: Mr. Zappia, what do you think about that proposal?

Zappia: Saturday is fine, but I work that day so I won't be there. However, I'd prefer to be billed directly for my portion from the tree specialist with a breakdown of the fee on the billing. So, instead of paying Spriggs, I'll pay the tree professional.

Mediator: Mr. Spriggs, how do you feel about that?

Spriggs: Fine with me.

Mediator: I think you have achieved a very positive resolution so far. Now, you need to discuss the issue of who will be responsible for the care of the trees and the leaves in the future. In other words, should the branches of the trees cause problems in the future, who will be responsible for tending to them, and when the leaves fall from the trees, who will be responsible for raking them? Since I started with Mr. Spriggs last time, I would like to start with Mr. Zappia this time. Do you have any suggestions Mr. Zappia?

Zappia: I'd like to see those branches kept trimmed at all times so

BOX 10-5 *(continued)*

this doesn't happen again. That will also keep most of the leaves out of my yard and reduce the problem with the birds.

Mediator: Define "trimmed" for me.

Zappia: I'd like the branches not to cross the property line.

Mediator: Who would be responsible for keeping them trimmed?

Zappia: Since they are Spriggs's trees, I think it's only fair that he keeps them trimmed.

Mediator: So, you are saying that you want Mr. Spriggs to be responsible for keeping the trees trimmed to the property line?

Zappia: Right.

Mediator: Mr. Spriggs, how do you respond to that?

Spriggs: This is quite an expense, but I guess I won't have to trim them that often. I'll go along with that, but I also want assurance that he won't cut the trees again when he sees them crossing the property line. I think thirty days notice would be fair.

Mediator: How do you want Mr. Zappia to notify you if he thinks a problem is developing?

Spriggs: In writing.

Mediator: Let me see if I understand you correctly. You will be responsible for trimming the trees. If Mr. Zappia notices that a problem is developing, he should notify you in writing and give you thirty days to trim the trees.

Spriggs: Right. But I'd like him to notify me through certified mail to make sure I get the request.

Mediator: Mr. Zappia, what do you think of that proposal?

Zappia: Sounds OK to me.

Mediator: Very impressive work. One last issue to be discussed: What should be done about the leaves that gather in Mr. Zappia's yard? Mr. Spriggs, any suggestions?

Spriggs: Well, I can't be responsible for all the leaves in the neighborhood that blow into his yard. I mean, who knows if they are from my trees or not. If he doesn't want leaves from other neighbors' trees blowing in his yard, he might consider putting in leaf guards along his property line. They're cheap and work well.

Mediator: Mr. Zappia, what do you think about installing leaf guards along your property line?

Zappia: Well, to tell you the truth, I never thought of that. I guess leaf guards would be a good idea.

Mediator: Mr. Spriggs, is there anything else you would like to discuss today?

Spriggs: No.

Mediator: Mr. Zappia?

Zappia: No.

of action. If the parties experience difficulty in this process, the mediator might advance some suggestions; however, as previously noted, the mediation process centers on the concept of self-determination. The parties produce the "best" solutions themselves, since their own solutions are more likely to be ones to which they have a personal sense of commitment. Huff-Arneson (1988) suggests that mediators pay particularly close attention to the wording of disputant proposals, especially in cases where the language and phrasing used is "if . . . then," since such phrasing usually marks a willingness to work collaboratively.

The mediator's responsibility during the option-generation stage underscores that the solutions being proposed meet the disputants' criteria. That is, as they have talked through their perspectives on the problem, each of the disputants has described one or more "needs" that, if met, will result in a satisfactory agreement for managing the conflict. "Ideal" solutions address the needs of both (all) parties, are practical, and are enforceable.

Unfair or unbalanced agreements present a difficult paradox for the mediator. On the one hand, mediators are ethically bound to remain neutral and impartial throughout the process; that is, the mediator should not act as an advocate for one party against the other or for one particular solution, even if that solution seems better in the eyes of the mediator. However, mediators are also ethically bound to help disputants reach fair solutions (often defined in terms of what would be acceptable within a court of law and/or as being responsive to the needs of each disputant). If, in the mediator's best judgment, the solution being proposed and agreed to by the disputants does not meet the standards of fairness (as defined, admittedly, by the mediator), then most defined standards of practice for mediators indicate that the mediator needs to make his or her concerns known (Academy of Family Mediators, 1985; American Bar Association, 1984; Association of Family and Conciliation Courts, 1989; Bush, 1992; National Association of Social Workers, 1991; Society of Professionals in Dispute Resolution, 1987). This action on the part of the mediator might not keep the parties from going forward with their decision; however, it at least alerts the parties to the mediator's concerns. The mediator then needs to decide whether she or he could or should continue to be part of the mediation process.

The kinds of decisions we are discussing are not simple, nor are there in all cases clear guidelines. Critics of mediation (especially Grillo, 1991) argue, implicitly if not explicitly, in favor of mediators' assuming activist roles, ensuring that the rights and position of any disadvantaged participant is protected. At the same time, though, any attempt to define a single, "right" answer for all situations would ignore possible cultural differences or other factors that might argue for more sensitive attention to situational and relational distinctions.

Stage 5: Writing the Agreement

Assuming that the disputants have been able to generate and come to agreement concerning an acceptable solution, the mediator writes up that agreement (see Box 10-6). The agreement itself should be written in precise, positive, and balanced language. By "precise," we mean that the agreement should clearly indicate the who, what, where, when, and how of the actions to which the disputants have committed themselves. Most agreements also have a "what if" clause that specifies what will happen should one of the disputants violate the provisions of the agreement. The agreement should be phrased in a positive manner. That is, the agreement should focus on what the parties agree to do (for example, respect each other's property) rather than on

---

BOX 10-6

MEDIATION—STAGE 5: WRITING THE AGREEMENT

Mediator: Let me just see if I can summarize what we have agreed to today. If I miss anything or if you have any second thoughts or concerns, please feel free to let me know. Mr. Spriggs will have the tree professional come over on Saturday to trim the trees. He will have the tree specialist bill him for $30 for the trimming, $22.50 for half of the spraying, and $37.50 for half of the labor. Mr. Spriggs will have the tree specialist bill Mr. Zappia $37.50 for half of the labor and $22.50 for half of the spraying. In the future, if the branches from the maple trees cross the property line, Mr. Zappia will notify Mr. Spriggs of that fact in writing and will have the letter sent by certified mail to make sure that Mr. Zappia receives it. Mr. Spriggs will attend to the problem within thirty days. Finally, Mr. Zappia has agreed to install leaf guards to prevent the leaves from the neighbors' yards from blowing into his yard. Mr. Spriggs, is that your understanding of the total agreement?

Spriggs: Yes, it is.

Mediator: Mr. Zappia, is that your understanding of what you have agreed to today?

Zappia: Yes.

Mediator: Okay. I would like to thank both of you for coming to mediation today and for all of your hard work. I think you have reached a very positive solution. Our mediation center will be contacting both of you in a few weeks to make sure this agreement is working out for you. If you have any questions or concerns before we contact you, please feel free to call the center at any time. Thank you for coming.

what they agree not to do (for example, not intruding on each other's property), and the agreement should not point a finger of guilt at either of the parties. Finally, the written agreement should be balanced. For example, to the extent possible, "we" language should be used, and if one of the disputants is going to do three things, then if at all possible the other party should do three things as well.

Once written, the agreement is reviewed by the parties and, if found acceptable, signed by both parties and perhaps by the mediator as witness to the agreement. Because of the confidential nature of mediations, the only document that results from the mediation is the written agreement. In the Zappia-Spriggs case, because the mediation was mandated by the courts, a copy of the agreement would typically be forwarded to the judge. Otherwise, the disputants and the mediation center (assuming that the mediation was conducted through a community mediation service) would be the only individuals or agencies to retain a copy of the agreement.

WHAT SKILLS AND KNOWLEDGE CONTRIBUTE TO COMPETENCE ON THE PART OF MEDIATORS?

The universal model just described might be referred to as the interventionist, or control-based, model (Burrell, Donohue & Allen, 1990). The primary characteristic of this model is its highly structured process. The mediator facilitates discussion and seeks to empower the parties to address the issues under dispute rather than solving their problems for them. An interventionist mediator structures the interaction by controlling turn taking, equalizing talk time, balancing power, maintaining or changing the topic, and helping the disputants identify both the key issues involved and the potential solutions to their problems. Honeyman (1990) suggests that the best mediators are capable of (1) identifying and seeking out information relevant to the issues in dispute, (2) demonstrating empathy for all parties, (3) exhibiting ability at persuasion and presentation of ideas, (4) reducing tensions at appropriate times, (5) managing the interaction by coping with conflicts and developing effective strategies for the interaction, and (6) demonstrating expertise (as needed) concerning the issues in dispute.

There are some things that mediators are *not*. As already explained, a mediator is *not* a judge. Some people mistakenly believe that mediators determine who is right, who is wrong, and hand down decisions. However, the role of mediator does not involve such activities. The rules of evidence and procedure that exist within a court do not exist within a mediation. Mediators do not (or should not) offer legal advice, represent clients, dictate courses of action, or champion the cause of one of the disputants against the other.

Nor are mediators therapists. Occasionally, people seeking mediation should really be seeking the help of family or personal counselors. While a mediator is not a therapist or a counselor, conversations during a mediation can help an individual or a couple decide whether counseling is needed. Many psychologists, social workers, and other counseling professionals are adding mediation to the list of services they provide. However, the professional associations that attempt to describe standards of ethics for these professionals (for example, the National Association of Social Workers, 1991) caution their members that any attempts to act *both* as a counselor for a client *and* as a mediator for a dispute involving that client will probably be viewed as a conflict of interest.

In a recent discussion of mediation ethics, Robert A. Baruch Bush (1992) outlined nine types of dilemmas faced by dispute mediators (see Table 10-1). We do not have sufficient space here to discuss each of these dilemmas in depth. However, as you examine them, you will discover that each calls for the mediator not only to examine carefully and monitor her or his own behavior within the mediation, but to be aware of the definitions others might apply to those behaviors and to the way in which the mediation was conducted.

Although it might be easy, in the absence of experience, to provide an answer for each of the dilemmas that Professor Bush's research identified, each mediation provides its own set of challenges. Mediators must learn from each of their mediations, being honest with themselves both about what they did "right" and areas where they should have responded differently (that is, in a more appropriate and effective manner).

Occasionally, obstacles make it difficult for all the participants in a mediation to meet the criteria of appropriateness and effectiveness in their participation. One such obstacle is that of power imbalances. Power is the ability of a person to effect outcomes (costs or benefits) in an interpersonal context (Thibaut & Kelley, 1959). Power imbalances within a mediation mean that one party has more influence or control over the other party or over the outcome.

Davis and Salem (1984) argue that power imbalances within a mediation context can have extreme adverse effects on the process. They argue that the mediator has a responsibility to interrupt intimidating behaviors within the mediation; otherwise, it will not be possible to reach a fair agreement. Whereas Davis and Salem believe that a mediator can equalize power within a mediation, Auerbach (1983) argues against mediation when a power imbalance is present. He believes that the only fair way to equalize power is to address the issue in a court of law.

As you might expect, this issue is hotly debated, perhaps in part because there are various ways of defining power and because truly equal power between disputants is probably a false hope. It is the responsibility of the mediator not only to understand that power imbalances exist and to appreciate how such imbalances might affect the mediation, but also to be familiar with techniques for trying to balance power (such as having an advocate present for the weaker party) and to be willing to call a halt to the mediation sessions should the situation be one in which the imbalance simply cannot be overcome.

TABLE 10-1
DILEMMAS FOR MEDIATORS*

---

1. Keeping within the limits of competence:
   Recognizing when either the mediator's own ability to diagnose a problem or a disputant's ability (skill) to participate in the mediation process is not sufficient

2. Preserving impartiality:
   Recognizing when prior associations with or personal reactions to the parties during the mediation either impair the ability of the mediator to act impartially or create questions concerning the mediator's impartiality
   Exercising caution with respect to the development of any type of relationship (even a professional relationship) with the disputants *after* the mediation is concluded

3. Maintaining confidentiality:
   With respect to outsiders, distinguishing between information that should be kept confidential and information (such as allegations of child abuse or criminal activities) that must be reported
   With respect to the parties, determining how a confidential disclosure should be handled

4. Ensuring informed consent:
   Recognizing when a party either does not possess the information necessary to make an informed decision or does not possess the ability (intellect) to make an informed decision

5. Preserving self-determination/maintaining nondirectiveness:
   Determining how to respond to situations in which the parties want the mediator to make a decision for them
   Determining how to respond to situations in which the decision reached by the parties is illegal, unfair to a weaker party, unwise, or unfair to an outside party (for example, the children of a divorcing couple)

6. Separating mediation from counseling and legal advice:
   Recognizing when the parties need expert information or guidance, or therapy and counseling

7. Avoiding exposure of a party to harm as a result of mediation:
   Recognizing when mediation might make a bad situation worse

8. Preventing party abuse of the mediation process:
   Recognizing when a party is not participating in good faith (perhaps concealing information, lying, or engaging in intimidation)

9. Handling conflicts of interest:
   Recognizing when relationships with the courts, referral agencies, lawyers, or other professionals might create the reality or the appearance of a conflict of interest on the part of the mediator

---

*Adapted from Bush (1992).

WHAT SKILLS AND KNOWLEDGE CONTRIBUTE TO COMPETENCE ON THE PART OF DISPUTANTS?

Many practitioners involved in mediation assume that by providing the right structure and techniques, a mediator can help disputing parties reach mutually satisfactory agreements. The need for effective performance of appropriate conflict management behaviors is not, however, limited to the mediator. Although mediators garner the majority of research attention, much of the credit for the success (or failure) of any mediation rests with the disputants. Just as the mediator does, they must bring something to the mediation if that process is to achieve its desired goal.

No universally established and agreed-to disputant qualities or skills guarantee a successful mediation. However, it seems reasonable to argue that characteristics (or capabilities) that typically contribute to the perception that someone is a competent communicator probably significantly increase the chances of a positive mediation experience for all involved. As a negative example, disputants who deviate from the established rules by refusing to negotiate in good faith, by breaking turn-taking rules or by refusing to listen to the contributions of the other disputant will probably be viewed not only as less competent but as less trustworthy by the others involved in the session (including the mediator).

Examination of each of the stages of mediation suggests different skills or abilities that might contribute to a successful mediation experience. The initial stage (the intake process) requires that the disputants be capable of explaining their problem to the intake professional and, with the assistance of that individual, assessing whether mediation is a suitable venue for talking through their conflict(s). During Stage 1 of the mediation, the disputants must be capable of focusing on the mediator's instructions and, again, of making a decision about their willingness to commit to the mediation process. In Stage 2 (story telling), the disputants must possess the communication skills to share, in a coherent fashion, their perspectives on the issues in dispute. Although the mediator might assist in the development of the story (by asking questions, reflecting back what he or she hears the disputant saying, helping the disputant clarify points that might be vague or select a more precise and effective way of phrasing his or her point), the mediator cannot tell the story for the disputant. At Stage 3 (issue identification), the disputants must work with the mediator to define their underlying needs. In some situations, disputants should express disagreement with the mediator—for example, if the mediator misidentifies the key issues. Stage 4 (option generation) requires that disputants participate in creative problem solving, again expressing their needs and evaluating proposals in terms of those needs. Finally, Stage 5 (the written agreement) requires that each of the disputants understand the nature of the commitments being entered into and have the power (or authority) to enter into those commitments.

At each stage, disputants are asked to listen (to the intake professional, to the mediator, to the other disputant). During all stages, disputants are encouraged to consider the point of view of the other party and to look at the dispute from a perspective different from their own. Clearly, disputants whose communication skills and cognitive capacities have not developed sufficiently to allow them to participate fully in the process should not be forced (or allowed[4]) to enter into mediation as the venue for handling their disputes. At the same time, we remind you that peer mediation programs have been introduced and are operating successfully in many elementary schools throughout the country. Nonetheless, mediators must help protect against situations in which an individual who is not capable of representing himself or herself—especially as an equal—is asked to take part in a mediation.

SUMMARY

We have, necessarily, presented a very general picture of mediation. In presenting this picture, we have only hinted at or given basic descriptions of the challenges that face mediators and disputants involved in dispute mediation. Recently, a variety of authors (see, for example, Folger & Bush, 1994; Jones, 1994) have written about the potential of mediation to transform and/or reframe the relationship that exists between the disputants. In the picture that we have presented, we have not fully explored this transformative potential. Were we to do so, one of the things we would do in the Zappia-Spriggs case is spend much more time in the mediation exploring the disputants' understandings of what it means to be a neighbor and what is desired from that relationship. The mediator would work toward a situation in which the neighbors are capable of communicating directly as opposed to via registered mail.

Our decision to develop the Zappia-Spriggs case as we did does not repudiate the call for transformative mediations. Instead, while acknowledging the imperfections of the approach presented, we hoped to convey in part the fact that mediators must deal with the solutions that the disputants believe to be best. It is the disputants—and not the mediator—who must live with the results of the mediation.

As mediators, we have experienced situations in which we either identified a particular issue as more important (central to the dispute) than did our disputants, and mediations in which the disputants enthusiastically embraced courses of action that we would not have preferred for ourselves. We have tried to convey a sense in which such situations can be problematic for mediators. On the one hand, mediators should help disputants exercise autonomous

---

[4] The word *allowed* is used here on purpose. At least within the private sector, mediators do not have to accept every disputant who crosses their doorstep. Even within the public sector, though, there are disputants whose situations are inappropriate for mediation.

decision-making ability. On the other hand, mediators should help establish a process in which the disputants act as equals, reaching agreements that are fair and responsive to their individual needs.

We began this chapter by referring to an "ideal" world. In such a world, individuals in conflict collaborate to find ways of managing their conflicts. When people lack the ability to collaborate, mediation is an important mechanism for trying to work through problems and, ultimately, finding the elusive solution to those problems. In comparison to other dispute management processes that rely on the involvement of a third party, the clear advantage of mediation is that the disputants retain decision-making power with respect to issues of substance. The process is not perfect—no process is. However, mediation offers a realistic potential for transforming even the most stressful and contentious of conflict situations into a circumstance where collaboration and mutual problem solving are fully possible.

DISCUSSION QUESTIONS

1 The benefit of mediation, in comparison to other forms of dispute management, is that the disputants retain decision-making power with respect to issues of substance. Why is this desirable? Under what circumstances would it be undesirable for disputants to retain decision-making power?

2 Some mediators believe that the primary goal of mediation is to reach agreement regarding the substantive issues of dispute. Others believe that the primary goal is to help parties deal with emotional and relational issues, and that resolution of substantive issues is secondary (see Figure 10-1). Which approach to mediation do you favor? Explain why. What are the pros and cons of your preferred approach?

3 Mediators are supposed to be fair, neutral, and impartial. Does this imply that their mediation behavior is not influenced by distal and proximal influences? What are some distal and proximal factors that might influence the mediator's behavior?

4 In what ways does the behavior of a mediator affect the communication competence of disputants? How does it enhance disputants' appropriateness and effectiveness? How could it detract from the perceived competence of one or more of the disputants? Does a good mediator attempt to compensate for a disputant who is less communicatively competent than his or her adversary? How so? Would doing so violate the principle of being impartial? Explain your answer.

5 To be communicatively competent, mediators presumably need to possess knowledge, motivation, and skill if they are to be successful at helping disputants resolve their differences. What knowledge, motivations, and skills in particular does a competent mediator need to have? Are these any different from the characteristics that any of us should possess for managing our everyday (nonmediated) interpersonal conflicts? Please explain.

11

LOOKING FORWARD TO FUTURE CONFLICTS

We do not mean to imply with this chapter title that conflicts should become enjoyable. Instead, now that interpersonal conflict has been described and reviewed in different contexts, we think it is necessary to conclude with a look toward future interactions. In doing so, we emphasize the theme of competence in managing conflict. We begin by discussing implications of the inevitability of conflict. Then we summarize the value of a competence approach to interpersonal conflict and comment on the ethical ramifications of our approach. Finally, we synthesize some of the recurring suggestions in this text in the form of general guidelines for managing conflict.

THE INEVITABILITY OF CONFLICT

As Chapter 1 indicated, interpersonal conflict is pervasive. From the time you are a toddler, you experience interpersonal conflict and its social functions. *Conflict enables people to understand their personal and social boundaries, to develop ideas, and to coordinate actions and activities.* Because no two people see the world identically, there will always be disagreements. Although you may sometimes avoid direct confrontation, you cannot eliminate the experience of conflict.

Why is conflict so ubiquitous? Disagreement per se is not abnormal. Conflict is a natural ingredient of interpersonal interaction. Whenever you and someone else communicate, the two of you become at least partially interdependent. Moreover, you do not restrict your conflicts to dissimilar or disliked others. Ironically, the more you know and like another person, the *greater* the opportunities for conflict! Intimacy in relationships creates greater interdependence and, usually, more frequent interaction (Braiker & Kelley, 1979). These very conditions increase the propensity for disagreements. Whenever you interact with others, you risk the possibility of interpersonal conflict.

We usually think about conflict in terms of its overt expression—that is, the communication of disagreement. But conflict is not confined neatly to overt confrontation. If you feel dissatisfied with your roommate's behavior but avoid discussing it, your roommate may not realize that your anger and annoyance are escalating. On the other hand, confronting your roommate and negotiating an amicable agreement does not preclude the possibility that the issue of disagreement will crop up again later.

Some conflict issues are not easily "resolved"; they recur again and again, and you must manage them temporarily. You and your close friends probably disagree in some unresolvable ways. In such cases, you will agree to disagree if the relationship can tolerate it. If the issue overshadows the relationship, however, the ongoing disagreement can dissolve the relationship.

THE VALUE OF COMPETENCE IN MANAGING INTERPERSONAL CONFLICT

This book has focused on how to respond in a competent manner during conflict interactions—that is, ways of appropriately and effectively managing disagreements with others. Throughout this book, then, competence has served as a unifying framework to discuss processes and products of conflict interaction. A critical underlying assumption is that people *should* behave in appropriate and effective ways, for ethical as well as practical reasons.

The competence approach to managing conflict does not specify a set of behaviors that invariably lead to positive outcomes (although the research indicates that certain behaviors are destructive, more often than not, when compared to alternative behaviors). No one can offer a magic formula that guarantees success. However, possessing knowledge about conflict management and developing communication skills that help you translate your goals into actions can increase your chances for managing conflict competently. Being motivated to handle conflicts competently also will help you realize success.

Competence *does* imply an *ethic* for managing conflict—a set of principles regarding conduct that is considered preferable and good. Competent interaction involves appropriateness as well as effectiveness. Appropriateness *modifies* effectiveness. That is, *socially and interpersonally agreed-upon principles should guide the behaviors you employ to satisfy your individual needs and pursue your individual goals.* If effectiveness entails successful control of your environment (and hence others in that environment) so that you get your way, then appropriateness embodies the ethical means of exercising that control.

We do not presume to know what is ethical and what is unethical in managing every conflict. But we do believe that you should *approach conflict ethically;* that is, *you should have a sense of moral responsibility when dealing with conflict,* and that responsibility should be reflected in both your attitude and your behavior.

The standards for judging behavior vary considerably across individuals, communities, and cultures. Still, as Parks indicated,

> There is also a remarkable level of consensus about what constitutes incompetence. We can agree that it is a mark of incompetence when . . . self-esteem is damaged, and when physical health is threatened. We can also agree that socially inappropriate and violent behavior is usually undesirable. (1994, p. 589)

Standards of appropriateness contribute to competent conflict management for several reasons. On philosophical grounds, we contend that appropriateness promotes social values of civility and respect. What constitutes respect is not universally held, but the human desire for it is. Regardless of cultural and social differences, people everywhere learn "to have pride, honor, and dignity, to have considerateness, to have tact and a certain amount of poise" (Goffman, 1967, p. 44). Even in the face of serious disagreements, people expect to affirm these fundamental human values.

Fostering mutual respect and meeting minimal expectations for appropriate behavior promote collaboration that is necessary to sustain civilized interaction. By "civilized" we mean the coordinated efforts of individuals through communication (Pearce & Cronen, 1980). Without the ability to coordinate efforts through communication, social behavior would become anarchic and unpredictable—especially in situations where people disagree. People engaging in destructive or avoidant messages could understand the anarchy they could cause with messages, and they might purposefully create uncertainty to limit others' ability to coordinate actions.

Providing reasonable excuses for acting incompetently does not help much in coordinating future activities ("I didn't tell you the truth because I knew you would get angry with me"). Unreasonable excuses for incompetence during conflict provide even less confidence in coordinating future events ("I hit you because you wanted me to").

Competent communicators appreciate the fact that "there are limits to how much any given situation or person can be controlled. Expecting to influence others in unrealistic ways is a mark of incompetence" (Parks, 1994, p. 613). When your attempts to resolve disagreements become coercive rather than persuasive, you are seeking personal effectiveness at the expense of appropriateness. Wiemann explained that "*effectiveness* in an intrapersonal sense— that is, the accomplishment of an individual's goals—may be incompetent in an interpersonal sense if such effectiveness precludes the possibility of others accomplishing their own goals" [italics in original] (1977, p. 196).

Similarly, it is unethical to minimize the partner's goals or to hurt the partner when one is frustrated from obtaining rewards—that is, when one is ineffective. In the clearest form, this behavior involves physical aggression. But aggression often serves the simple purpose of venting anger: People sometimes feel better when they hurt others who frustrate them (Berkowitz, 1993). And people often do not know the source of their own ineffectiveness and frustrations and may be hurting someone without cause. For example, people with low self-efficacy and an external locus of control (see Chapter 4) believe they can't manage difficult problems. Such people may give up too soon and blame the partner for their task failures and relational frustrations, thereby justifying verbal or physical harm to the partner. In other words, people sometimes blame their own incompetence on their partners. Of course, few people would agree that being incompetent justifies punishing other people.

The criterion of appropriateness makes sense pragmatically as well as ethically. Codes of appropriate behavior not only constrain our pursuit of personal effectiveness; they also provide a means of being effective and they represent a product of effectiveness (Parks, 1994). As we have stressed throughout this book, you always possess multiple goals. Competence involves your ability to recognize and balance those goals. Pursuing one goal in a socially inappropriate manner is incompetent to the extent that you undermine your ability to achieve equally or more important goals. So, if you get your friend to loan you money by threatening to tell secrets about him if he doesn't comply, you may get the money, but you may also lose a friend and develop a reputation for being an unscrupulous bully. You have scored the classic *Pyrrhic victory:* You have won one battle, but with staggering overall losses.

Appropriate behavior is also desirable simply because it typically promotes the achievement of your own goals. Appropriateness *is* pragmatic.

Competent communicators know that displaying appropriateness is often most effective. When you are engaged in interaction, particularly in conflict situations, your outcomes intertwine with the outcomes of others. In other words, each person has some degree of control over what happens to the other. Thwarting the goals of others to get your own way can easily backfire. "People who consistently fail to satisfy their goals are likely to display more anger, to be violent, to be more exploitative, to be less generous, and to be less cooperative" (Parks, 1994, p. 611). Thus, facilitating the effectiveness of others can enable your own effectiveness. Parks offers this summary:

> Competent communicators recognize that they usually have a vested interest in maintaining the rules of social conduct because they recognize, however dimly, that their ability to pursue their own goals often depends on the freedom of others to pursue their goals. (1994, p. 613)

To get their way, some people don't seem to mind hurting others—of course, until the tables are turned. (CALVIN AND HOBBES© 1994, 1995 Watterson Dist. by Universal Press Syndicate. Reprinted with permission. All rights reserved.)

GUIDELINES FOR MANAGING INTERPERSONAL CONFLICT

In this section, we offer some general guidelines for managing conflict. We do not believe in micromanaging conflict behavior. In our experience, students can quickly learn how-to formulas and forget them following an examination. Accordingly, we do not offer prescriptions of particular communication skills that you should employ whenever in conflict. (Besides, many of these skills would sound ridiculous when conflicts actually arise.) Instead, we attempt to provide guidelines that you can adapt to your own conflict encounters.

The Question Is Not If, but How

Believing that you can avoid conflict places blinders on your understanding of how people work and live together. The question is not whether you will have conflicts with others—you will. The question is *how* you manage your conflicts through communication.

If you wanted to bet on how you should manage conflict, you should bet on constructive messages. *People engage in constructive or destructive conflict* (Deutsch, 1973). Constructive conflict, as its name implies, focuses on reaching positive and creative outcomes for both parties. Some features of constructive conflict messages have been implied in previous chapters. The following features presume that the conflict interactions involve no serious, physically threatening circumstances:

1 *Combine the parties' resources to solve the problem.* Both parties' talents are maximized to achieve beneficial results instead of being used for combat. When both parties' talents are used to maximize each person's outcomes, we can see the conflict as a win-win situation, instead of a competitive win-lose situation.

2 *Free the avenues of exchange between parties.* Both parties share their thoughts about the causes, definitions, and solutions for the problem in a balanced manner, giving each the same opportunity to present views and to propose and evaluate solutions.

3 *If parties cannot agree, they should agree to disagree.* Compromise could be utilized if the parties cannot pool their resources and work together. Although compromise may not maximize what each party obtains, it can ensure at least some gain and can minimize losses. For example, couples who compromise during mediation do not have to sell their homes to pay divorce lawyers who litigated their cases.

4 *Adopt a nonviolent stance.* Once a person uses coercion, force, or violence, she or he loses the ability to use problem-solving communication to manage the conflict productively. By definition, aggression involves harming another person.

5 *Flee the scene of a crime before it occurs.* If you cannot engage in productive conflict, then at a minimum, refrain from engaging in destructive conflict. Such restraint may appear nearly impossible, but it is worth it in the long run. If only to preserve your sense of dignity, you should avoid doing things you will regret later.

Avoid Reciprocating Negative Affect

The reciprocation of negative emotion powerfully affects your relationships. Nothing appears to affect a relationship as adversely as the reciprocation and escalation of negative messages (see Chapter 6).

BOX 11-1

THE THREE RULES FOR LIFE

You can make lots of money providing quick and easy how-to formulas for people. Bookstores, magazine racks, and TV commercials provide hundreds of such formulas, contained within titles such as "How to Get Rich without Working Hard or Risking Anything," "Ten Secrets to a Successful Relationship," and "How to Act Like a Man without Offending Women." Instead of presenting our own checklist of how-to items, we provide more general and abstract principles, which you can apply to your own conflicts.

If asked to summarize how to manage conflict, we would borrow the words of a former teacher and good friend of one of the authors, Dr. George Enell, who likes to recite the following "three rules for life" (which are themselves paraphrased from Brendan Gil):

There are three, and only three, rules for life:
Rule 1: Be as happy as you possibly can.
Rule 2: Try not to make others unhappy.
Rule 3: There are no other rules.

The urge to respond in like manner directly and powerfully affects people—especially in conflict episodes. Gottman (1994), however, argued that satisfied couples and dissatisfied couples appear to focus on different elements of the same message. Satisfied couples focus more on the content of the message and how to resolve the problem indicated by the partner, whereas dissatisfied couples tend to react to the negative features of the message, such as a disapproving and whining voice, a rejecting stare, or the inequity in a complaint. As Chapter 6 showed, negative conflict behaviors (especially criticism, disgust, and contempt) appear to affect people and relationships immediately as well as cumulatively over time.

How you choose to live your life is reflected in the way you manage conflicts with other people. Do you choose to remain patient, asking for the other person's view and reasons for their frustration? Do you routinely decide to avoid disagreement and accommodate other people whenever possible? Or do you give an "eye for an eye" and meet aggression with aggression? If you selected the latter, understand that this response mode works *against* most people's goals. The reason is that people view others who engage in such negative behaviors as inept, both in terms of work and play, and as socially undesirable. Hence, although you may stand up for your rights, you can easily lose your objective if you use negative messages. Instead of reciprocating negative messages, you should consider unilaterally using more constructive or even avoidant messages to stop the conflict escalation.

Respond Proactively to Anger

People can react in anger to many negative events (see Chapter 5). In addition, people have initial cognitive and physiological reactions and higher-ordered cognitive reactions. The "anger script" most people think of, for example, requires that social actors become either enraged or avoidant. But you should not be surprised when you experience anger in various situations—for example, when you are depressed or someone else gets their way unfairly. Instead, you should develop a plan for responding to anger provocations so that you are not caught in a reactive state.

In developing your plan, consider the social expectations regarding anger. Averill (1993, pp. 182–184) provided the following rules for expressing anger:

1 One has the right to become angry at intentional wrongdoing and at unintended misdeeds—if those misdeeds can be corrected (for example, negligence).

2 One should direct anger at objects or people who are responsible for the action(s).

3 One should not vent anger on innocent third parties, "nor should it be directed at the target for reasons other than the instigation."

4 The objective should be to correct the problem and restore fairness—not to create a sense of fear in the other person.

5 One's response to anger should match the instigation; it should not "exceed what is necessary to correct the situation, restore equity, or prevent the instigation from happening again."

6 One's expression of anger should follow the provoking event as soon as possible; it should not last longer than the time needed to remedy the problem.

7 One's expression of anger should involve a commitment to solve the problem, including any necessary follow-through.

"If you are patient in one moment of anger, you will escape a hundred days of sorrow," concluded Tavris in a review of the effects of anger (1994, p. 188). The saying was taken from a fortune cookie. Nevertheless, this quote represents more than conventional wisdom; it reflects a guideline that is supported by the research. Counting to ten or even more when you are very angry and want to crush someone you find extremely offensive can work to your benefit in the long run.

Do Not Inadvertently Reinforce Aggressive Behaviors

This is a tough guideline to adopt, for many reasons. For example, Bandura's (1973) analysis showed that people rely on aggression because over time they have learned to do so and that they view aggression as effective in obtaining rewards.

For example, someone who has learned how to slander others continues to use slander to obtain goals. Over time, the aggressor stops feeling remorse for his or her actions, for example, by gradually becoming desensitized to the pain he or she inflicts. Sometimes the aggressor desensitizes him- or herself by discounting the victim's feelings ("It's a cruel world, friend, so you better get used to this kind of treatment"). Bandura (1973) observed that one can stop aggression by modeling alternative behaviors, by providing positive rewards for different behaviors, and by punishing aggression. In this manner, the expectations for positive outcomes when using aggressive behaviors (such as slander) could be reduced. Accordingly, one way to discourage the use of slander and malicious gossip is simply not to say anything, thereby not providing any reward (such as laughter) for that behavior.

Save Face

All people want to have their identities supported when they interact (see Chapter 6). Unfortunately, and for various reasons, conflict situations are particularly ripe for face threats. As conflict escalates, we seem to worry more about protecting our own face and we exhibit less concern than usual with preserving the face of our disputant.

Face loss can make you feel awkward, confused, guilty, ashamed, embarrassed, angry, and defensive (Cupach & Metts, 1994). These feelings do not tend to promote constructive management of conflict. Instead, they often lead to behaviors that exacerbate the loss of face. Ironically, the relationships with the greatest intimacy are probably the ones in which we display the least amount of tact, the greatest amount of impoliteness, and the most distressing forms of disrespect.

The key is to maintain your own face *and* the faces of others, even during disagreement. Saving face requires conscious effort during conflict, and it should be something you try to make habitual.

Notarius and Markman (1993) devised a "no-nonsense guide to politeness." They recommend that during conflict discussions, you imagine that you have a sack over your shoulder that contains all the infinitely different things you could say to your partner. The sack contains statements that can be divided into "zingers" or polite remarks. During conflict, imagine reaching into the sack for something to say. If you pull out a zinger, throw it back and keep reaching into the sack until you have something polite to say. (Remember, being polite does not prevent you from disagreeing.) Notarius and Markman (1993), on the basis of decades of research and clinical experience, offer seven specific guidelines for recognizing and eschewing zingers and finding politeness during conflicts with relational partners:

1 When asked to do something, say what you can or want to do rather than what you can't or don't want to do. For example, if your partner asks if you want to go to the movies and you are feeling tired, you might say, "I'd love to go to the movies tomorrow" rather than "I'm too tired."

2 When you first notice that your partner has done a chore, always show appreciation for the job even if there are aspects of the way in which it was done that do not meet with your approval. Say "Thanks for washing the counter" rather than "You missed a spot." If you routinely don't like the way your partner does a task, you should have a discussion about it at a time specially set aside for this purpose.

3 Take note of departures from and reunions with your partner. Always greet each other with an acknowledgment and warm hello, and mark a leaving with a tender good-bye. You should not come home, go to bed, or leave the house in si-

---

BOX 11-2

CASE STUDY: CONFRONTATION IN THE PARKING LOT

"Boomer" and Helen had been dating for several months when they decided to live together. Boomer earned his nickname on the wrestling squad in high school, where he lettered three years in the heaviest weight class. Boomer became a bartender at an exclusive restaurant where Helen worked as a wine steward. Helen was quite attractive.

Helen knew that being attractive was good not only for her image, but also for the restaurant. So she wore flattering outfits, and she instinctively showed affiliation toward customers by smiling, listening, and sometimes touching them on the arm. This affiliation attracted Boomer to Helen, but it was now driving him crazy.

Boomer found himself trying to see if Helen was flirting with male customers, and there were so many of them that he could not keep track of them all. Many times he thought he had caught her and interrogated her about specific customers. One in particular, a corporate lawyer, was clearly interested in Helen and often dined there on Friday nights. At first, when Boomer asked her about it, Helen assured him nothing was wrong. After a few weeks of interrogation and bickering, however, both Boomer and Helen grew tired of his spying and constant questioning.

So Boomer and Helen started working different days and nights, in hopes that Boomer would not be so jealous of male customers. He worked Monday through Thursday nights, and she worked mainly on weekends, when the restaurant was busiest. Still, Boomer had a tough time keeping away, and he would call or drop by around closing. Helen saw through his "spontaneous" visits and decided to flirt whenever she could.

One Friday night, Boomer somehow sensed the lawyer would be there. He was right, and he saw Helen flirting with the man. Boomer returned home and waited outside for her. As soon as she entered the apartment parking lot, he confronted her:

"I knew you were unfaithful!" Boomer screamed.

"What are you talking about?" Helen asked, although she knew, from previous scenes like this one.

BOX 11-2 *(continued)*

"You know what I'm talking about. I saw you flirting with your lawyer friend," he replied.

She tried to reason with him: "Look, nothing happened."

Boomer felt his heart in his throat, "Yeah, but how do I know that?"

"Well, don't you drive me to it!" she replied.

"Me? I've only been thoughtful of you, you #$%@! And this is how you treat me?! I should kick your @#(*&%!" Boomer yelled.

Helen was quite afraid. "If you lay a hand on me, I'll call the police!"

Boomer couldn't believe this was happening. "I would never hurt you!"

Helen knew Boomer was totally irrational at this point. "Just leave me alone," she demanded.

Boomer panicked, "Listen, honey, I would never hurt you. Please don't leave me." He reached out for her.

"Stop it!" screamed Helen. "Just let me be!"

Boomer worried that he had gone too far. "Helen, listen, I would never hurt you!" This time he grabbed her by the wrist.

"No!" She wrangled to break free. "Help me!" she cried out.

Boomer couldn't believe his ears. "Help you? Help you?!?" he shouted. "Help me, please someone HELP ME!!!" He let go of Helen's wrist to plead with the rest of the apartment complex.

Helen now knew for sure that Boomer had lost all ability to reason. She was mad at herself for ever getting involved with him. "Look, I'm leaving you!"

He continued his plea, "Help me, please someone! My baby's leaving me, help me!!"

Helen just shook her head.

Helen ran into the apartment and Boomer followed her, begging for someone to help him. It was quite a sight—this 240-pound athlete imploring someone half his size to help him. Not until she agreed to talk things over did he stop pleading.

This story may sound too melodramatic, but it is largely true. (One of the authors lived next door to "Boomer" and "Helen.") Perhaps even more amazing is the fact that Helen and Boomer replayed a similar scene every two to three weeks. Every time, Helen forgave Boomer and they returned to their usual routine—until Boomer caught Helen flirting with someone else.

Discussion Questions:

1 What advice would you give Helen?
2 What advice would you give Boomer?

tender good-bye. You should not come home, go to bed, or leave the house in silence.

4 Avoid being a "psychopest." Psychopests try to offer insight into their partner's behavior under the guise of being helpful when in fact they are merely being critical. Don't say things like "You're behaving just like your mother" or "Do you know you're being anal retentive about the den?"

5 Always speak for yourself and avoid speaking for your partner. Say "I really want to go to the picnic" rather than "I know you will have a good time at the company picnic."

6 When you have an opinion on something, say what it is rather than fishing around with questions to get your partner to guess what it is. Try "I'd really like to eat at Captain Bob's tonight" instead of "Do you want to eat out tonight?"

7 When all else fails, fall back on the ancient wisdom: "If you don't have anything nice to say, don't say anything." (1993, pp. 77–78)

Maximize Happiness: Pursue Your Goals in View of Other People's Goals

A common cause of conflict is the perception that another person blocks you from achieving a valued goal. You can feel frustrated and angry, especially if the objective is important to you. Similarly, your conflict partner probably feels that you are frustrating his or her valued objectives. You should realize that you pursue your goals in the context of the other person's pursuit of his or her goals.

People routinely pursue instrumental, relational, and self-presentation goals. One goal may be primary (for example, to increase credibility), whereas other goals remain secondary in importance (for example, to obtain permission to use the car). Regardless, you should keep in mind that some combination of these three goals motivates people, and that each person must clarify for him- or herself the priorities of these goals.

Some goals seem so appealing that people lose sight of other goals. For example, in the film *Wall Street,* the hero (Bud Fox) becomes so absorbed in obtaining financial wealth that he is willing to break laws, manipulate friends and relatives, and alter his public image (he buys an expensive apartment and decorates it in art he doesn't understand). Bud Fox's obsession with the goal of being wealthy costs him dearly. Likewise, during conflict, people can become so preoccupied with one goal that they ruin their chances at other important goals. As Papa and Papa showed in Chapter 8, people who bargain in a overly tough manner, without concern for the greater good or the other person's goals, may obtain their goal for the short term but lose in the long haul.

The nearsighted, inflexible pursuit of a goal can be heard following the conflict in complaints about the inflexible behavior. For example:

"No, don't invite her—she only likes to talk about herself and doesn't care about other people."

"I will never go back to that music store, because that guy ripped me off!"

"You can't believe a word he tells you, because he'll agree to do one thing and then do whatever he wants."

"She is so competitive that I never want to work out with her again!"

"He always needs to be right—I need to find someone else to date."

Recognize the Systems You Create

Recognizing that you are part of a system allows you to understand your partner's behavior as a function of your behavior, and vice versa. For example, you see that your partner's withdrawal relates to your confrontation and vice versa, so you do not become angry at the partner for being avoidant or silent. Moreover, you realize that two people are making similar kinds of attributions about the conflict, such that you will rarely find "right" versus "wrong" explanations of conflict causes. This knowledge not only permits you to become more circumspect in analyzing the conflict issue; it also provides flexibility in terms of how you should respond (for example, you do not have to play judge and execute a just response).

Recognizing that you are part of a system allows you to see that your current behavior is a function of your own previous behaviors. People should acknowledge that they have created their own relational patterns, and that these patterns are self-reinforcing. In social systems, there are no causes and effects as we ordinarily think of causes and effects. Research indicates that a person's present behavior has an effect on his or her own later behavior (Ting-Toomey, 1983a).

If a dysfunctional system cannot be restructured by the adoption of new rules for interaction, then it might need to be redefined through entropy. A relational system is dysfunctional if it impedes someone's growth (for example, adult children who still depend on their elderly parents) or even hurts an individual (for example, physical abuse). Professor Spitzberg's look at physical aggression (see Chapter 9) shows that abusive relationships are not uncommon, and many people appear to be caught in individually destructive relationships. In our view, a person has an ethical obligation (and in some cases, a legal one) to change the system. If the system cannot be changed, and the person continues to suffer, then the system—not the person—should terminate. As Hocker and Wilmot put it, "you have a responsibility to protect yourself from verbal abuse" (1995, p. 179). Of course, we would argue that this statement extends to physical abuse as well.

SUMMARY

We hope that you understand that your communication during conflict is more important than the mere occurrence or frequency of your disagreements. Communication competence in conflict requires that you communicate in ways that are appropriate as well as effective. Competent communicators are able to influence others successfully, but they attempt to do so in ethical ways. Appropriateness fosters respect and civility, and it mitigates contempt and chaos. Moreover, appropriateness fosters effectiveness insofar as it helps prioritize goals. Competent communication embraces the notion that getting your way usually depends on getting along with others.

No checklist of communication behavior can guarantee your success in handling conflict. Competent communicators are aware of the distal and proximal factors that affect conflict interaction, and they take these into account when making choices about how to handle specific instances of disagreement. We have offered in this chapter some guidelines that we feel will be useful as you make these choices. In particular, we suggest that you avoid reciprocating negative messages and affect, respond proactively to anger, and save face. Above all, recognize that when you interact with others you are part of a communication system. Collaborating with others in that system and adapting your behavior according to the context are hallmarks of the competent communicator.

DISCUSSION QUESTIONS

1 We have argued that ethical codes are part of appropriateness and should guide conflict management. Are there any exceptions, or is this value absolute? Does this statement assume that the relevant moral codes are fair and just? When, if ever, do you think it is justifiable to be socially inappropriate? Can you give examples? In cases where inappropriateness seems justified, would the behavior be competent? Ethical?

2 Do you agree that checklists of how-to behavior offer little insight about how to manage conflicts when they arise? Why or why not?

3 We stated that the relationships with the greatest intimacy are probably the ones in which we display the least amount of tact, the greatest amount of impoliteness, and the most distressing forms of disrespect. How would you explain this paradox?

4 Pick a close relationship you are currently in. Describe the rules of politeness that you follow (or would like to follow) when you and the other person in this relationship have conflict.

5 We claim that if a system harms the individual, the system should be redefined. We also claim that if the system's rules for interaction do not change, the system should be terminated. What are the critical points that indicate when a system needs to be terminated? How do these compare to times when people need to sacrifice themselves for the sake of their relationships, their organization, or their nation?

6 The fact that you and another person constitute a system when you interact suggests that you never have complete control of what happens to the system—you are only a part of it. Do you agree or disagree? Explain your answer. Can someone else *make you incompetent* during conflict? Or do you have complete control over your own competence?

REFERENCES

Academy of Family Mediators. (1985). *Standards of practice for family and divorce mediation.* Eugene, Oreg.: Academy of Family Mediators.

Alberts, J. K. (1988). An analysis of couples' conversational complaints. *Communication Monographs, 55,* 184–197.

Alberts, J. K. (1989). A descriptive taxonomy of couples' complaint interactions. *Southern Communication Journal, 54,* 125–143.

Alberts, J. K., and Driscoll, G. (1992). Containment versus escalation: The trajectory of couples' conversation complaints. *Western Journal of Communication, 56,* 394–412.

Alexander, J. F. (1973). Defensive and supportive communications in normal and deviant families. *Journal of Consulting and Clinical Psychology, 40,* 223–231.

Altman, I., and Taylor, D. A. (1973). *Social penetration: The development of interpersonal relationships.* Austin, Tex.: Holt, Rinehart, & Winston.

American Bar Association. (1984). Standards of practice for family mediators (adopted August, 1984). *Family Law Quarterly, 17,* 455–468.

Andes, R. H. (1992). Message dimensions of negotiation. *Negotiation Journal, 8,* 125–130.

Andrews, B. (1992). Attribution processes in victims of marital violence: Who do women blame and why? In J. H. Harvey, T. L. Orbuch, and A. L. Weber (Eds.), *Attributions, accounts, and close relationships* (pp. 176–193). New York: Springer-Verlag.

Argyle, M., and Henderson, M. (1984). The rules of friendship. *Journal of Social and Personal Relationships, 1,* 211–237.

Arias, I., and Johnson, P. (1989). Evaluations of physical aggression among intimate dyads. *Journal of Interpersonal Violence, 4,* 298–307.

Association of Family and Conciliation Courts. (1989). Model standards of practice for family and divorce mediation. In N. H. Rogers and C. A. McEwen (Eds.), *Mediation law, policy, practice.* Deerfield, Ill.: Clark, Boardman, Callaghan.

Auerbach, J. S. (1983). *Justice without laws: Resolving disputes without lawyers.* New York: Oxford University Press.

Auwal, M. A., Papa, M. J., and Singhal, A. (1994). *Organizing productive micro-enterprises for social change: A multi-theoretic study of the Grameen Bank.* Paper presented at the International Communication Association Conference, Sydney, Australia.

Auwal, M. A., and Singhal, A. (1992). The diffusion of the Grameen Bank in Bangladesh: Lessons learned about alleviating rural poverty. *Knowledge: Creation, Diffusion, Utilization, 14*(1), 7–28.

Averill, J. R. (1993). Illusions of anger. In R. B. Felson and J. T. Tedeschi (Eds.), *Aggression and violence: Social interactionist perspectives* (pp. 171–193). Washington, D.C.: American Psychological Association.

Axelrod, R., and Keohane, R. O. (1986). Achieving cooperation under anarchy: Strategies and insinuations. In K. A. Oye (Ed.), *Cooperation under anarchy* (pp. 226–254). Princeton, N.J.: Princeton University Press.

Bach, G. R., and Goldberg, H. (1974). *Creative aggression.* Garden City, N.Y.: Doubleday.

Bach, G. R., and Wyden, P. (1968). *The intimate enemy: How to fight fair in love and marriage.* New York: Avon Books.

Bachman, R. (1994). *Violence against women: A national crime victimization survey report (NCJ-145325).* Washington, D.C.: U.S. Dept. of Justice.

Bandura, A. (1973). *Aggression: A social learning analysis.* Englewood Cliffs, N.J.: Prentice-Hall.

Barnlund, D. (1989). *Communicative styles of Japanese and Americans: Images and realities.* Belmont, Calif.: Wadsworth.

Baron, R. A. (1984). Reducing organizational conflict: An incompatible response approach. *Journal of Applied Psychology, 69,* 272–279.

Baron, R. A. (1985). Reducing organizational conflict: The role of attributions. *Journal of Applied Psychology, 70,* 434–441.

Baucom, D. H., Sayers, S. L., and Duhe, A. (1989). Attributional style and attributional patterns among married couples. *Journal of Personality and Social Psychology, 56,* 596–607.

Baumeister, R. F., Stillwell, A., and Wotman, S. R. (1990). Victim and perpetrator accounts of interpersonal conflict: Autobiographical narratives about anger. *Journal of Personality and Social Psychology, 59,* 994–1005.

Baxter, L. A. (1986). Gender differences in the heterosexual relationship rules embedded in break-up accounts. *Journal of Social and Personal Relationships, 3,* 289–306.

Berk, S. F. (1985). *The gender factory: The apportionment of work in American households.* New York: Plenum.

Berkowitz, L. (1983). The goals of aggression. In D. Finkelhor, R. J. Gelles, G. T. Hotaling, and M. A. Straus (Eds.), *The dark side of families: Current family violence research* (pp. 166–181). Newbury Park, Calif.: Sage.

Berkowitz, L. (1993). Towards a general theory of anger and emotional aggression: Implications of the cognitive-neoassociationistic perspective for the analysis of anger and other emotions. In R. S. Wyer, Jr., and T. K. Srull (Eds.), *Perspectives on anger and emotion: Advances in social cognition,* vol. 6 (pp. 1–46). Hillsdale, N.J.: Erlbaum.

Bernal, G., and Golann, S. (1980). Couple interaction: A study of the punctuation process. *International Journal of Family Therapy, 2,* 47–56.

Berryman-Fink, C., and Brunner, C. C. (1987). The effects of sex of source and target on interpersonal conflict management styles. *Southern Speech Communication Journal, 53,* 38–48.

Betancourt, H., and Blair, I. (1992). A cognition (attribution)-emotional model of violence in conflict situations. *Personality and Social Psychology Bulletin, 18,* 343–350.

Billingham, R. E. (1987). Courtship violence: The patterns of conflict resolution strategies across seven levels of emotional commitment. *Family Relations, 36,* 283–289.

Billingham, R. E., and Sack, A. R. (1986). Courtship violence and the interactive status of the relationship. *Journal of Adolescent Research, 1,* 315–325.

Billingham, R. E., and Sack, A. R. (1987). Conflict tactics and the level of emotional commitment among unmarrieds. *Human Relations, 40,* 59–74.

Billings, A. (1979). Conflict resolution in distressed and nondistressed married couples. *Journal of Consulting and Clinical Psychology, 47,* 368–376.

Birchler, G. R., and Webb, L. J. (1977). Discriminating interaction behaviors in happy and unhappy marriages. *Journal of Consulting and Clinical Psychology, 45,* 494–495.

Bird, G. W., Stith, S. M., and Schladale, J. (1991). Psychological resources, coping strategies, and negotiation styles as discriminators of violence in dating relationships. *Family Relations, 40,* 45–50.

Bjorkqvist, K. (1994). Sex differences in physical, verbal, and indirect aggression: A review of recent research. *Sex Roles, 30,* 177–188.

Blake, R. R., and Mouton, J. S. (1964). *The managerial grid.* Houston, Tex.: Gulf.

Blake, R. R., and Mouton, J. S. (1970). The fifth achievement. *Journal of Applied Behavioral Science, 6,* 413–426.

Bookwala, J., Frieze, I. H., Smith, C., and Ryan, K. (1992). Predictors of dating violence: A multivariate analysis. *Violence and Victims, 7,* 297–311.

Bradbury, T. N., and Fincham, F. D. (1990). Attributions in marriage: Review and critique. *Psychological Bulletin, 107,* 3–33.

Bradley, P. H. (1980). Sex, competence, and opinion deviation: An expectation states approach. *Communication Monographs, 47,* 101–110.

Braiker, H. B., and Kelley, H. H. (1979). Conflict in the development of close relationships. In R. L. Burgess and T. L. Huston (Eds.), *Social exchange in developing relationships* (pp. 135–168). New York: Academic Press.

Brenders, D. A. (1987). Perceived control: Foundations and directions for communication research. In M. L. McLaughlin (Ed.), *Communication yearbook 10* (pp. 86–116). Newbury Park, Calif.: Sage.

Brown, C. (1994). Fair share of the economic pie. *New York Times,* February 14, B9.

Brown, D. (1982). Divorce and family mediation: History, review, future directions. *Conciliation Courts Review, 20,* 1–37.

Brown, P., and Levinson, S. (1987). *Politeness: Some universals in language usage.* Cambridge: Cambridge University Press.

Burggraf, C. S., and Sillars, A. L. (1987). A critical examination of sex differences in marital communication. *Communication Monographs, 54,* 276–294.

Burgoon, J. K., Buller, D. B., and Woodall, W. G. (1989). *Nonverbal communication: The unspoken dialogue.* New York: Harper & Row.

Burke, P. J., Stets, J. E., and Pirog-Good, M. A. (1989). Gender identity, self-esteem, and physical and sexual abuse in dating relationships. In M. A. Pirog-Good and J. E. Stets (Eds.), *Violence in dating relationships: Emerging social issues* (pp. 72–93). New York: Praeger.

Burman, B., Margolin, G., and John, R. S. (1993). America's angriest home videos: Behavioral contingencies observed in home reenactments of marital conflict. *Journal of Consulting and Clinical Psychology, 61,* 28–39.

Burrell, G., and Morgan, G. (1979). *Sociological paradigms and organizational analysis.* London: Heinemann.

Burrell, N. A., Donohue, W. A., and Allen, M. (1990). The impact of disputants' expectations of mediation: Testing an interventionist model. *Human Communication Research, 17,* 104–139.

Burt, M. R. (1991). Rape myths and acquaintance rape. In A. Parrot and L. Bechhofer (Eds.), *Acquaintance rape: The hidden crime* (pp. 26–40). New York: Wiley.

Busby, D. M. (1991). Violence in the family. In S. J. Bahr (Ed.), *Family research: A sixty-year review, 1930–1990,* vol. 1 (pp. 335–386). New York: Lexington.

Bush, R. A. B. (1992). *The dilemmas of mediation practice: A study of ethical dilemmas and policy implications.* Washington, D.C.: National Institute for Dispute Resolution.

Buss, A. H., and Perry, M. (1992). The aggression questionnaire. *Journal of Personality and Social Psychology, 63,* 452–459.

Campbell, A., and Muncer, S. (1987). Models of anger and aggression in the social talk of women and men. *Journal for the Theory of Social Behaviour, 17,* 489–511.

Campbell, L. E. G., and Johnston, J. R. (1986). Impasse-directed mediation with high conflict families in custody disputes. *Behavioral Sciences & the Law, 4,* 217–241.

Canary, D. J., and Cody, M. J. (1994). *Interpersonal communication: A goals-based approach.* New York: St. Martin's.

Canary, D. J., Cunningham, E. M., and Cody, M. J. (1988). Goal types, gender, and locus of control in managing interpersonal conflict. *Communication Research, 15,* 426–446.

Canary, D. J., and Cupach, W. R. (1988). Relational and episodic characteristics associated with conflict tactics. *Journal of Social and Personal Relationships, 5,* 305–325.

Canary, D. J., Cupach, W. R., and Messman, S. J. (1995). *Relationship conflict: Conflict in parent-child, friendship, and romantic relationships.* Thousand Oaks, Calif.: Sage.

Canary, D. J., and Spitzberg, B. H. (1987). Appropriateness and effectiveness perceptions of conflict strategies. *Human Communication Research, 14,* 93–118.

Canary, D. J., and Spitzberg, B. H. (1989). A model of perceived competence of conflict strategies. *Human Communication Research, 15,* 630–649.

Canary, D. J., and Spitzberg, B. H. (1990). Attribution biases and associations between conflict strategies and competence outcomes. *Communication Monographs, 57,* 139–151.

Canary, D. J., Spitzberg, B. H., and Semic, B. (In press). The experience and expression of anger in interpersonal settings. In P. A. Andersen and L. K. Guerrero (Eds.), *Communication and emotion: Theory, research, and applications.* San Diego: Academic Press.

Canary, D. J., Weger, H., Jr., and Stafford, L. (1991). Couples' argument sequences and their associations with relational characteristics. *Western Journal of Speech Communication, 55,* 159–179.

Cate, R. M., Henton, J. M., Koval, J., Christopher, F. S., and Lloyd, S. (1982). Premarital abuse: A social psychological perspective. *Journal of Family Issues, 3,* 79–90.

Caulfield, M. B., and Riggs, D. S. (1992). The assessment of dating aggression: Empirical evaluation of the conflict tactics scale. *Journal of Interpersonal Violence, 7,* 549–558.

Chapin, D. (1993). They love this game. *Street & Smith's Pro Basketball, 24*(1), 6–8.

Christopher, F. S., Owens, L. A., and Stecker, H. L. (1993). Exploring the dark side of courtship: A test of a model of male premarital sexual aggressiveness. *Journal of Marriage and the Family, 55,* 469–479.

Chua, E., and Gudykunst, W. (1987). Conflict resolution style in low- and high-context cultures. *Communication Research Reports, 4,* 32–37.

Clark, R. A., and Delia, J. (1979). *Topoi* and rhetorical competence. *Quarterly Journal of Speech, 65,* 187–206.

Clore, G. L., and Ortony, A. (1991). What more is there to emotion concepts than prototypes? *Journal of Personality and Social Psychology, 60,* 48-50.

Clore, G. L., Ortony, A., Dienes, B., and Fujita, F. (1993). Where does anger dwell? In R. W. Wyer and T. K. Srull (Eds.), *Perspectives on anger and emotions,* vol. 6 (pp. 57–88). Hillsdale, N.J.: Erlbaum.

Cloven, D. H., and Roloff, M. E. (1993). The chilling effect of aggressive potential on the expression of complaints in intimate relationships. *Communication Monographs, 60,* 199–219.

Cody, M. J., Canary, D. J., and Smith, S. W. (1994). Compliance-gaining goals: An inductive analysis of actor's goal types, strategies, and successes. In J. Daly and J. Wiemann (Eds.), *Communicating strategically* (pp. 33–90). Hillsdale, N.J.: Erlbaum.

Cohen, R. (1991). *Negotiating across cultures: Communication obstacles in international diplomacy.* Washington, D.C.: U.S. Institute of Peace.

Coleman, D. H., and Straus, M. A. (1986). Marital power, conflict, and violence in a nationally representative sample of American couples. *Violence and Victims, 1,* 141–157.

Conrad, C. (1991). Communication in conflict: Style-strategy relationships. *Communication Monographs, 58,* 135–155.

Coogler, O. J. (1978). *Structured mediation in divorce settlements.* Lexington, Mass.: Heath.

Cook, S. L. (1995). Acceptance and expectation of sexual aggression in college students. *Psychology of Women Quarterly, 19,* 181–194.

Cooks, L. M., and Hale, C. L. (1994). Communication ethics within dispute mediation. *Mediation Quarterly, 12,* 55–76.

Coser, L. (1956). *The functions of social conflict.* New York: Free Press.

Cross, S. E., and Markus, H. R. (1993). Gender in thought, belief, and action: A cognitive approach. In A. E. Beall and R. J. Sternberg (Eds.), *The psychology of gender* (pp. 55–98). New York: Guilford.

Cupach, W. R., and Canary, D. J. (1995). Managing conflict and anger: Investigating the sex stereotype hypothesis. In P. J. Kalbfleisch and M. J. Cody (Eds.), *Gender, power, and communication in human relationships* (pp. 233–252). Hillsdale, N.J.: Erlbaum.

Cupach, W. R., and Metts, S. (1994). *Facework.* Thousand Oaks, Calif.: Sage.

Darley, J. M., and Batson, C. D. (1973). From Jerusalem to Jericho: A study of situational and dispositional variables in helping behavior. *Journal of Personality and Social Psychology, 27,* 100–108.

Davis, A. M., and Salem, R. A. (1984). Dealing with power imbalances in the mediation of interpersonal disputes. In J. A. Lemmon (Ed.), *Procedures for guiding the divorce mediation process.* San Francisco: Jossey-Bass.

Davitz, J. R. (1969). *The language of emotion.* New York: Academic Press.

Deal, J. E., and Wampler, K. S. (1986). Dating violence: The primacy of previous experience. *Journal of Social and Personal Relationships, 3,* 457–471.

Deaux, K., and Lewis, L. L. (1984). The structure of gender stereotypes: Interrelationships among components and gender label. *Journal of Personality and Social Psychology, 46,* 991–1004.

deTurck, M. A. (1987). When communication fails: Physical aggression as a compliance-gaining strategy. *Communication Monographs, 54,* 106–112.

Deutsch, M. (1973). *The resolution of conflict: Constructive and destructive processes.* New Haven, Conn.: Yale University Press.

Dillard, J. P. (1990). Primary and secondary goals in interpersonal influence. In M. J. Cody and M. L. McLaughlin (Eds.), *The psychology of tactical communication* (pp. 70–90). Clevedon, England: Multilingual Matters.

Dillard, J. P., Segrin, C., and Harden, J. M. (1989). Primary and secondary goals in the production of interpersonal influence messages. *Communication Monographs, 56,* 19–38.

Dobash, R. E., and Dobash, R. (1979). *Violence against wives: A case against the patriarchy.* New York: Free Press.

Dobash, R. E., and Dobash, R. P. (1984). The nature and antecedents of violent events. *British Journal of Criminology, 24,* 269–288.

Dreyfuss, J. (1990). Get ready for the new workforce. *Fortune,* April 23, 165–181.

Dunn, J., and Munn, P. (1987). Development of justification in disputes with another sibling. *Developmental Psychology, 23,* 791–798.

Dunn, J., and Slomkowski, C. (1992). Conflict and the development of social understanding. In C. U. Shantz and W. W. Hartup (Eds.), *Conflict in child and adolescent development* (pp. 70–92). New York: Cambridge University Press.

Duran, R. (1985). Communicative adaptability: A measure of social communicative competence. *Communication Quarterly, 31,* 320–326.

Duran, R. (1992). Communicative adaptability: A review of conceptualization and measurement. *Communication Quarterly, 40,* 253–268.

Eagly, A. (1987). *Sex differences in social behavior: A social role interpretation.* Hillsdale, N.J.: Erlbaum.

Eagly, A. H., and Chaiken, S. (1993). *The psychology of attitudes.* New York: Harcourt Brace Jovanovich.

Eisenberg, A. R. (1992). Conflicts between mothers and their young children. *Merrill-Palmer Quarterly, 38,* 21–43.

Ellis, D. (1989). Male abuse of a married or cohabiting female partner: The application of sociological theory to research findings. *Violence and Victims, 4,* 235–255.

Epstein, N., Pretzer, J. L. and Fleming, B. (1987). The role of cognitive appraisal in self-reports of marital communication. *Behavior Therapy, 18,* 51–69.

Ernst, D., and Bleeke, J. (1993). *Collaborating to compete.* New York: McKinsey.

Evarts, W. R., Greenstone, J. L., Kirkpatrick, G. J., and Leviton, S. C. (1983). *Winning through accommodation: The mediator's handbook.* Dubuque, Iowa: Kendall/Hunt.

Falbo, T., and Peplau, L. A. (1980). Power strategies in intimate relationships. *Journal of Personality and Social Psychology, 38,* 618–628.

Felmlee, D. H. (1995). Fatal attractions: Affection and disaffection in intimate relationships. *Journal of Social and Personal Relationships, 12,* 295–311.

Felson, R. B. (1981). An interactionist approach to aggression. In J. T. Tedeschi (Ed.), *Impression management theory and psychological research* (pp. 181–199). New York: Academic Press.

Felson, R. B. (1984). Patterns of aggressive interaction. In A. Mummendey (Ed.), *Social psychology of aggression: From individual behavior to social interaction* (pp. 107–126). New York: Springer-Verlag.

Felson, R. B. (1993). Motives for sexual coercion. In R. B. Felson and J. T. Tedeschi (Eds.), *Aggression and violence: Social interactionist perspectives* (pp. 233–253). Washington, D.C.: American Psychological Association.

Ferraro, K. J., and Johnson, J. M. (1983). How women experience battering: The process of victimization. *Social Problems, 30,* 325–339.

Feshbach, S. (1986). Reconceptualizations of anger: Some research perspectives. *Journal of Social and Clinical Psychology, 4,* 123–132.

Filley, A. C. (1975). *Interpersonal conflict resolution.* Glenview, Ill.: Scott, Foresman.

Fincham, F. D., Beach, S. R. H., and Nelson G. (1987). Attribution processes in distressed and nondistressed couples: 3. Causal and responsibility attributions for spouse behavior. *Cognitive Therapy and Research, 11,* 71–86.

Fincham, F. D., and Bradbury, T. N. (1987). The impact of attributions in marriage: A longitudinal analysis. *Journal of Personality and Social Psychology, 53,* 510–517.

Fincham, F. D., and Bradbury, T. N. (1992). Assessing attributions in marriage: The relationship attribution measure. *Journal of Personality and Social Psychology, 62,* 457–468.

Fincham, F. D., Bradbury, T. N., and Scott, C. K. (1990). Cognition in marriage. In F. D. Fincham and T. N. Bradbury (Eds.), *The psychology of marriage: Basic issues and applications* (pp. 118–149). New York: Guilford.

Fine, M. G. (1991). New voices in the workplace: Research directions in multicultural communication. *Journal of Business Communication, 23,* 259–275.

Fisher, B. A. (1978). *Perspectives on human communication.* New York: Macmillan.

Fisher, D. (1993). *Communication in organizations* (2d ed.). St. Paul, Minn.: West.

Fisher, R., and Brown, S. (1988). *Getting together: Building relationships as we negotiate.* New York: Penguin.

Fisher, R., and Ury, W. (1981). *Getting to yes: Negotiating agreement without giving in.* Boston: Houghton Mifflin.

Fisher, R., and Ury, W. (1983). *Getting to yes: Negotiating agreement without giving in.* New York: Penguin.

Fitness, J., and Fletcher, G. J. O. (1993). Love, hate, anger, and jealousy in close relationships: A prototype and cognitive appraisal analysis. *Journal of Personality and Social Psychology, 65,* 942–958.

Fitzpatrick, M. A. (1988a). *Between husbands and wives: Communication in marriage.* Newbury Park, Calif.: Sage.

Fitzpatrick, M. A. (1988b). Negotiation, problem-solving, and conflict in various types of marriages. In P. Noller and M. A. Fitzpatrick (Eds.), *Perspectives on marital interaction* (pp. 245–270). Philadelphia: Pa.: Multilingual Matters.

Fitzpatrick, M. A., Fallis, S., and Vance, L. (1982). Multifunctional coding of conflict resolution strategies in marital dyads. *Family Relations, 31,* 61–70.

Fitzpatrick, M. A., and Winke, T. (1979). You always hurt the one you love: Strategies and tactics in interpersonal conflict. *Communication Quarterly, 27,* 3–11.

Flanzer, J. P. (1993). Alcohol and other drugs are key causal agents of violence. In R. J. Gelles and D. R. Loseke (Eds.), *Current controversies on family violence* (pp. 171–181). Newbury Park, Calif.: Sage.

Folberg, J., and Taylor, A. (1984). *Mediation: A comprehensive guide to resolving conflicts without litigation.* San Francisco: Jossey-Bass.

Folger, J. P., and Bush, R. A. B. (1994). Ideology, orientations to conflict, and mediation discourse. In J. P. Folger and T. S. Jones (Eds.), *New directions in mediation* (pp. 3–25). Thousand Oaks, Calif.: Sage.

Folger, J. P., Poole, M. S., and Stutman, R. K. (1993). *Working through conflict: Strategies for relationships, groups, and organizations* (2d ed.). New York: Harper Collins.

Follingstad, D. R., Rutledge, L. L., Polek, D. S., and McNeill-Hawkins, K. (1988). Factors associated with patterns of dating violence toward college women. *Journal of Family Violence, 3,* 169–182.

Follingstad, D. R., Wright, S., Lloyd, S., and Sebastian, J. A. (1991). Sex differences in motivations and effects in dating violence. *Family Relations, 40,* 51–57.

Freud, S. (1949). *An outline of psychoanalysis* (J. Stracyey, Trans.). New York: Norton.

Freud, S. (1953). *The interpretation of dreams* (J. Stracyey, Trans.). London: Hogarth. (Original work published 1900).

Frijda, N. H., Kuipers, P., and ter Shure, E. (1989). The relationships between emotion, appraisal, and emotional action readiness. *Journal of Personality and Social Psychology, 57,* 212–228.

Frost, W. D., and Averill, J. R. (1982). Differences between men and women in the everyday experience of anger. In J. R. Averill (Ed.), *Anger and aggression: An essay on emotion* (pp. 281–316). New York: Springer-Verlag.

Fuglesang, A., and Chandler, D. (1988). *Participation as process—What can we learn from the Grameen Bank?* Dhaka, Bangladesh: Grameen Bank.

Gayle, B. M., Preiss, R. W., and Allen, M. (1994). *Gender differences in conflict management strategy selection: A meta-analytic review.* Unpublished manuscript. University of Portland, Portland, Oregon.

Geis, F. L. (1993). Self-fulfilling prophecies: A social psychological view of gender. In A. E. Beall and R. J. Sternberg (Eds.), *The psychology of gender* (pp. 9–54). New York: Guilford.

Gergen, K. J. (1984). Aggression as discourse. In A. Mummendey (Ed.), *Social psychology of aggression: From individual behavior to social interaction* (pp. 51–68). New York: Springer-Verlag.

Gibb, J. R. (1961). Defensive communication. *Journal of Communication, 3,* 141–148.

Goffman, E. (1967). *Interaction ritual: Essays on face-to-face behavior.* New York: Pantheon.

Goldaper, S. (1983). N.B.A. strike averted with accord on 4-year pact. *New York Times,* April 1, A19–A20.

Gondolf, E. W. (1988). Who are those guys? Toward a behavioral typology of batterers. *Violence and Victims, 3,* 187–203.

Goodchilds, J. D., and Zellman, G. L. (1984). Sexual signaling and sexual aggression in adolescent relationships. In N. M. Malamuth and E. Donnerstein (Eds.), *Pornography and sexual aggression* (pp. 233–243). New York: Academic Press.

Goodstadt, B. E., and Hjelle, L. A. (1973). Power to the powerless: Locus of control and the use of power. *Journal of Personality and Social Psychology, 27,* 190–196.

Gottman, J. M. (1979). *Marital interaction: Experimental investigations.* New York: Academic Press.

Gottman, J. M. (1982). Emotional responsiveness in marital conversations. *Journal of Communication, 32,* 108–120.

Gottman, J. M. (1994). *What predicts divorce? The relationship between marital processes and marital outcomes.* Hillsdale, N.J.: Erlbaum.

Gottman, J. M., and Krokoff, L. J. (1989). Marital interaction and marital satisfaction: A longitudinal view. *Journal of Consulting and Clinical Psychology, 57,* 47–52.

Gottman, J. M., and Levenson, R. W. (1988). The social psychophysiology of marriage. In P. Noller and M. A. Fitzpatrick (Eds.), *Perspectives on marital interaction* (pp. 182–200). Philadelphia, Pa.: Multilingual Matters.

Gottman, J. M., and Levenson, R. W. (1992). Marital processes predictive of later dissolution: Behavior, physiology, and health. *Journal of Personality and Social Psychology, 63,* 221–233.

Graham, E. E., and Papa, M. J. (1993). Gender and function-oriented discourse in small groups: An examination of problem-solving processes and outcomes. In C. Berryman-Fink, D. Ballard-Reisch, and L. H. Newman (Eds.), *Communication and sex-role socialization* (pp. 311–336). New York: Garland.

Greenblat, C. S. (1983). A hit is a hit is a hit . . . or is it? Approval and tolerance of the use of physical force by spouses. In D. Finkelhor, R. J. Gelles, G. T. Hotaling, and M. A. Straus (Eds.), *The dark side of families: Current family violence research* (pp. 235–260). Newbury Park, Calif.: Sage.

Grillo, T. (1991). The mediation alternative: Process dangers for women. *Yale Law Journal, 100,* 15–45.

Gryl, F. E., Stith, S. M., and Bird, G. W. (1991). Close dating relationships among college students: Differences by use of violence and by gender. *Journal of Social and Personal Relationships, 8,* 243–264.

Gudykunst, W., and Ting-Toomey, S. (1988). *Culture and interpersonal communication.* Newbury Park, Calif.: Sage.

Guerrero, L. K. (1994). "I'm so mad I could scream": The effects of anger expression on relational satisfaction and communication competence. *Southern Communication Journal, 59,* 125–141.

Gulliver, P. H. (1979). *Disputes and negotiations: A cross-cultural perspective.* New York: Academic Press.

Haefner, P. T., Notarius, C. I., and Pellegrini, D. S. (1991). Determinants of satisfaction with marital discussions: An exploration of husband-wife differences. *Behavioral Assessment, 13,* 67–82.

Hall, E. T. (1976). *Beyond culture.* New York: Doubleday.

Hall, E. T. (1983). *The dance of life.* New York: Doubleday.

Hall, E., and Hall, M. (1987). *Hidden differences: Doing business with the Japanese.* Garden City, N.Y.: Anchor/Doubleday.

Hall, J. A. (1984). *Nonverbal sex differences: Accuracy of communication and expressive style.* Baltimore: Johns Hopkins University Press.

Hammock, G. S., Richardson, D. R., Pilkington, C. J., and Utley, M. (1990). Measurement of conflict in social relationships. *Personality and Individual Differences, 11,* 577–583.

Hample, D., and Dallinger, J. M. (1995). A Lewinian perspective on taking conflict personally: Revision, refinement, and validation of the instrument. *Communication Quarterly, 43,* 297–319.

Harris, L. M., Alexander, A., McNamee, S., Stanback, M., and Kang, K.-W. (1984). Forced cooperation: Violence as a communicative act. In S. Thomas (Ed.), *Studies in communication,* vol. 2 (pp. 20–32). Norwood, N.J.: Ablex.

Harris, L. M., Gergen, K. J., and Lannamann, J. W. (1986). Aggression rituals. *Communication Monographs, 53,* 252–265.

Haynes, J. M. (1982). A conceptual model of the process of family mediation: Implications for training. *American Journal of Family Therapy, 10*(4), 5–16.

Heavey, C. L., Layne, C., and Christensen, A. (1993). Gender and conflict structure in marital interaction: A replication and extension. *Journal of Consulting and Clinical Psychology, 61,* 16–27.

Henderson, D. C. (1965). *Conciliation and Japanese law: Tokugawa and modern.* Seattle: University of Washington Press.

Henton, J., Cate, R., Koval, J., Lloyd, S., and Christopher, S. (1983). Romance and violence in dating relationships. *Journal of Family Issues, 4,* 467–482.

Hirokawa, R. Y. (1985). Discussion procedures and decision-making performance: A test of a functional perspective. *Human Communication Research, 12,* 203–224.

Hirokawa, R. Y. (1988). Group communication and decision-making performance: A continued test of the functional perspective. *Human Communication Research, 14,* 487–515.

Hobart, C. (1991). Relationships between the formerly married. *Journal of Divorce & Remarriage, 14,* 1–23.

Hochschild, A. (1989). *The second shift: Working parents and the revolution at home.* New York: Viking.

Hocker, J. L., and Wilmot, W. W. (1985). *Interpersonal conflict* (2d ed.). Dubuque, Iowa: Wm. C. Brown.

Hocker, J. L., and Wilmot, W. W. (1991). *Interpersonal conflict* (3d ed.). Dubuque, Iowa: Wm. C. Brown.

Hocker, J. L., and Wilmot, W. W. (1995). *Interpersonal conflict* (4th ed.). Dubuque, Iowa: Wm C. Brown.

Hofstede, G. (1980). *Culture's consequences: International differences in work-related values.* Beverly Hills, Calif.: Sage.

Hofstede, G. (1991). *Cultures and organizations: Software of the mind.* London: McGraw-Hill.

Holt, R. R. (1970). On the interpersonal and intrapersonal consequences of expressing or not expressing anger. *Journal of Consulting and Clinical Psychology, 35,* 8–12.

Holtzworth-Munroe, A., and Anglin, K. (1991). The competency of responses given by maritally violent versus nonviolent men to problematic marital situations. *Violence and Victims, 6,* 257–269.

Holtzworth-Munroe, A., Waltz, J., Jacobson, N. S., Monaco, V., Fehrenbach, P. A., and Gottman, J. M. (1992). Recruiting nonviolent men as control subjects for research on marital violence: How easily can it be done? *Violence and Victims, 7,* 79–88.

Honeycutt, J. M., Woods, B. L., and Fontenot, K. (1993). The endorsement of communication conflict rules as a function of engagement, marriage and marital ideology. *Journal of Social and Personal Relationships, 10,* 285–304.

Honeyman, C. (1990). On evaluating mediators. *Negotiation Journal, 6,* 23–36.

Howat, G., and London, M. (1980). Attributions of conflict management strategies in supervisor-subordinate dyads. *Journal of Applied Psychology, 65,* 172–175.

Huff-Arneson, R. (1988). *A language of leaders.* Paper presented at the annual convention of the American Library Association, New Orleans.

Huston, T. L., Surra, C. A., Fitzgerald, N. M., and Cate, R. M. (1981). From courtship to marriage: Mate selection as an interpersonal process. In S. Duck and R. Gilmour (Eds.), *Personal relationships 2: Developing personal relationships* (pp. 53–88). London: Academic Press.

Infante, D. A., Chandler, T. A., and Rudd, J. E. (1989). Test of an argumentative skill deficiency model of interpersonal violence. *Communication Monographs, 56,* 163–177.

Infante, D. A., and Rancer, A. S. (1982). A conceptualization and measurement of argumentativeness. *Journal of Personality Assessment, 46,* 72–80.

Infante, D. A., Riddle, B. L., Horvath, C. L., and Tumlin, S. A. (1992). Verbal aggressiveness: Messages and reasons. *Communication Quarterly, 40,* 116–126.

Infante, D. A., Sabourin, T. C., Rudd, J. E., and Shannon, E. A. (1990). Verbal aggression in violent and nonviolent marital disputes. *Communication Quarterly, 38,* 361–371.

Infante, D. A., Trebing, J. D., Shepard, P. E., and Seeds, D. E. (1984). The relation of argumentativeness to verbal aggression. *Southern Speech Communication Journal, 50,* 67–77.

Infante, D. A., and Wigley, C. J. Jr. (1986). Verbal aggressiveness: An interpersonal model and measure. *Communication Monographs, 53,* 61–69.

Jenson, J. K. (1991). If only . . . In B. Levy (Ed.), *Dating violence: Young women in danger* (pp. 45–49). Seattle: Seal.

Jones, E., and Gallois, C. (1989). Spouses' impressions of rules for communication in public and private marital conflicts. *Journal of Marriage and the Family, 51,* 957–967.

Jones, K. (1992). Competing to learn in Japan. *McKinsey Quarterly, 1,* 45–57.

Jones, R. E., and White, C. S. (1985). Relationships among personality, conflict resolution styles, and task effectiveness. *Group & Organization Studies, 10,* 152–167.

Jones, T. S. (1994). A dialectical reframing of the mediation process. In J. P. Folger and T. S. Jones (Eds.), *New directions in mediation* (pp. 26–47). Thousand Oaks, Calif.: Sage.

Jones, W. H., and Burdette, M. P. (1994). Betrayal in relationships. In A. L. Weber and J. H. Harvey (Eds.), *Perspectives on close relationships* (pp. 243–262). Boston: Allyn and Bacon.

Kanin, E. J. (1984). Date rape: Unofficial criminals and victims. *Victimology, 9,* 95–108.

Kasian, M., and Painter, S. L. (1992). Frequency and severity of psychological abuse in a dating population. *Journal of Interpersonal Violence, 7,* 350–364.

Katz, D., and Kahn, R. L. (1978). *The social psychology of organizations* (2d ed.). New York: Wiley.

Kelley, H. H. (1979). *Personal relationships: Their structure and processes.* Hillsdale, N.J.: Erlbaum.

Kelley, H. H., Cunningham, J. D., Grisham, J. A., Lefebvre, L. M., Sink, C. R., and Yablon, G. (1978). Sex differences in comments made during conflict within close heterosexual pairs. *Sex Roles, 4,* 473–492.

Kiecolt-Glaser, J. K., Malarkey, W. B., Chee, M. A., Newton, T., Cacioppo, J. T., Mao, H. Y., and Glaser, R. (1993). Negative behavior during marital conflict is associated with immunological down-regulation. *Psychosomatic Medicine, 55,* 395–409.

Kiely, L. S., and Crary, D. R. (1986). Effective mediation: A communication approach to consubstantiality. In J. A. Lemmon (Ed.), *Emerging roles in divorce mediation* (pp. 37–50). San Francisco: Jossey-Bass.

Kilmann, R. H., and Thomas, K. W. (1977). Developing a forced-choice measure of conflict-handling behavior: The "MODE" instrument. *Educational and Psychological Measurement, 37,* 309–325.

Kim, U., Triandis, T., Kagitcibasi, C., Choi, S.-C., and Yoon, G. (Eds.). (1994). *Individualism and collectivism: Theory, method, and applications.* Thousand Oaks, Calif.: Sage.

Kipnis, D., and Schmidt, S. M. (1982). *Respondent's guide to the Kipnis-Schmidt profiles of organizational influence strategies.* Beverly Hills, Calif.: University Associates.

Koralewski, M. A., and Conger, J. C. (1992). The assessment of social skills among sexually coercive college males. *Journal of Sex Research, 29,* 169–188.

Koren, P., Carlton, K., and Shaw, D. (1980). Marital conflict: Relations among behaviors, outcomes and distress. *Journal of Consulting and Clinical Psychology, 48,* 460–468.

Koss, M. P. (1989). Hidden rape: Sexual aggression and victimization in a national sample of students in higher education. In M. A. Pirog-Good and J. E. Stets (Eds.), *Violence in dating relationships: Emerging social issues* (pp. 145–168). New York: Praeger.

Koss, M. P. (1993). Detecting the scope of rape: A review of prevalence research methods. *Journal of Interpersonal Violence, 8,* 198–222.

Laner, M. R. (1989). Competitive vs. noncompetitive styles: Which is most valued in courtship? *Sex Roles, 20,* 165–172.

Laner, M. R. (1990). Violence or its precipitators: Which is more likely to be identified as a dating problem? *Deviant Behavior, 11,* 319–329.

Langer, E. (1989). *Mindfulness.* Reading, Mass.: Addison-Wesley.

Larzelere, R. E., and Huston, T. L. (1980). The dyadic trust scale: Toward understanding interpersonal trust in close relationships. *Journal of Marriage and the Family, 42,* 595–604.

Laursen, B. (1993). The perceived impact of conflict on adolescent relationships. *Merrill-Palmer Quarterly, 39,* 535–550.

Lefcourt, H. M. (1982). *Locus of control: Current trends in theory and research* (2d ed.). Hillsdale, N.J.: Erlbaum.

Lei, D., and Slocum, J. W. (1992). Global strategy, competence-building and strategic alliances. *California Management Review, 26*(4), 81–97.

LeResche, D. (Ed.). (1993). Special issue: Native American perspectives on peace-making. *Mediation Quarterly, 10*(4), 321–422.

Lerman, L. G. (1984). Mediation of wife abuse cases: The adverse impact of informal dispute resolution on women. *Harvard Women's Law Journal, 7,* 57–113.

Leung, K. (1987). Some determinants of reactions to procedural models for conflict resolution: A cross-national study. *Journal of Personality and Social Psychology, 53,* 898–908.

Leung, K. (1988). Some determinants of conflict avoidance. *Journal of Cross-Cultural Psychology, 19,* 125–136.

Leung, K., and Bond, M. (1984). The impact of cultural collectivism on reward allocation. *Journal of Personality and Social Psychology, 47,* 793–804.

Leung, K., and Iwawaki, S. (1988). Cultural collectivism and distributive behavior. *Journal of Cross-Cultural Psychology, 19,* 35–49.

Levenson, R. W., Carstensen, L. L., and Gottman, J. M. (1994). The influence of age and gender on affect, physiology, and their interrelations: A study of long-term marriages. *Journal of Personality and Social Psychology, 67,* 56–68.

Levinson, D. (1989). *Family violence in cross-cultural perspective.* Newbury Park, Calif.: Sage.

Lewicki, R. J., and Litterer, J. (1985). *Negotiation.* Homewood, Ill.: Irwin.

Lie, G.-Y., Schilit, R., Bush, J., Montagne, M., and Reyes, L. (1991). Lesbians in currently aggressive relationships: How frequently do they report aggressive past relationships? *Violence and Victims, 6,* 121–135.

Lipton, D. N., McDonel, E. C., and McFall, R. M. (1987). Heterosocial perception in rapists. *Journal of Consulting and Clinical Psychology, 55,* 17–21.

Lloyd, S. A. (1987). Conflict in premarital relationships: Differential perceptions of males and females. *Family Relations, 36,* 290–294.

Lloyd, S. A. (1990). Conflict types and strategies in violent marriages. *Journal of Family Violence, 5,* 269–284.

Lloyd, S. A., and Emery, B. C. (1993). *Physically aggressive conflict in romantic relationships.* Paper presented at the Iowa Network in Personal Relationships conference, Milwaukee, Wisconsin.

Loden, M., and Rosener, J. (1991). *Workforce America! Managing employee diversity as a vital resource.* Homewood, Ill.: Business One Irwin.

London, M., and Howat, G. (1978). The relationships between employee commitment and conflict resolution behavior. *Journal of Vocational Behavior, 13,* 1–14.

Long, G. M., and McNamara, J. R. (1989). Paradoxical punishment as it relates to the battered woman syndrome. *Behavior Modification, 13,* 192–205.

Lubit, R., and Russett, B. (1984). The effects of drugs on decision-making. *Journal of Conflict Resolution, 28,* 85–102.

Lund, M. (1985). The development of investment and commitment scales for predicting continuity of personal relationships. *Journal of Social and Personal Relationships, 2,* 3–23.

Maccoby, E. E., and Jacklin, C. N. (1974). *The psychology of sex differences,* vol. 1: *Text.* Stanford, Calif.: Stanford University Press.

Mahoney, E. R., Shively, M. D., and Traw, M. (1986). Sexual coercion & assault: Male socialization and female risk. *Sexual Coercion & Assault, 1,* 2–8.

Makepeace, J. M. (1983). Life events, stress, and courtship violence. *Family Relations, 30,* 97–102.

Makepeace, J. M. (1986). Gender differences in courtship violence victimization. *Family Relations, 35,* 383–388.

Makepeace, J. M. (1989). Dating, living together, and courtship violence. In M. A. Pirog-Good and J. E. Stets (Eds.), *Violence in dating relationships: Emerging social issues* (pp. 94–107). New York: Praeger.

Malamuth, N. M. (1984). Aggression against women: Cultural and individual causes. In N. M. Malamuth and E. Donnerstein (Eds.), *Pornography and sexual aggression* (pp. 19–52). New York: Academic Press.

Malarkey, W. B., Kiecolt-Glaser, J. K., Perl, D., and Glaser, R. (1994). Hostile behavior during marital conflict alters pituitary and adrenal hormones. *Psychosomatic Medicine, 56,* 41–51.

Margolin, G., John, R. S., and Gleberman, L. (1988). Affective responses to conflictual discussions in violent and nonviolent couples. *Journal of Consulting and Clinical Psychology, 56,* 24–33.

Margolin, G., and Wampold, B. E. (1981). Sequential analysis of conflict and accord in distressed and nondistressed marital partners. *Journal of Consulting and Clinical Psychology, 49,* 554–567.

Markus, H., and Kitayama, S. (1991). Culture and the self: Implications for cognition, emotion, and motivation. *Psychological Review, 2,* 224–253.

Marshall, L. L. (1994). Physical and psychological abuse. In W. R. Cupach and B. H. Spitzberg (Eds.), *The dark side of interpersonal communication* (pp. 281–311). Hillsdale, N.J.: Erlbaum.

Marshall, L. L., and Rose, P. (1987). Gender, stress, and violence in the adult relationships of a sample of college students. *Journal of Social and Personal Relationships, 4,* 299–316.

Marshall, L. L., and Rose, P. (1988). Family of origin and courtship violence. *Journal of Counseling and Development, 66,* 414–418.

Marshall, L. L., and Vitanza, S. A. (1994). Physical abuse in close relationships: Myths and realities. In A. L. Weber and J. H. Harvey (Eds.), *Perspectives on close relationships* (pp. 263–284). Boston: Allyn and Bacon.

Mason, A., and Blankenship, V. (1987). Power and affiliation motivation, stress, and abuse in intimate relationships. *Journal of Personality and Social Psychology, 52,* 203–210.

Mathes, E. W., and Verstraete, C. (1993). Jealous aggression: Who is the target, the beloved or the rival? *Psychological Reports, 72,* 1071–1074.

McDonel, E. C., and McFall, R. M. (1991). Construct validity of two heterosocial perception skill measures for assessing rape proclivity. *Violence and Victims, 6,* 17–30.

McGonagle, K. A., Kessler, R. C., and Gotlib, I. H. (1993). The effects of marital disagreement style, frequency, and outcome on marital disruption. *Journal of Social and Personal Relationships, 10,* 385–404.

McIsaac, H. (1983). Court-connected mediation. *Conciliation Courts Review, 21,* 49–59.

McNeely, R. L., and Robinson-Simpson, G. (1987). The truth about domestic violence: A falsely framed issue. *Social Work, 32,* 485–490.

Mead, D. E., Vatcher, G. M., Wyne, B. A., and Roberts, S. L. (1990). The comprehensive areas of change questionnaire: Assessing marital couples' presenting complaints. *American Journal of Family Therapy, 18,* 65–79.

Mesquita, B., and Frijda, N. (1992). Cultural variations in emotions: A review. *Psychological Bulletin, 112,* 179–204.

Metts, S. (1994). Relational transgressions. In W. R. Cupach and B. H. Spitzberg (Eds.), *The dark side of interpersonal communication* (pp. 217–239). Hillsdale, N.J.: Erlbaum.

Millar, F. E., and Rogers, L. E. (1987). Relational dimensions of interpersonal dynamics. In M. E. Roloff & G. R. Miller (Eds.), *Interpersonal processes: New directions in communication research* (pp. 117–139). Newbury Press, Calif.: Sage.

Miller, J. L., and Miller, J. G. (1992). Greater than the sum of its parts. I. Subsystems which process both matter-energy and information. *Behavioral Science, 37,* 1–9.

Miller, P. C., Lefcourt, H. M., Holmes, J. G., Ware, E. E., and Saleh, W. E. (1986). Marital locus of control and marital problem solving. *Journal of Personality and Social Psychology, 51,* 161–169.

Mills, C. S., and Granoff, B. J. (1992). Date and acquaintance rape among a sample of college students. *Social Work, 37,* 504–509.

Milne, A. (1978). Custody of children in a divorce process: A family self-determination model. *Conciliation Courts Review, 16,* 1–16.

Montemayor, R. (1986). Family variation in parent-adolescent storm and stress. *Journal of Adolescent Research, 1,* 15–31.

Moore, C. W. (1986). *The mediation process: Practical strategies for resolving conflict.* San Francisco: Jossey-Bass.

Morley, I., and Shockley-Zalabak, P. (1986). Conflict avoiders and compromisers: Toward an understanding of their organizational communication style. *Group and Organizational Behavior, 11*(4), 387–402.

Morrill, C., and Thomas, C. K. (1992). Organizational conflict management as disputing process: The problem of social escalation. *Human Communication Research, 18,* 400–425.

Morton, T. C., Alexander, J. F., and Altman, I. (1976). Communication and relationship definition. In G. R. Miller (Ed.), *Explorations in interpersonal communication* (pp. 105–126). Beverly Hills, Calif.: Sage.

Muehlenhard, C. L., and Falcon, P. L. (1990). Men's heterosocial skill and attitudes toward women as predictors of verbal sexual coercion and forceful rape. *Sex Roles, 23,* 241–259.

Muehlenhard, C. L., Goggins, M. F., Jones, J. M., and Satterfield, A. T. (1991). Sexual violence and coercion in close relationships. In K. McKinney and S. Sprecher (Eds.), *Sexuality in close relationships* (pp. 155–176). Hillsdale, N.J.: Erlbaum.

Muehlenhard, C. L., and Linton, M. A. (1987). Date rape and sexual aggression in dating situations: Incidence and risk factors. *Journal of Personality and Social Psychology, 34,* 186–196.

Mummendey, A., Linneweber, V., and Loschper, G. (1984). Aggression: From act to interaction. In A. Mummendey (Ed.), *Social psychology of aggression: From individual behavior to social interaction* (pp. 69–106). New York: Springer-Verlag.

Mumpower, J. L. (1991). The judgment policies of negotiators and the structure of negotiation problems. *Management Science, 37,* 1304–1324.

Murnen, S. K., Perot, A., and Byrne, D. (1989). Coping with unwanted sexual activity: Normative responses, situational determinants ,and individual differences. *Journal of Sex Research, 26,* 85–106.

Murphy, C. M., and O'Leary, K. D. (1989). Psychological aggression predicts physical aggression in early marriage. *Journal of Consulting and Clinical Psychology, 57,* 579–582.

Murphy, W. D., Coleman, E. M., and Haynes, M. R. (1986). Factors related to coercive sexual behavior in a nonclinical sample of males. *Violence and Victims, 1,* 255–278.

Nance, R. (1995a). League, players race deadline for labor deal. *USA Today,* August 9, 1C.

Nance, R. (1995b). NBA player reps OK agreement 25-2. *USA Today,* September 14, 1C.

Naotsuka, R., Sakamoto, N., Hirose, T., Hagihara, H., Ohta, J., Maeda, S., Hara, T., and Iwasaki, K. (1981). *Mutual understanding of different cultures.* Tokyo: Taishukan.

National Association of Social Workers. (1991). *Standards of practice for social work mediators.* Washington, D.C.: National Association of Social Workers.

Newell, S. E., and Stutman, R. K. (1988). The social confrontation episode. *Communication Monographs, 55,* 266–285.

Newton, D. A., and Burgoon, J. K. (1990a). Nonverbal conflict behaviors: Functions, strategies, and tactics. In D. D. Cahn (Ed.), *Intimates in conflict: A communication perspective* (pp. 77–104). Hillsdale, N.J.: Erlbaum.

Newton, D. A., and Burgoon, J. K. (1990b). The use and consequences of verbal influence strategies during interpersonal disagreements. *Human Communication Research, 16,* 477–518.

Noller, P., Feeney, J. A., Bonnell, D., and Callan, V. J. (1994). A longitudinal study of conflict in early marriage. *Journal of Social and Personal Relationships, 11,* 233–252.

Notarius, C., and Markman, H. (1993). *We can work it out: Making sense of marital conflict.* New York: Putnam.

Nunamaker, J. F., Dennis, A. R., Valacich, J. S., and Vogel, D. R. (1991). Information technology for negotiating groups: Generating options for mutual gain. *Management Science, 37,* 1325–1345.

Nussbaum, J. F. (Ed.). (1989). *Life-span communication: Normative processes.* Hillsdale, N.J.: Erlbaum.

Ohbuchi, K.-I., Kameda, M., and Agarie, N. (1989). Apology as aggression control: Its role in mediating appraisal of and response to harm. *Journal of Personality and Social Psychology, 56,* 219–227.

O'Leary, K. D. (1993). Through a psychological lens: Personality traits, personality disorders, and levels of violence. In R. J. Gelles and D. R. Loseke (Eds.), *Current controversies on family violence* (pp. 7–30). Newbury Park, Calif.: Sage.

O'Leary, K. D., Barling, J., Arias, I., Rosenbaum, A., Malone, J., and Tyree, A. (1989). Prevalence and stability of physical aggression between spouses: A longitudinal analysis. *Journal of Consulting and Clinical Psychology, 57,* 263–268.

Ostermeyer, M. (1991). Conducting the mediation. In K. G. Duffy, J. W. Grosch, and P. V. Olczak (Eds.), *Community mediation* (pp. 91–104). New York: Guilford.

Pagelow, M. D. (1984). *Family violence.* New York: Praeger.

Papa, M. J., and Canary, D. J. (1995). Conflict in organizations: A competence-based perspective. In A. M. Nicotera (Ed.), *Conflict in organizations: Communicative processes* (pp. 153–179). Albany, N.Y.: State University of New York Press.

Papa, M. J., and Graham, E. E. (1990). *A test of the ecological validity of the functional communication perspective of small group decision-making.* Paper presented at the annual meeting of the International Communication Association, Dublin, Ireland.

Papa, M. J., and Pood, E. A. (1988a). Coorientational accuracy and differentiation in the management of conflict. *Communication Research, 15,* 400–425.

Papa, M. J., and Pood, E. A. (1988b). Coorientational accuracy and organizational conflict: An examination of tactic selection and outcome satisfaction. *Communication Research, 15,* 3–28.

Parkhe, A. (1991). Interfirm diversity, organizational learning, and longevity in global strategic alliances. *Journal of International Business Studies, 22,* 579–601.

Parkhe, A. (1993). Strategic alliance structuring: A game theoretic and transaction cost examination of interfirm cooperation. *Academy of Management Journal, 36,* 794–829.

Parks, M. R. (1994). Communicative competence and interpersonal control. In M. L. Knapp and G. R. Miller (Eds.), *Handbook of interpersonal communication* (2d ed., pp. 589–618). Thousand Oaks, Calif.: Sage.

Pavitt, C., and Haight, L. (1985). The "competent communicator" as a cognitive prototype. *Human Communication Research, 12,* 225–242.

Pearce, W. B. (1976). The coordinated management of meaning: A rules-based theory of interpersonal communication. In G. R. Miller (Ed.), *Explorations in interpersonal communication* (pp. 17–35). Beverly Hills, Calif.: Sage.

Pearce, W. B., and Conklin, F. (1979). A model of hierarchical meanings in coherent conversations and a study of "indirect responses." *Communication Monographs, 46,* 75–87.

Pearce, W. B., and Cronen, V. (1980). *Communication, action, and meaning.* New York: Praeger.

Pedullah, T. (1995). With decertification settled, issue is unity among players. *USA Today,* September 13, p. 2C.

Perlman, D., and Fehr, B. (1987). The development of intimate relationships. In D. Perlman and S. Duck (Eds.), *Intimate relationships* (pp. 13–42). Newbury Park, Calif.: Sage.

Perrow, L. R. (1979). *Complex organizations.* Glenview, Ill.: Scott, Foresman.

Peterson, D. R. (1983). Conflict. In H. H. Kelley, E. Berscheid, A. Christensen, J. H. Harvey, T. L. Huston, G. Levinger, E. McClintock, L. A. Peplau, and D. R. Peterson (Eds), *Close relationships* (pp. 360–396). New York: W. H. Freeman.

Pfeiffer, S. M., and Wong, P. T. (1989). Multidimensional jealousy. *Journal of Social and Personal Relationships, 6,* 181–196.

Phillips, E., and Cheston, R.(1979). Conflict resolution: What works? *California Management Review, 21*(4), 76–83.

Pierce, C. P. (1995). The NBA's ship of fools. *Sports Illustrated,* August 14, 78.

Pike, G. R., and Sillars, A. L. (1985). Reciprocity of marital communication. *Journal of Social and Personal Relationships, 2,* 303–324.

Pondy, L. R. (1967). Organizational conflict: Concepts and models. *Administrative Science Quarterly, 12,* 296–320.

Ponzetti, J. J., Cate, R. M., and Koval, J. E. (1982). Violence between couples profiling the male abuser. *Personnel and Guidance Journal, 61,* 221–224.

Prince, J. E., and Arias, I. (1994). The role of perceived control and the desirability of control among abusive and nonabusive husbands. *American Journal of Family Therapy, 22,* 126–134.

Putnam, L. L., and Bullis, C. (1984). *Intergroup relations and issue redefinition in teacher bargaining.* Paper presented at the annual meeting of the International Communication Association, San Francisco.

Putnam, L. L., and Jones T. S. (1982). Reciprocity in negotiations: An analysis of bargaining interaction. *Communication Monographs, 49,* 171–191.

Putnam, L. L., and Poole, M. S. (1987). Conflict and negotiation. In F. Jablin, L. Putnam, K. Roberts, and L. Porter (Eds.), *The handbook of organizational communication* (pp. 549–599). Beverly Hills, Calif.: Sage.

Putnam, L. L., and Wilson, C. E. (1982). Communicative strategies in organizational conflicts: Reliability and validity of a measurement scale. In M. Burgoon (Ed.), *Communication yearbook 6* (pp. 629–652). Beverly Hills, Calif.: Sage.

Rahim, M. A. (1983). A measure of styles of handling interpersonal conflict. *Academy of Management Journal, 26,* 368–376.

Raush, H. L., Barry, W. A., Hertel, R. J., and Swain, M. A. (1974). *Communication, conflict, and marriage.* San Francisco: Jossey-Bass.

Renwick, P. A. (1975). Perception and management of superior-subordinate conflict. *Organizational Behavior and Human Performance, 13,* 444–456.

Renzetti, C. M. (1992). *Violent betrayal: Partner abuse in lesbian relationships.* Newbury Park, Calif.: Sage.

Resick, P. A. (1993). The psychological impact of rape. *Journal of Interpersonal Violence, 8,* 223–255.

Retzinger, S. M. (1991). *Violent emotions: Shame and rage in marital quarrels.* Newbury Park, Calif.: Sage.

Rifkin, J., Millen, J., and Cobb, S. (1991). Toward a new discourse for mediation: A critique of neutrality. *Mediation Quarterly, 9,* 151–164.

Riggs, D. S. (1993). Relationship problems and dating aggression: A potential treatment target. *Journal of Interpersonal Violence, 8,* 18–35.

Riggs, D. S., O'Leary, K. D., and Breslin, F. C. (1990). Multiple correlates of physical aggression in dating couples. *Journal of Interpersonal Violence, 5,* 61–73.

Riordan, C. A., Marlin, N. A., and Kellogg, R. T. (1983). The effectiveness of accounts following transgression. *Social Psychology Quarterly, 46,* 213–219.

Robin, A. L., and Foster, S. L. (1989). *Negotiating parent-adolescent conflict: A behavioral systems approach.* New York: Guilford.

Rodenburg, F. A., and Fantuzzo, J. W. (1993). The measure of wife abuse: Steps toward the development of a comprehensive assessment technique. *Journal of Family Violence, 8,* 203–228.

Rogers, E. M. (1983). *The diffusion of innovations* (3d ed.). New York: Free Press.

Roloff, M. E., and Janiszewski, C. A. (1989). Overcoming obstacles to interpersonal compliance: A principle of message construction. *Human Communication Research, 16,* 33–61.

Roscoe, B. (1985). Courtship violence: Acceptable forms and situations. *College Student Journal, 19,* 389–393.

Roscoe, B., and Benaske, N. (1985). Courtship violence experienced by abused wives: Similarities in patterns of abuse. *Family Relations, 34,* 419–424.

Roscoe, B., and Kelsey, T. (1986). Dating violence among high school students. *Psychology, 23,* 53–59.

Ross, R. G., and DeWine, S. (1988). Assessing the Ross-DeWine conflict management message style (CMMS). *Management Communication Quarterly, 1,* 414–429.

Ruane, J. M. (1993). Tolerating force: A contextual analysis of the meaning of tolerance. *Sociological Inquiry, 63,* 293–304.

Rusbult, C. E. (1987). Responses to dissatisfaction in close relationships: The exit-voice-loyalty-neglect model. In D. Perlman and S. Duck (Eds.), *Intimate relationships: Development, dynamics, and deterioration* (pp. 209–337). Newbury Park, Calif.: Sage.

Rusbult, C. E., Drigotas, S. M., and Verette, J. (1994). The investment model: An interdependence analysis of commitment processes and relationship maintenance phenomena. In D. J. Canary and L. Stafford (Eds.), *Communication and relational maintenance* (pp. 115–139). New York: Academic Press.

Rusbult, C. E., Johnson, D. J., and Morrow, G. D. (1986). Predicting satisfaction and commitment in adult romantic relationships: An assessment of the generalizability of the investment model. *Social Psychological Quarterly, 49,* 81–89.

Rusbult, C. E., Verette, J., Whitney, G. A., Slovik, L. F., and Lipkus, I. (1991). Accommodation processes in close relationships: Theory and preliminary empirical evidence. *Journal of Personality and Social Psychology, 60,* 53–78.

Russell, D. E. H. (1982). *Rape in marriage.* New York: Collier.

Russell, J. (1991). Culture and the categorizations of emotions. *Psychological Bulletin, 110,* 426–450.

Russell, J. A., and Fehr, B. (1994). Fuzzy concepts in a fuzzy hierarchy: Varieties of anger. *Journal of Personality and Social Psychology, 67,* 186–205.

Samter, W., Cupach, W. R., and Nathanson, A. (1995). *Friendly fire: Topical variations in conflict among same- and cross-sex friends.* Paper presented at the Central States Communication Association convention, Indianapolis.

Sander, F. E. A., and Goldberg, S. B. (1994). Fitting the forum to the fuss: A user-friendly guide to selecting an ADR procedure. *Negotiation Journal, 10,* 49–68.

Saunders, D. G. (1986). When battered women use violence: Husband-abuse or self-defense? *Victims and Violence, 1,* 47–60.

Schaap, C., Buunk, B., and Kerkstra, A. (1988). Marital conflict resolution. In P. Noller and M. A. Fitzpatrick (Eds.), *Perspectives on marital interaction* (pp. 203–224). Philadelphia: Multilingual Matters.

Schacter, S., and Singer, J. E. (1962). Cognitive, social, and physiological determinants of emotional state. *Psychological Review, 69,* 379–399.

Scheff, T. J., and Retzinger, S. M. (1991). *Emotions and violence: Shame and rage in destructive conflicts.* Lexington, Mass.: Lexington.

Schlenker, B. R. (1980). *Impression management: The self-concept, social identity, and interpersonal relations.* Monterey, Calif.: Brooks/Cole.

Schönbach, P. (1990). *Account episodes: The management or escalation of conflict.* Cambridge: Cambridge University Press.

Schutte, N. S., Malouff, J. M., and Doyle, J. S. (1988). The relationship between characteristics of the victim, persuasive techniques of the batterer, and returning to a battering relationship. *Journal of Social Psychology, 128,* 605–610.

Selman, R. L. (1980). *The growth of interpersonal understanding: Developmental and clinical analyses.* New York: Academic Press.

Sereno, K. K., Welch, M., and Braaten, D. (1987). Interpersonal conflict: Effects of variations in manner of expressing anger and justifications for anger upon perceptions of appropriateness, competence, and satisfaction. *Journal of Applied Communication Research, 15,* 128–143.

Serrin, W. (1983). N.B.A. agreement is acclaimed. *New York Times,* April 1, A19–A20.

Shafer, P., Schwartz, D., Kirkson, D., and O'Connor, C. (1987). Emotion knowledge: Further exploration of a prototype approach. *Journal of Personality and Social Psychology, 52,* 1061–1086.

Shan, W. (1990). An empirical analysis of organizational strategies by entrepreneurial high-technology firms. *Strategic Management Journal, 11,* 129–139.

Shantz, C. U. (1987). Conflicts between children. *Child Development, 58,* 283–305.

Shehabuddin, R. (1992). *Empowering rural women: The impact of Grameen Bank in Bangladesh.* Dhaka, Bangladesh: Grameen Bank.

Shepard, M. F., and Campbell, J. A. (1992). The abusive behavior inventory: A measure of psychological and physical abuse. *Journal of Interpersonal Violence, 7,* 291–305.

Sherman, S. (1992). Are strategic alliances working? *Fortune,* September 21, 77–78.

Shields, N. M., McCall, G. J., and Hanneke, C. R. (1988). Patterns of family and nonfamily violence: Violent husbands and violent men. *Violence and Victims, 3,* 83–97.

Shimanoff, S. (1980). *Communication rules: Theory and research.* Beverly Hills, Calif.: Sage.

Shupe, A., Stacey, W. A., and Hazlewood, L. R. (1987). *Violent men, violent couples: The dynamics of domestic violence.* Lexington, Mass.: Lexington.

Siegman, A. W. (1994). Cardiovascular consequences of expressing and repressing anger. In A. W. Siegman & T. W. Smith (Eds.), *Anger, hostility, and the heart* (pp. 173–197). Hillsdale, N.J.: Erlbaum.

Sigelman, C. K., Berry, C. J., and Wiles, K. A. (1984). Violence in college students' dating relationships. *Journal of Applied Social Psychology, 5,* 530–548.

Sillars, A. L. (1980a). The sequential and distributional structure of conflict interactions as a function of attributions concerning the locus of responsibility and stability of conflicts. In D. Nimmo (Ed.), *Communication Yearbook 4* (pp. 217–235). New Brunswick, N.J.: Transaction.

Sillars, A. L. (1980b). The stranger and the spouse as target persons for compliance-gaining strategies: A subjective expected utility model. *Human Communication Research, 6,* 265–279.

Sillars, A. L. (1981). Attributions and interpersonal conflict resolution. In J. H. Harvey, W. Ickes, and R. F. Kidd (Eds.), *New directions in attribution research,* vol. 3 (pp. 281–306). Hillsdale, N.J.: Erlbaum.

Sillars, A. L., Coletti, S. F., Parry, D., and Rogers, M. A. (1982). Coding verbal conflict tactics: Nonverbal and perceptual correlates of the "avoidance-distributive-integrative" distinction. *Human Communication Research, 9,* 83–95.

Sillars, A. L., and Parry, D. (1982). Stress, cognition, and communication in interpersonal conflicts. *Communication Research, 9,* 201–226.

Sillars, A. L., and Weisberg, J. (1987). Conflict as a social skill. In M. E. Roloff and G. R. Miller (Eds.), *Interpersonal processes: New directions in communication research* (pp. 140–171). Newbury Park, Calif.: Sage.

Sillars, A. L., Weisberg, J., Burggraf, C. S., and Zietlow, P. H. (1990). Communication and understanding revisited: Married couples' understanding and recall of conversations. *Communication Research, 17,* 500–532.

Sillars, A. L., and Wilmot, W. W. (1989). Marital communication across the life-span. In J. F. Nussbaum (Ed.), *Life-span communication: Normative processes* (pp. 225–253). Hillsdale, N.J.: Erlbaum.

Sillars, A. L., and Wilmot, W. W. (1994). Communication strategies in conflict and mediation. In J. A. Daly and J. M. Wiemann (Eds.), *Strategic interpersonal communication* (pp. 163–190). Hillsdale, N.J.: Erlbaum.

Sitkin, S. B., and Bies, R. J. (1993). Social accounts in conflict situations: Using explanations to manage conflict. *Human Relations, 46,* 349–370.

Smetana, J. G. (1988). Adolescents' and parents' conceptions of parental authority. *Child Development, 59,* 321–335.

Smetana, J. G. (1989). Adolescents' and parents' reasoning about actual family conflict. *Child Development, 60,* 1052–1067.

Smith, A., and Aldrich, H. E. (1991). *The role of trust in the transaction cost economics framework.* Paper presented at the annual meeting of the Academy of Management, Miami.

Society of Professionals in Dispute Resolution. (1987). Ethical standards of professional responsibility for the Society of Professionals in Dispute Resolution (adopted June 2, 1986; re-adopted June 2, 1991). In *Dispute Resolution Forum.* Washington, D.C.: National Institute for Dispute Resolution.

Sorenson, S. B., Siegel, J. M., Golding, J. M., and Stein, J. A. (1991). Repeated sexual victimization. *Violence and Victims, 6,* 299–308.

Spitzberg, B. H., and Canary, D. J. (1985). Loneliness and relationally competent communication. *Journal of Social and Personal Relationships, 2,* 387–402.

Spitzberg, B. H., Canary, D. J., and Cupach, W. R. (1994). A competence-based approach to the study of interpersonal conflict. In D. D. Cahn (Ed.), *Conflict in personal relationships* (pp. 183–202). Hillsdale, N.J.: Erlbaum.

Spitzberg, B. H., and Cupach, W. R. (1984). *Interpersonal communication competence.* Beverly Hills, Calif.: Sage.

Spitzberg, B. H., and Cupach, W. R. (1989). *Handbook of interpersonal competence research.* New York: Springer-Verlag.

Spitzberg, B. H., and Duran, R. L. (1994). *Toward an ideological deconstruction of communication competence.* Paper presented at the International Communication Association Conference, Sydney, Australia.

Spitzberg, B. H., and Hecht, M. L. (1984). A component model of relational competence. *Human Communication Research, 10,* 575–599.

Sprey, J. (1971). On the management of conflict in families. *Journal of Marriage and the Family, 33,* 722–731.

Stafford, L., and Bayer, C. L. (1993). *Interaction between parents and children.* Newbury Park, Calif.: Sage.

Stafford, L., and Daly, J. A. (1984). Conversational memory: The effects of recall mode and memory expectancies on remembrances of natural conversations. *Human Communication Research, 10,* 379–402.

Sternberg, R. J., and Dobson, D. M. (1987). Resolving interpersonal conflicts: An analysis of stylistic consistency. *Journal of Personality and Social Psychology, 52,* 794–812.

Sternberg, R. L., and Soriano, L. J. (1984). Styles of conflict resolution. *Journal of Personality and Social Psychology, 47,* 115–126.

Stets, J. E. (1990). Verbal and physical aggression in marriage. *Journal of Marriage and the Family, 52,* 501–514.

Stets, J. E. (1992). Interactive processes in dating aggression: A national study. *Journal of Marriage and the Family, 54,* 165–177.

Stets, J. E., and Pirog-Good, M. A. (1987). Violence in dating relationships. *Social Psychology Quarterly, 50,* 237–246.

Stets, J. E., and Pirog-Good, M. A. (1989). Patterns of physical and sexual abuse for men and women in dating relationships: A descriptive analysis. *Journal of Family Violence, 4,* 63–76.

Stewart, E., and Bennett, M. (1991). *American cultural patterns: A cross-cultural perspective.* Yarmouth, Maine: Intercultural Press.

Storms, M. D. (1973). Videotape and the attribution process: Reversing actors' and observers' points of view. *Journal of Personality and Social Psychology, 27,* 165–175.

Straus, M. A. (1979). Measuring intrafamily conflict and violence: The conflict tactics (CT) scales. *Journal of Marriage and the Family, 41,* 75–88.

Straus, M., Gelles, R., and Steinmetz, S. (1980). *Behind closed doors: Violence in the American family.* New York: Doubleday.

Struckman-Johnson, C. (1988). Forced sex on dates: It happens to men, too. *Journal of Sex Research, 24,* 234–241.

Struckman-Johnson, C., and Struckman-Johnson, D. (1992). Acceptance of male rape myths among college men and women. *Sex Roles, 27,* 85–100.

Sugarman, D. B., and Hotaling, G. T. (1989). Dating violence: Prevalence, context, and risk markers. In M. A. Pirog-Good and J. E. Stets (Eds.), *Violence in dating relationships: Emerging social issues* (pp. 3–32). New York: Praeger.

Sumner, W. (1940). *Folkways.* Boston: Ginn.

Swan, R. (1995). Agents step up campaign against NBA union deal. *Sports Industry News, 13*(4), 233.

Sycara, K. P. (1991). Problem restructuring in negotiation. *Management Science, 37,* 1248–1268.

Tavris, C. (1984). On the wisdom of counting to ten: Personal and social dangers of anger expression. *Review of Personality and Social Psychology, 5,* 170–191.

Thalhofer, N. N. (1993). Intergroup differentiation and reduction of intergroup conflict. *Small Group Research, 24*(1), 28–43.

Thibaut, J., and Kelley, H. (1959). *The social psychology of groups*. New York: Wiley.

Thompson, E. H., Jr. (1991). The maleness of violence in dating relationships: An appraisal of stereotypes. *Sex Roles, 24,* 261–277.

Ting-Toomey, S. (1983a). An analysis of verbal communication patterns in high and low marital adjustment groups. *Human Communication Research, 9,* 306–319.

Ting-Toomey, S. (1983b). Coding conversation between intimates: A validation study of the intimate negotiation coding system (INCS). *Communication Quarterly, 31,* 68–77.

Ting-Toomey, S. (1985). Toward a theory of conflict and culture. In W. Gudykunst, L. Stewart, and S. Ting-Toomey (Eds.), *Communication, culture, and organizational processes*. Beverly Hills, Calif.: Sage.

Ting-Toomey, S. (1988). Intercultural conflict styles: A face-negotiation theory. In Y. Kim and W. Gudykunst (Eds.), *Theories in intercultural communication*. Newbury Park, Calif.: Sage.

Ting-Toomey, S. (Ed.). (1994a). *The challenge of facework: Cross-cultural and interpersonal issues*. Albany, N.Y.: State University of New York Press.

Ting-Toomey, S. (1994b). Managing conflict in intimate intercultural relationships. In D. Cahn (Ed.), *Intimate conflict in personal relationships*. Hillsdale, N.J.: Erlbaum.

Ting-Toomey, S. (1994c). Managing intercultural conflicts effectively. In L. Samovar and R. Porter (Eds.), *Intercultural communication: A reader* (7th ed.). Belmont, Calif.: Wadsworth.

Ting-Toomey, S., Gao, G., Trubisky, P., Yang, Z., Kim, H. S., Lin, S.-L., and Nishida, T. (1991), Culture, face maintenance, and styles of handling interpersonal conflict: A study in five cultures. *International Journal of Conflict Management, 2,* 275–296.

Tjosvold, D. (1982). Effects of approach to controversy on supervisors' incorporation of subordinates' information in decision making. *Journal of Applied Psychology, 67,* 189–191.

Tjosvold, D. (1983). Effect of supervisor's influence orientation on their decision making controversy. *Journal of Psychology, 113,* 175–182.

Tjosvold, D., and Chia, L. C. (1989). Conflict between managers and workers: The role of cooperation and competition. *Journal of Social Psychology, 129,* 235–247.

Tracy, K. (1990). The many faces of facework. In H. Giles and W. P. Robinson (Eds.), *Handbook of language and social psychology* (pp. 209–226). New York: Wiley.

Triandis, H. (1990). Theoretical concepts that are applicable to the analysis of ethnocentrism. In R. Brislin (Ed.), *Applied cross-cultural psychology*. Newbury Park, Calif.: Sage.

Triandis, H. (1994). *Culture and social behavior*. New York: McGraw-Hill.

Triandis, H. (1995). *Individualism and collectivism*. Boulder, Colo.: Westview.

Trubisky, P., Ting-Toomey, S., and Lin, S.-L. (1991). The influence of individualism-collectivism and self-monitoring on conflict styles. *International Journal of Intercultural Relations, 15,* 65–84.

Tuppen, C. J. S., and Gaitan, A. (1989). Constructing accounts of aggressive episodes. *Social Behaviour, 4,* 127–143.

Umbreit, M. S. (1989). Violent offenders and their victims. In M. Wright and B. Galaway (Eds.), *Mediation and criminal justice* (pp. 99–112). Newbury Park, Calif.: Sage.

Umbreit, M. S. (1993). Juvenile offenders meet their victims: The impact of mediation in Albuquerque, New Mexico. *Family and Conciliation Courts Review, 31,* 90–100.

U.S. Department of Justice. (1994). *Violence between intimates.* Bureau of Justice Statistics, Selected Findings (NCJ-149259). Washington, D.C.: U.S. Department of Justice.

Utley, M. E., Richardson, D. R., and Pilkington, C. J. (1989). Personality and interpersonal conflict management. *Personality and Individual Differences, 10,* 287–293.

van de Vliert, E., and Euwema, M. C. (1994). Agreeableness and activeness as components of conflict behaviors. *Journal of Personality and Social Psychology, 66,* 674–687.

Vangelisti, A. L. (1994). Messages that hurt. In W. R. Cupach and B. H. Spitzberg (Eds.), *The dark side of interpersonal communication* (pp. 53–82). Hillsdale, N.J.: Erlbaum.

Vincent, J. P., Weiss, R. L., and Birchler, G. R. (1975). A behavioral analysis of problem-solving in married and stranger dyads. *Behavior Therapy, 6,* 475–487.

Vivian, D., Langhinrichsen-Rohling, J. (1994). Are bi-directionally violent couples mutually victimized? A gender-sensitive comparison. *Violence and Victims, 9,* 107–124.

Vuchinich, S. (1986). On attenuation in verbal family conflict. *Social Psychology Quarterly, 49,* 281–293.

Vuchinich, S. (1987). Starting and stopping spontaneous family conflicts. *Journal of Marriage and the Family, 49,* 591–601.

Vuchinich, S. (1990). The sequential organization of closing in verbal family conflict. In A. D. Grimshaw (Ed.), *Conflict talk: Sociolinguistic investigations of arguments in conversations* (pp. 118–138). New York: Cambridge University Press.

Walton, R. E. (1969). *Interpersonal peacemaking: Confrontations and third party consultation.* Reading, Mass.: Addison-Wesley.

Walton, R. E., and McKersie, R. B. (1965). *A behavioral theory of labor negotiations: An analysis of a social interaction system.* New York: McGraw-Hill.

Watzlawick, P., Beavin, J., and Jackson, D. D. (1967). *Pragmatics of human communication.* New York: Norton.

Weinstein, E. A. (1969). The development of interpersonal competence. In D. A. Goslin (Ed.), *Handbook of socialization theory and research* (pp. 753–775). Chicago: Rand McNally.

Weiss, R. L., and Summers, K. J. (1983). Marital interaction coding system-III. In E. E. Filsinger (Ed.), *Marriage and family assessment: A sourcebook for family therapy* (pp. 85–115). Beverly Hills, Calif.: Sage.

White, J. W., and Koss, M. P. (1991). Courtship violence: Incidence in a national sample of higher education students. *Violence and Victims, 6,* 247–256.

White, J. W., and Kowalski, R. M. (1994). Deconstructing the myth of the nonaggressive woman. *Psychology of Women Quarterly, 18,* 487–508.

Wiemann, J. M. (1977). Explication and test of a model of communicative competence. *Human Communication Research, 3,* 195–213.

Witteman, H. (1992). Analyzing interpersonal conflict: Nature of awareness, type of initiating event, situational perceptions and management styles. *Western Journal of Communication, 56,* 248–280.

Witteman, H., and Fitzpatrick, M. A. (1986). Compliance-gaining in marital interaction: Power bases, processes, and outcomes. *Communication Monographs, 53,* 130–143.

Wolf-Smith, J. H., and La Rossa, R. (1992). After he hits her. *Family Relations, 41,* 324–329.

Woolpert, S. (1991). Victim-offender reconciliation programs. In K. G. Duffy, J. W. Grosch, and P. V. Olczak (Eds.), *Community mediation: A handbook for practitioners and researchers* (pp. 275–298). New York: Guilford.

Zillmann, D. (1988). Cognition-excitation interdependence in aggressive behavior. *Aggressive Behavior, 14,* 51–64.

Zillmann, D. (1990). The interplay of cognition and excitation in aggravated conflict among intimates. In D. D. Cahn (Ed.), *Intimates in conflict: A communication perspective.* Hillsdale, N.J.: Erlbaum.

INDEX